RED HEELS & RED FLAGS

Red Heels & Red Flags

SCARLETT STEEL

Onion River Press
89 Church Street
Burlington, VT 05401
info@onionriverpress.com
www.onionriverpress.com

ISBN: 978-1-957184-93-7
Library of Congress Control Number: 2024922636

We've all been there. This is for you.

CONTENTS

Introduction

There are two sides to every story, and three sides to every triangle. While these stories don't include any love triangles, there are plenty of points in which they overlap or intersect. And as far as 'his' side vs. mine, I can only share mine. I'm sure, if asked, their version would sometimes differ, but all I can do is share from my perspective. I've done my best to tell these stories as I remember them. There is no malice in my tone, nor did I write this to hurt or embarrass anyone. But there's got to be a silver lining to my time in the dating world. Surely I've earned something with all the absurd and unhinged happenings I've had to endure. I've included details that don't necessarily paint me in the best light. Sure, I could've omitted these specifics, but in order to paint a fair and accurate picture of what happened and who these men were, I felt the need to include everything. Even the time I vindictively egged a guy's house, and the time (okay times, plural) that I got frisky in the backseat of a truck. Hell, one time I looked up and was surprised to see a dirty footprint on the roof of my car. Though I suppose I shouldn't have been surprised. #flipflopseason

In the two years after my divorce, I was determined to get back out there, but to not put myself in a position to have my heart broken again. Much like Julia Roberts' character in *The Runaway Bride*, I spent years identifying with the men I was in long term relationships with. I no longer knew how I liked my eggs, and damn if it wasn't my time to find out again. I decided to go on dates here and there with several men. Whoever I wanted to. As many as I wanted to. Nothing serious. Always casual. Never committed. And I was fair to these guys, always letting them know that we weren't exclusive, and that I was and would continue to see other men. Most were okay with this. Some asked me on date #2 or date #3 to be their girlfriend and to cut off ties with everyone else. That was the best part. There were no ties to cut! I wasn't obligated to anyone. I didn't owe anyone anything. That was a breath of fresh air and exactly what I needed for that season of my life. I had made myself a promise to take my time and figure out who I was and what I wanted. I wanted to date myself for a bit and fall back in love with my own company. I had nights of self-care and also nights of loneliness. I had adventures with friends, old and new, and solo adventures. I watched movies while holding hands, curled up under a blanket, and I also watched movies while painting my toes and applying a charcoal face mask. I learned to love myself again. To pay myself the respect those in my past had long since neglected to. I showed myself grace and forgiveness. I learned to walk again so I could once again enjoy dancing. And then boy, did I dance. I danced in the kitchen when making dinner. I danced away my sadness, my anger. I danced in the rain. Hell, I even danced when there was no music at all, just a song in my heart that no one else could hear. And damn it, I deserved every second. I don't have any regrets about taking the time I needed for me. I healed. I grew and rediscovered. I laughed, I loved... basic white bitch and all. It was everything I needed and included a lot of what I didn't, but it ultimately, taught me so many lessons I didn't know that I needed to learn.

I wrote this for so many reasons, but first and foremost for myself. Secondly, so you all could find some entertainment in my misadventures. I know you'll relate to some of these experiences, and I hope you'll learn from some of them. That you won't allow yourself to be subjected to some of the bullshit that I did. I hope my words encourage you to build a better fortress around your life but also give you the encouragement to let the right people in when the timing is right. I hope you give yourself grace and forgiveness. And please, extend that grace and forgiveness to me as well. Red flags are much easier to see once there are several, and much easier to see in the rearview mirror. It was a long path but by the end, I was stronger and smarter for it. And if nothing else, I hope you can laugh at the audacity of these men and the ridiculousness that ensued. Don't forget, these are true stories. These things truly happened. *Shudder.* Join me down this path lined with red flags and paved with regret.

With humility and sincerity
(and a whole lot of sarcasm),
Scarlett

P.S. If you're easily offended by strong language or sexual situations, I'd put this book down. It's not for you. If you don't mind a healthy dose of FBombs and 'shits' sprinkled about and stories of multiple orgasms and stolen panties, keep reading. You're in for a treat. Hopefully you enjoy reading this half as much as I enjoyed writing it.

| 1 |

The Vegan Saga (Part 1)

I remember the night I first created an online dating profile, or should I say "we". My ex and I decided to spice things up one night when we were three sheets to the wind, and of course we felt differently in the cold light of day. Though honestly, I would've maybe been open to the idea of adding someone to our bed if my was-band had actually been serious. We never used that profile... together. My picture, my name, no bio (God knows they don't read it anyway), and my age—58. In hindsight, we shouldn't have used his date of birth when setting this up, but I was always amused when those I matched with would reach out and proclaim, "There's no way you're 58!" No shit. Fast forward to me divorcing and finally swiping left with intent. Little did I know what was in store for me with unlimited men and their egos (and libidos) at my fingertips. Yum. This is where I introduce you to "The Vegan." Clear your calendar, make a cup of tea. Ensure no kids are present, as the words "What the fuck" are about to escape your lips. Multiple times (which is far more than the number of times this man ever pleasured me with his mouth). Once. Remember that number (see 'Post-its of passion').

* * *

We first met up innocently in a parking lot at the height of the pandemic, and the recommended 'six feet' rule perfectly masked my hesitation with getting close. He had made comments about wanting to run his fingers through my hair and that I was better looking in person. All good things, but still, I wasn't in a place to explore this, be it romantic or just physical. I was intrigued though, and ended up meeting up with him a week later in a more intimate setting. When I sat on his drab floral couch (that clearly he inherited from his grandmother or got for free on the side of the road), he made his move immediately. He not only pulled me into a straddling position on his lap in one swift move, but then tried to eat my entire face. Not kidding. I think he actually thought that was sexy. My cheeks hurt from the rub of his stubble, and my lips burned from the dragging of his teeth. And my pride hurt most of all. Looking back, I'm not entirely sure why I was putting myself through this if it wasn't enjoyable or something I was even intending to get involved with. As I tried to ignore the attack my face was under, I remembered the nude he had sent me just the week before. That sculpted ass was fine AF, and it was a refreshing alternative to the traditional dick pic. His determined smolder is what really sealed the deal, and what had me tolerating this saliva waterboarding. As I felt his... excitement... growing against my inner thigh, I realized that I would need to find an excuse to quickly leave or I'd soon be at his mercy, desperate for his touch. I'm a big fan of afternoon delight, huge fan. Any time of day, as many times a day as possible. I'm not saying I'm obsessed, but I have been called "addickted" before. Still, I wasn't ready to lay in this strange man's bed, sweaty and shameful in the light of the early afternoon. I clumsily tripped over my words as I gave one bogus excuse after the next and quickly made my escape.

The next time we met up within the safety of a local farm where we could walk and talk. Being in close proximity of other patrons didn't save me from being pinned against his truck, him begging me to let him get on his knees right there. He would've been discrete, I'm sure, but in the moment I panicked and shut him down. Even though this fling fizzled out as quickly as it began, the 802 is only so big, and I'd come to run into him all over town over the next couple of years. Months and months went by, and then our paths crossed again. I was finally in a different head space and ready to explore what could have been.

* * *

When my ex sold the house, I was given two weeks to move out. It was a whirlwind of tears, confusion, anger, and urgency. With days to pack up and get out, it was my turn to test positive for Covid. The fatigue hit hard, and I found it nearly impossible to pack my things and to prepare for the move. During this time, there were a few guys who reached out and made their presence known. The Vegan, being one of them, lived in the same town that I was about to vacate, and with only part-time teenage sons, he had time on his hands to be present. He brought me a wide array of soups, yogurts, and remedies (all organic of course, and vegan whenever possible) to help me onto the road to recovery.

The Vegan and I had reconnected while I was being thrown out of the house my ex and I shared, so my ex could go live his best midlife crisis in Florida. Things got messier and nastier the further along we got, like all divorces do, and he refused to even let me know where he was headed. By the end, this once loving man who had promised to grow old with me found himself calling me names under his breath. Then not under his breath. He even called me the dreaded C-word, knowing I had zero tolerance for it. I wish I could say that I didn't let it bother me, but it did. It really did. I was furious. A friend who was helping with the move provided me with a nip of whiskey to make the day more bearable. With a buzz (and some rage), I may or may not have put a piece of salmon in the saddle bag of my ex's prized Harley Davidson Road King. When the bourbon was wearing off, I had a smidge of remorse, but his bike had already been loaded into the moving truck, straps tight across the saddle bags. To remove the salmon at that point would mean admitting to him and his movers what I'd done. Instead, this little revenge prank of mine is definitely one for the ages, costing me a whopping $33,000. When he disappeared across state lines, I never heard from him again or received the remaining money he owed me from our dissolution. Silver lining though: I learned that his belongings stayed in that moving truck, in the hot sun, in Boston for a solid week before continuing on its way to hot and humid Florida. Worth every penny! Karma's a bitch, and apparently, so am I.

When The Vegan and I had connected initially, he made his intentions very clear. Sex. The whole sex and nothing but the sex. That's what he wanted. And I was now ready to indulge in some self-love by letting him indulge in me. *You're welcome, sir.* He had once said that I 'had a body worth exploring,' and I was ready to let him be my personal Magellan. Since my mindset had changed, when we finally experienced each other for the first time, I laid there in the afterglow, sweaty but without shame. Ladies, you do you. No apologies. No fucks given. But fucks given, ya know? (That's where the fun is.) Anyway, things *were* fun for a bit. He'd moved from the dingy basement apartment I met him in and was now the owner of a well-maintained house in a delightful little cul-de-sac. We'd sprinkle in outings like going for walks or making salsa from the sprawling garden that was his front yard. He took pride in sharing the fruits of his labor and I had no problem being the recipient. Even now, I miss devouring those scrumptious shishito peppers almost enough to reach back out. Almost. Although my physical needs were being somewhat met, and my taste buds were satisfied, our time together made it abundantly clear that he wasn't looking to develop feelings for me. Perhaps he wasn't even capable of developing real feelings of a romantic nature. I wasn't sure and never sought out clarification on what we were or where things were headed. We'd stroll down the dirt paths of Shelburne Farms, and I'd lock onto every word he said, asking questions and engaging. When it was my turn to converse, he was quick to say, "Can I get the abridged version?" Asshole. He would later explain that he was always joking when he would say this and assumed I knew it was just a joke. Man, the real joke ended up being him. Stay tuned.

I was able to justify my time and activities with him as a way to scratch an itch and allow me to date others. I had promised myself during my divorce that I wouldn't jump into a relationship. I wanted time to be single and rediscover myself. I not only wanted this time to heal and grow, but knew I desperately needed it. If I could fuck this guy (who didn't care about me as anything more than someone to enter), I wouldn't get hurt. And at the same time, I could date other men. All the men I wanted to, without any need to get physically intimate with them. And no one to answer to. In my defense, they all knew that there were others. Seeing several men at once would prevent me from falling in love and having my heart once again shattered into a million tiny pieces. And that's how I found myself in this place. Doing one man and dating the rest.

* * *

I remember the first time I stayed over. I woke up in the morning in his arms, and we went for round two. The sex was full of passion and passion-less all at the same time. The Vegan had a rhythm and stuck to it: the same circular motion, the same noises, no foreplay. In a way I suppose it was nice to know what to expect. Every. Single. Time. Hands didn't wander and positions rarely changed. He had a routine and he stuck to it. No wasted time. No inefficiencies. A means to an end. He liked the workout and when our frequency was down (I had to make time for all my dates, mind you), he often complained that he was missing out on part of his workout routine. I'd like to think that he was joking, but he wasn't. Many times he would lament about how he needed his yoga, his weight lifting, his rowing machine, his biking, and to ride me. If he didn't get his sweaty sessions of moving clockwise above me, I was ruining his exercise routine. I was keeping him from being the best version of himself by being a piece of gym equipment that was out of commission. Can you imagine being compared to an exercise bike or dumbbells? Ouch.

I should mention that although there were a lot of really odd things about The Vegan, there were also some really great redeeming qualities. He was there during some dark times and deserves a shout out for that. Maybe even a star sticker (one of the passed-over red ones, but definitely not a gold star). He even brought me to the ER when I was suffering from one of the worst migraines I've ever had. Once they had me connected to the IV and were pumping me full of pain meds and fluids, I was able to find some relief from the agony. Instead of reading or playing on his phone as most would, he remained completely silent in the dark, staying with me in presence and staying present in his own thoughts. It was almost off-putting. There he was in complete silence, staring off in the absolute darkness while I slept. He made trips to the store and the pharmacy. He bought my medications and cooked for me, and for a second, I thought maybe, just maybe, he was catching feelings for me. In retrospect, I think he liked having my dog around more than he liked having me around. He would take Wells with him for the day, mountain biking and going on hikes. The Vegan was big on things that were practical and logical, so having my dog in tow brightened his day. Gave him purpose.

Anyway, back to our first time. This particular morning, I woke up at his place and hadn't planned to spend the night. I had no extra clothes with me and would have to put on yesterday's daisy dukes and black V-neck. This isn't a fit I was worried about wearing in front of him or for a trip to the park, but nothing I would wear with any chance of running into anyone respectable. After finishing and collapsing onto his back, he quickly realized that he'd overslept and was late to pick up his friend. He had committed to helping him move a piece of equipment in the morning and needed to head out right away. Instead of staying behind, he insisted I come with him. I shimmied into my shorts and ran into the bathroom, trying to not hold him up. I ran a hand through my hair and attempted to look somewhat put together, trying and failing to wipe away last night's mascara. There was no way I was hiding this walk of shame as we ventured out to meet his pal.

We pulled up to the apartment building and I was horrified when his friend stepped out of his door and headed toward The Vegan's truck. It wasn't one of those times you know you know someone but you can't place it. This was one of those times you know *exactly* who you're making eye contact with. I remember those eyes looking up at me from between my legs, many times. I could feel the blood drain from my face and my palms begin to sweat. I was mortified, especially dressed like this, clearly having had my body ravaged the night before. Hell, even a half hour ago! What are the odds that his best friend, the man he promised to help out that very morning, was my very own OBGYN?! And yet here he was, Dr. C., climbing into the backseat, knowing damn well that I had spread my legs for his buddy just the night before. Ugh. He was my favorite doctor at that practice and had delivered one of my sons. He had provided great care for years and even removed my IUD surgically. I'm not saying we had matching friendship bracelets, but as far as patient/doctor relationships go, we go way back. Hell, in an especially embarrassing visit, he'd rolled away on his stool to grab something, and I flinched nervously, sending the speculum he'd left in place careening toward the wall. He failed to stifle his laugh completely and said he'd never seen that before. I was mortified (and grateful that I wasn't billed for the dent I left in the wall). #truestory. In typical doctor fashion, he was professional and didn't out me in front of The Vegan. After helping to move his old ultrasound machine to a new office, we headed back to drop him off. He kept our familiarity a secret until he was back home and had closed the truck door. With a smirk and a wink, he looked at The Vegan, then at me, and back to The Vegan. "So, you two are spending time together, huh?!" It only took that one second for my face to return to red and remain that way as we pulled out of the driveway and away from my embarrassment. Man, do I know how to pull off a walk of shame like nobody else.

| 2 |

Day Drinking Like a Pro

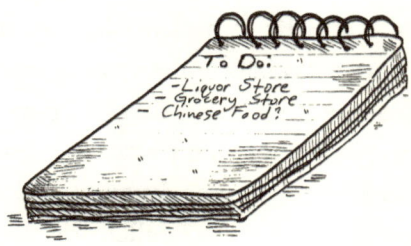

Guy #2. Disappointment #2. He held the door for me as I exited the liquor store, and at the same time we exchanged the same greeting. "Happy Thanksgiving." It certainly was not a rare phrase that day, but we were both a little tickled to have said it at the same time (him more than me). I climbed into my car, dressed for the holiday with nowhere to go. My sister and I have always dressed up for Thanksgiving and Christmas, and even now I dress to celebrate even if I don't have a gathering to attend. This was my first Thanksgiving since my was-band and I had separated, and the family all had their own plans that day. My To-Do list was small, being that most places were closed. Priorities. *Am I right?*

I sat in my car for a minute, searching on my phone to see if the grocery store was open or if I would have to eat Chinese food for dinner. *Aww, shucks! Spicy beef and broccoli for one. I guess. If I have to.* Since we met at a liquor store, we then referred to it as 'the bookstore.' If we hit it off, I didn't want to tell people that we met buying booze alone on a holiday. It was even sadder than it sounds. By the time I drove out of the parking lot, he'd exited the store as well. We pulled out onto the main road at the same time and headed north in separate lanes. He kept looking over at me, smiling, making his interest apparent. When I reached the grocery store, I turned left into the parking lot and he continued straight. It was flattering, and for a second I felt a little less alone.

The store was very obviously closed, so I pulled into a spot and pulled up the website for the chinese restaurant. I wasn't alone for long. With the parking lot so empty, it wasn't hard to spot the stark contrast across the way. There he was, the same black truck, idling in front of the store. I'm not sure how long he'd been there, but I did appreciate that he hadn't come closer before I had a chance to notice him. He slowly pulled up to my car, his driver side window parallel to mine with several feet between our vehicles. He had a black lab beside him, eager to make my acquaintance. "Stop following me!" he joked. I'm usually quicker, but he caught me off guard and I quickly began defending myself. "Actually, I was here first. I didn't follow you. I was just—," he cut me off. "I'm kidding. I decided to loop around and see if you were still here. I had to meet you." We talked for just a few short minutes, as he was hosting his family at his place and needed to continue on his way. He even used his adorable dog as bait. "We like cute girls, don't we, buddy?" *And I'm pissed at myself that that worked.* He asked if he could give me his number (one of the only things he did right). It's too bad that all of his right moves were used up on that very first day. Such a shame. Let's review, shall we?

1. He held the door for me
2. Wished me a Happy Thanksgiving
3. Didn't creep up on me in the parking lot
4. Kept a safe distance when he did pull up
5. Paid me a compliment

6. Gave me his number instead of asking for mine

That's basically where he stopped. It wasn't long before I texted him (I was lonely, don't judge). When he got home, he was busy preparing dinner for his folks. That didn't stop him from calling me though. He called me several times. I've worked in the kitchen and put on meals for my family gatherings. It's not all that manageable to be on the phone while preparing food, let alone an entire feast. Hell, just making dinner for my sons can be difficult while on the phone (and actually paying attention). It's my understanding that he basically ruined dinner, and if he had finished making it, they would have all sat down to eat around 10:00pm. The parents were upset, a fight ensued, and they left, never having eaten turkey or potatoes. Red flag #1. He cared more about flirting with a girl he had just met than fulfilling his commitment. He ruined his parents' Thanksgiving. That should have been all I needed to know to opt out right then and there. But naturally, you know I didn't.

We started spending time together and at first, I completely ignored how demanding he was. He didn't care if I had my sons on any given night, requesting that I meet up with him, even if just for a few minutes. He lived about ten minutes south of my house, and just the drive alone subtracted twenty minutes from my family time. It wasn't long before I put my foot down and refused to see him when I had my boys. When we would hang out, it was always at his place. He'd be drinking, and it always seemed that he'd started long before I got there. Maybe even during his work day. Many times, when I left, he was passed out, dead to the world but snoring loud enough to make the windows rattle. The one that really killed me though—he would often let his dog outside to use the bathroom and forget about him. We're talking during snowstorms, while it was raining, in below zero-degree weather. It didn't matter. He did this all the time, and that poor dog was outside, begging to be let back in. It broke my heart. He definitely deserved a better owner and honestly, this guy lucked out with such a good-hearted, obedient dog. *Such a shame.*

When I would show up to see him, his door would be locked. Of-tentimes, he wasn't yet home, or he'd fallen asleep on the couch. He always knew I was coming, yet he'd often neglect to unlock the door before hopping into the shower. I'd be waiting in my car for a solid half hour, waiting for him to finish up. I don't know if it was too hot a shower or what, but he would sweat profusely afterward, making me question why he would shower right before I would see him. He was so paranoid, in fact, that he kept the door locked at all times and didn't want me to be spotted by his neighbors. If they did see me, I wasn't supposed to make conversation with them, and definitely no eye contact. He had junk sprawled across and piled high in two of his three bedrooms. I haven't seen that much stuff in any given episode of *American Pickers*. It was a minefield of tetanus, and I quickly decided that there was no reason good enough to go into those rooms. I'd rather pee my pants. And don't even get me started on his boots. He wore these honkin' big work boots that most definitely should have been thrown out years ago. They smelled to high heaven, yet he re-fused to replace them. When they were within three feet of me, the smell was overwhelming. I contemplated buying him a new pair, but I didn't know this boy well enough to drop $300 on him. And if I did, I was worried that I'd be setting that expectation. *I'm nobody's sugar momma. Well, except for my kids'. And my dog's. But in their defense, they can't work.*

This guy was a total mess. Often, we would return to his house and he would have locked himself out. I'd wait for a solid 10-20 min-utes each time while he wrangled a way in. It got pretty old pretty quick. And somehow he managed to do this on the coldest nights of the year. Go figure. He was convinced he was dying and every other week would panic and head to the emergency room. The doctors never found anything though, other than the fact that he needed to lose some weight and cut back on his incessant drinking. And I don't have proof, of course, but I'm pretty sure he was spending his rent on expensive toys instead (anything with wheels or that could go up his nose). He had a fair amount of disposable income for someone who didn't often climb out of bed before 10:00am. He boasted that he was actually a really incredible cook, and he'd insist on cooking for me quite often. The meals I did have weren't terrible, some better than others, but usually edible. However, they were never served before 9:00pm. He didn't usually want my help making dinner, but he'd get distracted or head to the gas station to buy more alcohol or fall asleep. I knew if I was headed to his place that there was a good chance I'd leave hungry. It got really old, really fast. (At least The Vegan always fed me.) Fireball swore he'd given up smoking cigarettes (for me), but I'd often catch him reeking of those nasty things. And he always had some excuse—his employees were smoking, or his customers were smoking, and he was nearby. I would find lighters, matches and even cigarettes, but he'd do his best to lie his way out of that too. I'm not stupid, just far too lenient, I guess. I even found a line of what looked to be cocaine on his counter, but since I'm a virgin when it comes to drugs, I couldn't say for sure. It sort of looked like a sugar and salt mixture, but it was definitely in a straight line and covered by a baseball cap that looked to be intentionally placed over it. He feigned embarrassment that I found it, confusion as to what it was, and anger that someone would play a joke like that on him. His acting was transparent and didn't serve him one bit.

I knew there was no way he was running a legitimate, above-the-table business, but luckily, answers were at my fingertips. One quick internet search revealed that he was a scammy handyman at best. He would constantly overcharge for his shoddy work, which was never done in a timely fashion or to any kind of reasonable standard. The former job sites he was proud of and pointed out on our outings ended up being jobs he worked on with other, larger companies—not his own. Not representative of his company. He would charge his accounts and homeowners through the nose and pay his employees such a small fraction. He didn't stop there. He did the same to his own father. He'd pay him scraps, but even worse, he'd make his father wait for weeks upon weeks to get paid. They were often feuding, and his father would get so frustrated, they'd stop speaking until he got what was owed to him. The cycle would repeat, again and again. Fireball advertised that he was insured, though he wasn't. He would sign on for bigger jobs than he could handle and fall flat, disappointing home-owners left and right. At the time, I knew of at least two lawsuits that had been filed against him, not to mention that he had had many court appearances in the past. Not only did he get fired by most, they wanted their money back (which, presumably, he'd already spent on his newest motorcycle or trailer). Between the neighbors, the land-lord, disgruntled employees, his family and friends he'd screwed over, and customers he'd wronged, it became very obvious why he was paranoid and always hid in his house. There was probably a support group for all those he had fucked over. *"Sorry, Honey. I can't take out the garbage right now. I have to get to Grudge Group. I shouldn't be out late."* —*former friend who's wife Fireball screwed (wishes to remain anonymous)*

* * *

The first time he asked to borrow my car, I was at work. He sug-gested he swing by and swap it out for his truck, claiming that his truck wasn't registered (or some shitty excuse like that) and that he needed to borrow my vehicle to head to the DMV. It was about an hour drive, and since I was busy working, I didn't really mind. The second time, he was headed to the DMV again to finish what he couldn't before. The third time, he said it was because he didn't want to spend all that money driving his gas-guzzling truck all that way. DMV again? Really?! He would never leave his keys, however, and if an emergency had arisen, I would have had no way to get from point A to point B. The next time he borrowed my car, he left his keys with me, but arrived back at my office at the end of my shift with his shit-faced employee in the car. My car. I'd met this guy before, but not in such a state as this. He wore the stench of cheap vodka better than The Vegan wore his judgment, which was saying something. When he stepped out of the car, he was stumbling and his speech was in-coherent. I was steaming mad. I couldn't believe that this jackass was driving around, allowing his employee to drink alcohol in my car. I couldn't believe how wreckless he was. The whole thing felt like a slap in the face. I felt used. We had a lengthy discussion about this, and he promised to do better. They always do. The very last time he borrowed my car, he promised to leave me his truck in case of an emergency. I had to pick up my boys after work and explained that he'd need to be back no later than 4:00pm. I was planning on leaving early and certainly didn't want to pick them up in his nasty ass, smoke-filled, dirty truck (not sure if it was legal, safe, or even his). Maybe he had coke in the console. I didn't know for sure, but I didn't want to find out. He swore he'd be back in plenty of time, and when I reached out during the day to touch base, he neglected to respond. 4:00pm rolled around, then 4:12pm, and before long, it was after 5:00pm. He showed up closer to 6:00pm and I was livid! I had waited onsite, unwilling to use his truck. That was the very last time he borrowed anything of mine. *All the swear words. All of them. Grrrr!*

* * *

One evening after work, I showed up to his place. As usual, he waited until I was thirty seconds out to hop into the shower. I waited for him for a while and ended up falling asleep on his bed. He woke me up angrily, having gone through my phone. He denied this, of course, and said that he had just seen a text come in, so he decided to see what else was being sent to me. What he was angry about was taken out of context, nor was it any of his business. He said his concern stemmed from me arriving freshly perfumed and wearing mismatched socks. "You'd never wear mismatched socks! Clearly you were at some other man's house before coming here. And you put on perfume?! What the fuck, Scarlett?!!" he screamed. *Right. I went to some man's house and put on mismatched women's no show socks. That makes complete sense. I made damn good time too; must've been a quickie. And the perfume I keep in the door of my car couldn't account for my newest application?* You better believe I changed my password immediately and made it perfectly clear that if he ever touched my phone again, he'd have a hell of a lot more to fear than me seeing another man. I was furious. That was also the last time I wore perfume around him. And you bet your ass I intentionally wore mismatched socks around him after that too.

* * *

One night, we'd both had a few drinks. He always drank more than me and often tried to coax me into drinking more than my share so I'd be forced to stay over. Shocker. On this particular night, however, I saw a change in him. He'd lost his damn mind. He heard a noise outside (which to this day, I'm convinced was just the wind). He ran outside so quickly that both dogs were on alert. I had retreated to the bedroom, a little bit scared and frankly, trying to figure out what the hell was going on. I heard gunshots—one and then a second. The dogs were cowering beside me and I was doing my best to comfort them, still having no idea what had just happened. I didn't know if he'd been shot by a neighbor. If he'd taken down an intruder. No idea. Just absolute fear. After what seemed like forever, he ran back inside frantically, slamming the door behind him and locking it immediately. He ran through the house, peering out several of the windows before returning to the bedroom. He explained that there was a bobcat outside and that it was approaching, so he fired at it, fearful for his own safety. He'd made mention of this wild cat more than once, yet I'd never seen it or any sign of its existence. I was angered that he'd run outside and shoot at this phantom cat without explaining anything to me. I had been afraid to venture outside, fearful that I'd see him lying on the ground in a pool of blood, an angry murderer coming up the stairs and heading for the rest of us. My anxiety was through the roof, but he didn't care. He was so focused on the ringing in his ears, complaining of how badly they hurt. *Good. Serves you right.* A little while had passed, and we had finally agreed to try and sleep since it was so late. The night's drama had been exhausting, and I wanted so badly to sober up and leave. Just as I was finally beginning to drift off, there was a loud knock on the door. He climbed through the darkness of one of the spare bedrooms and peeked out the window as discreetly as he could. The knock repeated, not once, but a third time. He ignored the door and refused to answer it, saying that the police were there. *Of course they were, you jackass! You fired a gun in a residential area in the middle of the night. I'm sure one of your 'horrible' neighbors called for backup. I'm pretty sure I know who the horrible neighbor is now.*

* * *

Then there's the night I woke up covered in his piss. Yup. Great night. No explanation. You deserve one, of course, I just don't have one.

* * *

Les Miserables was the first show I ever saw on Broadway. It hit hard and almost became a part of me. I learned every song, knew every character, and was in love with the story and its symbolism. I was supposed to watch the movie years ago when it opened on Christmas Day, but long story short, it never happened. I had waited years to watch it, wanting everything to be perfect when I did—surround sound speakers, a big screen, the right snacks, no interruptions. Fireball knew this and decided he'd create the perfect movie night for us. He queued up the movie, set up a mattress on his living room floor, and tested his speakers. I had thoroughly explained my hesitation, and he knew how important this was to me. The first half of the film was great—no interruptions, great story building and character development. Then, he took a phone call. A woman he'd slept with on occasion but was now friends with. Her gay best friend hopped on the video call and proceeded to hit on Fireball for the next half hour or so. I was so appalled by what happened next that I don't even remember what the segue was. He pulled my shirt up and flashed his gentleman friend. I was blown away and oh so pissed. When we finally got off the phone and through our fight, he quieted down and resumed the movie. Not more than twenty minutes later, he pulled down my pants and started kissing my thighs, begging me to let him make his way up. I turned off the movie immediately and went home. I was so disappointed. *I guess I'm just glad he didn't snore through it? Lame.* He was a horrible friend and a horrible person and I hated that he was such an immature fuck. It took another two years before the stars aligned and I watched that movie in full (see Chapter 25: The Bartender).

* * *

Another night, we headed about ten minutes south of his house to a local dive bar. After being served his usual rum and coke, he began complaining that the drink was weak. He claimed that the staff were refilling the bottles of top shelf spirits with inferior alcohol. That's a mighty accusation to bring into a bar that you frequent. The bartenders denied this, and Fireball became belligerent. He made it clear that he wouldn't be tipping them, and the look on his face was priceless when they outed him for never tipping. He downed his drink and slammed his glass down on the bar. He grabbed my keys and headed outside. I was mortified at his behavior. These female bartenders were worried about me. His reputation preceded him, always being a drunk asshole. Drinking in excess and giving them a hard time. And never tipping. While they were offering their advice and suggestions for an out, he walked back into the bar. It was very evident by our hushed tones that we were talking about him, and he knew it. They offered to bring me home, and one of the girls even made me take her number, worried he'd leave without me or retaliate when we left. We had taken my car though, so I didn't have a choice but to leave with him. *Another fun night. There isn't enough alcohol to deal with this behavior. Mostly because he drank it all.*

* * *

Then my birthday came. He took me to a nice dinner, to a place I'd driven past many times but had never gone to. The drive was pleasant, the ambience amazing. Every table had its own warmth from the glow of the candle atop. The restaurant was dimly lit and perfect for the occasion. The owner was lovely and I even asked to see their attached event space. Fireball paid the check and left it at the table, following the owner for a private tour. I saw his signature before the leather booklet closed and was so disappointed at how poorly he had tipped. *At least he tipped this time?* It was too late, however, and the owner had already nabbed us for the tour. When we left the restaurant, I knew that surely she saw the horrible tip we'd left. Although I'm sure she wouldn't remember me, I've never been back. I later heard that oftentimes, if someone else pays the bill in cash, he would wait until they left the table and steal most of the money. I can't say for certain, but I'm pretty sure I saw him do this one of the times I paid. *So pathetic.* Another time, when he was out with a friend, cash had been left to cover the bill and the tip in its entirety. I'm told that he took it all and the police were called for theft. He would even fill his prescription medication (that he received for free) and would sell it for $30 a pill. *What a class act.*

* * *

Since I'm apparently a glutton for punishment, there's more. The Super Bowl came, and the plan was for me to stay over. This would allow for alcohol consumption and given the late hour of the game, no need to drive home. I showed up, put on comfy pjs (admittedly, sexy pjs) and began prepping the snacks. We were nearly halfway through the game (and a couple of drinks in), when his friends from down the road called. They weren't able to stream the game and really wanted to watch it. He was hesitant, but I'm the nicest bitch you've ever met, and told him it was no big deal if they came by for the second half of the game. I was aware that he had had a threesome or two with them and did my best to ignore this fact when they arrived. The girlfriend showed up in an emotional drunk state, hysterical about her grandfather who had recently passed. I missed the halftime show (we're talking Eminem, Dr. Dre, Mary J. Blige, and the like) and about another 40 minutes of commercials. Then the entire third quarter. I humored her and calmed her down. Finally, she laid on the floor, relaxed and all-but-sleeping. I walked into the kitchen where the two guys were. This was the same employee who was day drinking on the regular, and he'd recently checked himself into rehab. He was sober and I was not going to miss the opportunity to encourage him. What a positive change he had made. I spoke with him for all of ninety seconds while I could feel Fireball eyeing us. He was with us the entire time. Only a mere two feet away. It's not like I was alone with him. Nothing unsavory was said. Fireball looked me square in the eye and said, "I think it's time for you to go." I'm pretty sure I blinked in slow motion. *Are you kidding me?! Up until a half hour ago, you were pushing the shots. Now, with alcohol in my system and YOUR friends (ex lovers?) over, I have to leave??* Turns out, he was insanely jealous that his friend had my attention at all, but even moreso, since I was wearing some very boob-forward pajamas. Ridiculous. With no other option, I headed home, praying for safe travels. *What. An. Asshole.*

For a month straight, that waste of my time sent me flowers. He sent me one bouquet every Monday for a month. When I learned that I could, I refused bouquets #3 and #4. *Pathetic. And gross.* He learned this from his mentor (see Chapters 3, 10, and 19: Toothless).

* * *

Not long after my least favorite Super Bowl in history, I ran into old friends around town. They had heard I was dating Fireball. They didn't waste any time warning me about him, telling me to break things off immediately. He was bad news. The worst news. He'd beaten ex-girlfriends and even thrown his parents around. He was into drugs and had some really shady business dealings. Nothing they said surprised me, and several things they said actually aligned with the fears I was having. He was day drinking everyday, consuming an insane amount of Fireball whiskey. *In perfect hypocritical fashion, he often accused me of drinking at work or on my way home. Way to deflect, buddy. No one can smell the cinnamon on your breath.* I was standoffish at first, but decided I wanted to confront him. He denied everything, of course, and even suggested that I reach out to one of his exes for reassurance. I didn't know her super well, but I'd met her years ago and we had hit it off. "Reach out to her," he said. "We're still on good

terms. She'll tell you what a good guy I am." With really no other options left, I took him up on the suggestion. I sent her a message and
she quickly responded, filling me in. She was not the great reference
he had expected her to be, but rather warned me as well. She recalled a
time that he threw her off the back of a pickup truck while they were
loading boxes for a move. She told me that they used to be into all
kinds of hard drugs, and that he'd done some really despicable things
surrounding them. She confirmed that he had gotten into physical al-
tercations with his father many times and had even thrown his own
mother around. I was sick to my stomach and needed to end things as
soon as possible. Ending things last week wasn't soon enough.

Weeks went by and he begged me for a chance to talk. Just talk. He
swore he wasn't trying to get back together. He just wanted a chance
to explain himself—more like defend himself and lie about everything
I'd discovered. I refused to meet him (aren't y'all proud of me?), but
had made the mistake of mentioning I had to go grocery shopping.
He showed up at the store I usually went to and was parked next to
my car when I exited the store. We sat in our separate vehicles, windows parallel (much like how our first talk went) and made super
awkward small talk. The whole thing was so damn uncomfortable.
He was angry because he had tried calling me and I didn't answer. To
avoid fighting, I simply said that I'd been on the phone with one of my
girlfriends. He knew of her and made a completely uncalled-for comment—racist and filled with unfounded hatred. I sped off, so angry at
who he had proven himself to be. When I reached the turn for my
house, I didn't turn. I kept going straight. A full ten minutes past my
house. I was seeing red when I pulled into his junk-filled driveway. I
reached into the back seat and pulled out three freshly purchased eggs.
I rounded the corner of his house and aimed for his screen door. My
accuracy has never been better. I watched the yolk drip down between
the house and the steps, proud of my handiwork. When he arrived
home, he (rightfully) assumed it was me. I was the person he most
recently pissed off. Power of deduction. He sent me a picture of the
mess. The remaining eggshell fragments were white. I took the eggs

I already had in the fridge and snapped a picture to send to him. The caption read, "My eggs are clearly brown. Idiot. Maybe you should stop being such an asshole and you'd have fewer suspects to choose from. Fuck off and don't reach out again."

* * *

For the next few weeks, he gave me space, but something didn't feel right. A few weeks quickly turned into a few months, and while I still hadn't heard from him, I had this unsettled feeling that I couldn't shake. Something wasn't right. During this hiatus, I had reconnected with an old friend from our highschool days. He lived just over the border in New York, and I decided to visit him for the weekend and find some respite. It was getting late and my phone started blowing up. "WHERE THE HELL ARE YOU??" it read. "WHY AREN'T YOU HOME?" Fireball couldn't possibly know that I wasn't home... unless he was watching my house. Had he been driving by, looking for my car? Yes. And he had been driving by my office, looking for me through the window. He had gone full-blown psycho, and little did I know, I hadn't seen the last of him.

| 3 |

Once A Liar...

DISCLAIMER: Not all of the men who earned a chapter in this book earned a date. This is one of them. **I DID NOT DATE THIS MAN.** He just told everyone I did, including himself.

If I was going to subtitle this chapter, it might read: "No teeth. All lies. Game Over." This should be an entertaining, yet disturbing, read. Make your snacks, grab a blanket, and get cozy. And don't forget to lock your door to keep the nut jobs out. I've learned my lesson.

* * *

If I could take back one night, it might be the night I met "Toothless." "You're way too short for me," he said. He was fat. Not a little fat, but huge. Bulbous. He had the figure of Mr. Potato Head and half the brains. He had tattoos covering his neck, his chest, his arms and even his legs. Some looked like the kind you'd get in prison, but a lady doesn't ask such questions, so I didn't. I just kept those thoughts to myself. His tatted knuckles were what really sent me though: "G.A.M.E. O.V.E.R." they read. *Ooh, I'm shaking.* His beard was unruly and unkempt and surely wasn't compelling women to form a line. And there was a smell... I never could quite place it, but it was pungent and consistent. And so unique. He was missing his incisors and what stumps and pieces he had left were rotten. Definitely could have used a personal trainer, nutritionist, oral surgeon, barber, stylist, and life coach, just to name a few. He wasn't winning any beauty pageants, is what I'm getting at. I'm not one to tear any-body down, mind you, but I was definitely gritting my teeth (ahem, all 32 of them) while he was telling me I wasn't his type because I was "too short." I didn't really care, I just didn't appreciate his callousness or unprovoked need to insult. I never asked if I was his cup of tea. In fact, I had only met him because of his friend (remember Chapter 2: Fireball?), who was still trying to win me back. Simultaneously, he was showing me picture after picture of the amazing women he's dated. Models. I'm not kidding you. There's no way this guy has been with this many drop dead gorgeous women. Not unless he paid for it. #escorts #punchcard #buytengetonefree

* * *

Toothless was Fireball's best friend. Hugest red flag ever. I shouldn't have walked away. I should have run. Broken a sprint, run faster than had a posse of clowns been chasing me. I met this loser when he and Fireball called me, begging me to go out with them. He was quite the character, taking over the call and trying to convince me to join them. He was funny and I liked the way he spoke. Defi-nitely a shyster, that was immediately obvious, but nevertheless en-tertaining. Although I was done with Fireball, I had nothing going on that night and was up for a night out. Why not? They picked me up and we headed downtown. The night was young and the music was bumpin'. It was an awkward situation—this guy doesn't dance and was sitting most of the time. Fireball was trying to dance, but I definitely wasn't feeling his moves... or him. I didn't want to give him false hope that anything might reignite between us. That, and he had a gray turtleneck on with shorts. It was such a weird look. And why a turtleneck? Was he hiding a hickey from a one night stand? I don't know, but knowing him, probably. I found two lovely ladies on the dance floor and brought my white lady dance moves over to their party. The pair didn't seem to mind and quickly became my BFFs for the night. We were getting down to some classic Salt-N-Pepa when I noticed the chaos erupting near the bar. Fireball was being escorted out, Toothless following behind them. Of course. I don't think that asshole could go anywhere without getting himself into some kind of trouble. Every. Damn. Time. I wanted no part of it. And since I'd arrived at the club with them, I wanted to leave as quickly as I could, before I got drawn into whatever drama they had created. And if they both got locked up, I'd need to find a ride home anyway.

I made my way downstairs and onto the street, and the police were already on the scene. Toothless was answering their questions and FB was nowhere to be seen. Of course. He runs and hides from cops. I forgot. I heard my name a few times but couldn't figure out where it was coming from. The door to the shiny black Escalade opened slightly and I could see FB inside. He was trying his damndest to get me to come over and talk to him. He had no intention of coming out on the street, where he could be nabbed by the officers who were surely looking for him. I wonder if there was a warrant out for his arrest, or if his license was suspended. Something like that. He was always getting in trouble with the police and always evading them. Something was definitely off, and I wanted no part of it.

I didn't stay to see how the night played out and ended up leaving in an Uber with my two new besties. They were as disappointed as I was and wanted to make sure I got home safely—and without those two losers. I'm telling you, for all the ladies who have given women a bad rap for our cattiness and shitty treatment of our fellow woman, there are still good women out there. Women who befriend perfect strangers. Women who tell you you have something in your teeth. Women who tear their only Kleenex in half, waiting in line at the port-o-potty and give half to the stranger behind them, knowing there's no toilet paper. True story. (You know who you are and I fucking love ya!) And then there are men like this, who are crazy, arrogant, and abusers of your feelings. Who don't give a shit about what their actions will do to you. Who turn you into the woman who eggs a man's house because he verbally attacked one of those amazing women.

The next night, Toothless reached out again. I was understandably pissed at how the previous night had unfolded and wanted nothing to do with either of them. He, in his best used car salesman voice, convinced me to swing by for an explanation and an apology. Nothing more. Ugh, stupid Scarlett. I shouldn't have gone, but of course I did. I got to Fireball's place and brought my own drink. Just one. I figured that'd be a great timer and excuse to leave. One and done. When I arrived, FB was face down on his couch, already visibly intoxicated. He was in the same gray turtleneck from the night before. Gross. He was mumbling to himself over and over again. It took me a few minutes to figure out what he was saying. He wanted me. He loved me. He was so sad that I wouldn't be with him. I'm not sure if this was another of his ploys, or if he didn't even realize I was there. Either way, it was pathetic and wasn't getting him anywhere with me. This is also the point where Toothless was tearing me down and telling me he could do better. "You're too short. No offense, but you're just not for me." *You could do better? Really?! You can't even find a good dentist.* FB interrupted my thoughts. "I love you, Scarlett. I love you. Why don't you love me? Just love me. Please. Just love me," he mumbled, eyes closed. He was even drunker than I originally thought. FB told me that the bartender was picking a fight with him, and that he was defending himself. Nothing more. Toothless' story differed. He told me that the bartender got a little too close to FB's drink, and FB thought the bartender was going to knock it over, so the former shoved the latter. That tracks. They had a little shoving match and were escorted out, and Toothless, being the faithful friend he was, followed them out. That's more likely what happened, but I suppose I'll never know for sure. Nor do I care.

* * *

Toothless was working at a hardware store in town, and I remember running into him one time when I was there. I was plant shopping, and he had made his way over to me to chat, ignoring the line that was forming at the customer service desk. I suggested he go help, but he said, and I quote, "That's not my job." That's one of my least favorite lines ever. Makes my blood boil. And here I am, feeling like shit, while these customers make eye contact with me and I'm seemingly keeping this associate from helping them. He ended up using his employee discount and buying me my succulent. By now, it was very obvious to me that despite his words, he was interested in more than being a helpful store associate or wingman to his friend. When we were alone, he asked me if I was really, truly done with his buddy. "Yes, I really am. He's shown me who he is, time and time again. And this time, I'm listening." *Ladies, when a man tells you who they are, listen. Don't waste your time hoping their words and actions are a misrepresentation and that they're a better version of themselves than they've shown you so far. It doesn't happen. Unless he's the Grinch. He had a hail Mary late in the game and turned out to be a cool dude, but normally, no. That shit doesn't happen.* Toothless followed up with, "Well, I lied when I told you I didn't find you attractive. I was just trying to be a good friend [to FB] and not go there. You're not too short for me. You're perfect. I just said that so he wouldn't think I was into you. He's super jealous, ya know." *Yes, I'm aware. He threw me out during the Super Bowl because I was talking to his friend while wearing cute pjs. He thought I was cheating because my socks didn't match. He was even jealous of my time with my children. Oh, I know. He gave jealous a whole new meaning.*

* * *

My divorce was hitting the tarmac hard and fast (not in the fun way), and my was-band informed me that he'd sold the house and I had two weeks to find another place to live. It was a crazy few weeks and to say I was overwhelmed would be an understatement. Toothless knew exactly what to say and reassured me that it wasn't an issue. In addition to an uncanny ability to get women who were solid 10s, he apparently had an unreasonably large bank account. He would go on to tell me this often, claiming that he had so much money that he could "sit on his dick for the rest of his life." Knowing I didn't want to have to leave my house, he told me he had put in a cash offer well over the asking price, and that surely he'd be able to overthrow the current offer. He suggested I start looking for something to rent, 'just in case.' I don't believe there was ever any offer, but wow, coming strong out of the gate. That's one way to manipulate and take advantage of someone going through a really vulnerable time. I'd made it clear to him that I had no intention of dating him and wanted to remain single for a while. He said he understood. What a good friend to have (half sarcasm). He was calling, texting, and messaging everyday. I couldn't even look at rentals without him by my side. The support was nice at first but quickly became too much. What's the term—stage 5 clinger? He was at least a 9. It was so over the top. I found a house to rent and the supposed offer on the house wasn't accepted, so there was nothing left to do but pack my things and get out. At the same time, I got myself a case of Covid. Remember The Vegan bringing me a care package full of organic soups, echinacea, and yogurt? Toothless brought me Slim Jims, candy, and cough drops. Between the two, though? I was covered.

Toothless hired movers and paid them in cash. He offered direction to these men but wasn't doing any of the heavy lifting himself. It was clear that he wasn't used to doing a lot of laborious things. He was the one who provided me the nip of Maker's Mark and then inspired me to put salmon in the saddle bag of my ex's Harley (after the ex had called me the C-word). Oops. This guy wasn't good news by any means, but I could use a friend, and he was making himself more than available. It was hard to say no to that. I needed a place to stay that night, as the new house wouldn't be available until the next day. He booked a hotel room for me and wouldn't even let me pay for it. I was so appreciative... until he showed up at the hotel, too, and came in with the intent of staying. He'd paid for the room, so I couldn't say no, but told him the couch had his name all over it. He fed me drinks (just like his buddy—I wonder who learned it from who) and I had to turn him down two drinks in. He would have had me shitfaced in no time, and I wasn't about to let my guard down like that. The next day, along with the movers, we got my things out of the truck and into the house. He was there all day directing these guys but not lifting anything. He broke a sweat simply because it was stupid hot out, not because he exerted himself whatsoever. After the crew had cleared out for the night, and I had scrubbed the bathtub, I decided to take a much needed shower. I was soaked, and my hair had curled from the humidity of the day. I was disgusting. I kind of figured he'd hit the road soon himself, as it was getting late. When I got out of the shower, he had a towel on his arm and was waiting for his turn. He was also disgusting (for so many other reasons) and wanted to wash the day away. He wasn't shy though, and left the bathroom door open as he climbed behind the clear plastic sheet. I had only put up a liner so far, and it was completely see-through. Regrets. I couldn't unsee that. Fuck. He had a tattoo on his ass cheek that read "Made in the USA." Apparently, he'd lost a bet and followed through with terms. When he had dried off and put on some fresh clothes, he sat down on my couch, clearly not planning to leave any time soon. *Ugh. Really dude?* He ended up staying on my couch that night, citing that it was too late to leave and that he was exhausted. On some level, I couldn't blame him. It had been a long two days. The next day he jumped in again, helping to unpack some of my things. I strongly suggested he leave, thanking him for his help, but reassuring him that I was all set and could take it from there. He left, begrudgingly, and I had the place to myself. I was a little shocked (and a lot annoyed), when he returned later that evening, dinner in hand. I had forgotten to eat all day and appreciated the gesture, albeit a bit presumptive. We ate dinner together, and then he stayed. And stayed some more. It was getting late and he was clearly planning to stay over again. I was firmer than I like to be and told him that I needed him to leave. He did.

* * *

The picture this guy had painted for me was pretty simple: He had been living in Florida for the last 16 years or so, owned his own home, and was living his best life. He had come back home to bond and spend time with his estranged father, who he was now living with (and who was dying from) cancer. In order to spend as much time with him as possible, he moved into his father's house. He had had a dog, the love of his life, who he'd left behind in Florida. His mother's home had been broken into a few years earlier, and he left his dog to protect her and look out for her. *Aww, my hero!* Here to take care of his dad, his dog there, to take care of his mom. These would be the first two of many, many lies this man would end up telling me. *"Why was he really here?" I wondered. Maybe he was running from the police. Maybe he had kids he didn't want to acknowledge. Maybe he'd pissed off the wrong people and needed to seek refuge for a while.* All I knew was that this guy was a mystery, but not the kind you didn't want to put down. The kind you *couldn't* put down.

* * *

Toothless was coming over often or convincing me to grab a meal out. It didn't matter the outlet; he was simply eager to have my time (and as much of it as he could get). I remember pointedly joking with him, "You know how to monopolize a girl's time. Are you just trying to make it impossible for me to date other men?" He'd laugh and reply, "Ha! Do I look worried?! There's no competition. You go ahead and get this out of your system. When you're ready, I'll be here." And boy was he ever. He was always there. Even on nights I told him I had plans, he'd want to know when I'd be free. Sometimes I'd get home and he'd be there, waiting. Other nights, he'd insinuate that my date would surely end early and that he'd just come on over afterward. He said he didn't care that I was dating multiple men because surely none of them felt about me the way he did, and none of them would show up for me the way he had and would continue to. So suffocating. Knowing my poison, he'd often bring bottles of whiskey or bourbon with him. He'd ask if I'd had 'this one' or 'that one' before, and when I wasn't familiar with one, he'd tell me it was decent and expensive. Usually a solid Benjamin Franklin, or more. And he found the end of the ball of yarn to my heart—my Beagle. He offered to take care of my dog if he had a vet appointment, needed meds, needed anything. He had found one of my biggest soft spots and was absolutely using it to his advantage. *Well played.* He'd pull on that yarn, a little pull here, a little tug there. Turns out he was a master crafter—meticulously maneuvering this heart string while simultaneously weaving tall tales. He knew exactly what he was doing and was doing it well. *Give that man an Oscar.*

* * *

He had two trucks—one white, one blue. He planned to have the white one painted, maybe an Army green. He mentioned this many times but there was always something that came up, preventing him from getting it done. In the time I knew him, his white truck had broken down several times. The fact that he could buy fancy trucks and pay in cash didn't jive with this truck he had, always breaking down but not being fixed or replaced. He was nice enough to let his father 'borrow' his blue truck sometimes. *How convenient.* He would often point out other vehicles that he wanted to buy. When he went back, they were gone—already sold. Unavailable. *How convenient.* At one point, he drove past a pristine BMW, shiny and pearly white, sitting in someone's driveway with a FOR SALE sign. He was determined to go back and pick it up for me. It was only 'pocket change' to him, and I deserved a nice car to match my career status. Naturally, I had major concerns about letting a guy I barely know buy me such an expensive gift, so I refused. Of course, he ignored my concerns, but sadly, the car had been sold when he went back to acquire it. This happened with many things: Louis Vuitton handbags, Jimmy Choo shoes, jewelry. Always a plan to buy me something extravagant, always unavailable when he'd go to get it. Always. *How convenient.*

And for someone who had all the money in the world (professional dick sitter, remember?), he didn't dress the part nor did he give off the impression that he had money busting out of his wallet. Untucked and unfucked. His clothes were in rough condition, but mostly because they were stretched out. It was always surprising to me, though, that the worst parts of his look were the parts he could control. His body was covered in ink. Not the kind of intentional tattoos that told a story or held meaning—the kind of tattoos that looked sloppy and rushed, as if he'd thrown money at an artist and had them done in one session, half-assed. Maybe his artist(s) were half in the bag. Either way, we all have regrets. I'm assuming he regretted at least *some* of the tattoos he'd received. He kept a red strip of fabric tied tightly around his wrist and never removed it. Honestly, he must've tied it on a few pants sizes ago, as it looked to be all but cutting off the circulation now. He told me this sad story about how his friend died in his arms and wanted him to keep a piece of him, so he snagged a piece of the red cotton t-shirt his friend was wearing when he took his last breath. He wiped away a tear and affixed it to his wrist. It was now faded and dingy and looked as dirty as he was. He often wore a ball cap (but slightly to the side), an oversized gold chain, and white sneakers. I'm not sure if he was going for 'gangster' or 'skater,' but either way, it wasn't a good look. If he was shooting for 'punk ass bitch,' he fucking nailed it. Definitely someone a bank would take seriously while putting a cash offer on a house. Definitely.

* * *

My phone rang and Toothless was on the other end. Apparently, his truck had died on a sidestreet while leaving my neighborhood. *Grrr. I thought I had gotten rid of him for the night. Ugh. I'm way too nice. Ladies, don't be this nice.* I picked him up and brought him home. He hopped on the phone, trying to get a tow and trying to get a ride home—or one in the same, if possible. He was on the phone, call after call with no luck. In hindsight, I don't believe he actually called 'friends' to come pick him up. I do believe he was doing everything he could think of to come up with a reason to stay. I made a few calls and quickly reached someone who had the availability to come tow his truck and bring his dumbass home. Shocker. *Thank God.* While I was busy trying to secure him a lift and secure my solitude at home, he apparently got ahold of another towing company. He spoke to the owner, and although he wouldn't be able to tow him until the next day, they talked for several minutes. Toothless was busy selling himself, explaining that he knew the business, was overqualified, and that this gent would be an idiot not to fire him. *Wow. Freudian slip, but so damn good that imma leave that right there.* Ahem—an idiot not to hire him. They talked some more, and within a few days, he had the job.

He began working for this trucking company, driving the nicest and newest tow truck in their fleet. Well, when he felt like showing up, that is. Surely that's why he lost his job at the hardware store. He claims he left on principle, having been passed up for a management position that was all but promised to him. But knowing how often he'd call out, no call no show, or show up whenever he felt like it, I wasn't surprised he no longer held employment there. I assumed that ultimately, he wasn't given a choice in the matter. One day, I received a few texts from him showing that very tow truck off the road and in a ditch. He'd wrecked it. A deer had 'come out of nowhere' and darted into the road in front of him. In an effort to avoid it, he managed to drive off the road. He didn't miss the deer though, and its impact caused damage to the front end of the rig as well. Apparently, his father had come to his rescue and brought him to the emergency room. The towing company was taking care of its truck. I never really got an answer as to why police and rescue were not dispatched. The whole thing was super shady, but Toothless was quick to redirect my attention to his supposed injuries. He claimed that his father had had to leave hours ago and he was now ready to leave the ER. I finished up my work day. I had had plans to meet up with a guy (see Chapter 19: Skater Boi) down by the waterfront, and this guy's accident didn't deter me. I took my time, we swung on the park bench and talked while taking in the view of the lake. Toothless wasn't my problem. He wasn't my responsibility. If he lacked a support system, it was probably of his own doing and selfish nature. He had no one to bring him home and couldn't go home to his place. With his dad sick with cancer and frail from the day, he'd need to come home with me so I could look after him and take care of him. The prognosis was good. Just a broken leg. I wasn't at all thrilled, but whatever, I could handle it for one day.

#earningmyseatinheaven

I pulled up to the entrance of the hospital and he was already outside, waiting patiently in an oversized wheelchair. No one was with him. No orderly. No attendant. No nurse. No dad. No brother. No friend. No one. I wondered how long he'd been waiting outside. Secretly, I admired the audacity of the employee who wheeled him outside and abandoned him. Those are some serious role model guts! Guts I wish I had. *(This is now a New Year's Resolution—I'm working on it.)*

The drive to my house isn't normally long from the hospital, but this time it felt like one helluva trek. In anticipation of what would surely prove to be a long night, I decided a stop at the liquor store was in order. When I pulled into a parking spot, the man in my passenger seat offered to run in. The same man who broke his leg and couldn't bear weight on it. The same man I had to wheel to my car. He was insistent on running in and picking up a bottle of bourbon. He didn't want me to have to go in, but I wasn't about to be the asshole waiting in the car while his mangled ass waddled down the aisles of the store. As soon as I entered and rounded the corner toward the brown liquor section, I saw an end cap of whiskey. It was a little display setup, showcasing three different varieties that were currently being featured. Two of which were familiar to me. And it only took me about 3.42 seconds to realize why. They were two of the bottles Toothless had recently purchased and proclaimed were over $100 each. Their prices were clearly posted—$32.99 and $29.99. Un-fucking-believable. *You really needed to make sure I wasn't familiar and then tell me it cost more than three times what it does? How pathetic. He must've remembered this lie just as we pulled up. That explains his desperation.* I ended up snapping a quick pic, making my purchase, and exiting the store. I have no poker face, but I did my best to hide my anger the entire ride home. When we arrived, I was a little less helpful getting this lying piece of shit out of my car and up the stairs. I made sure he was comfortable while asking what the doctors had said about his leg. It was broken (humongous, deep bruise for sure), and they'd prescribed him oxycodone for the pain. Lots of ice and rest. The break was on his shin below his knee, so when he could tolerate bearing weight, he could try. I put on a show for him, made him a plate of food, and when I was out of the room, I texted him the pic I'd taken. I. Was. Pissed. I stayed away for a bit, giving him a chance to formulate his next lie. When I came back into the living room, he addressed my text immediately. "That's crazy! I can't believe you found those for so cheap!" he pretended. "Crazy, right? Where'd you buy them anyway?" I asked. He's not an idiot (well, not a complete idiot), and told me they were purchased at the same store as one another, weeks apart. Of course, I know a lot of people, and this happened to be at a store with which I had a connection. I reached out and got confirmation from the owner. Their prices (as mandated by state law), were the same as every other liquor store in the state. Toothless' story about someone doctoring the signage and collecting additional money was bogus (though I didn't need a store owner to tell me that). And then, with amazing timing, they must have replaced the signage appropriately. Fat chance.

The next morning, as I was getting ready for work, I grabbed the hospital discharge instructions from the top of his backpack. Turns out this guy had an even worse condition than I could've imagined. He couldn't read! "Contusion = Broken leg." "Tylenol = Oxycodone." "Ice it when you can, if you need = bed rest." I was seeing red. Not pink, but the absolute deepest shade of crimson. Steam was pouring out of my ears. *What the actual fuck?!* I didn't have time to deal with his snoring, smelly, fat ass so I headed off to work. He had promised me that he'd have his father or a friend pick him up during the day and get him situated back at home, where he could continue his healing. He reached out several times that day (while enjoying my food, my home, my bed, and the comfort that came with it all). The third time I spoke with him (ugh, gag me), I found out he was still doing a great job holding down my couch. When I left the office, I headed straight for home. I did not pass 'Go.' I did not collect $200 (think of how many bottles of that whiskey I could've gotten with that though). I greeted him (way more politely than he deserved) and started gathering his things. I don't know if it was the stench of desperation or the lack of a shower in days, but he was filthy, and the smell was almost overwhelming. Much to his disappointment, I ushered him into my car and away we went, headed for his place. I couldn't wait to get him out of my car and out of my life. I may have even run a red light or two. Whoops. *Cuff me and take me away, Officer. It couldn't be any worse than this.*

* * *

I will give him props on one thing, though. He was a master manipulator. Though downright lying about every last thing certainly helps with that. And in typical fashion, he took advantage of my good nature and willingness to forgive. Maybe he had smalldickitis. Maybe lying about the money he didn't have gave him the confidence he didn't find from the size imprinted on his basketball shorts or his lack of chompers. I don't know what compelled him to lie. About everything. A pathological liar? Maybe he couldn't even help himself. He had tried his best to dig himself out of both holes—lying about the booze and lying about the extent of his injuries—and at some point (although I didn't believe him), I moved past it. Between work, my kids, my family, friends, all the men I was dating (don't judge), and life in general, I didn't have the bandwidth to lament over his BS. He was still coming around all the time and offering his services. Wells needed to get to the vet, and rather than allow me to miss time from work, he was adamant he'd bring him. He was on workman's comp from the accident and kept getting additional doctor's notes to keep him out a little bit longer. Ultimately, he was out of work for nearly two months. Let's not forget. For a bruise. A FUCKING BRUISE!! And something still didn't sit right with me about his whole 'deer' story. One day, when he wasn't paying much attention, I'd asked again. He admitted to dozing off at the wheel, 'ya know, like we all do from time to time. Not fully asleep. I mean, there was still a deer.' *What a lying sack of shit.*

With his newfound time off, he brought Wells to his appointment and safely back. He hired someone to mow my lawn. He'd buy groceries and start making dinner. This man was determined to play house until I let him call my place 'home.' That's taking the phrase "fake it til you make it" to a whole new level. Wow. I tried to deter him from time to time. Other times, I had to be direct and harsh AF. I hated doing that. He had a way of making me feel bad if I turned him away or made other plans. One time, he even went so far as to concoct this whole story about how his father had tested positive for Covid, so he needed a place to stay. He suggested that he'd swing home, pack a bag, and head my way for the better part of a week or so. "Absolutely not," I told him. "I'm sorry you're in a tough spot, but I won't have you exposing my household or my children to that. You'll have to figure out something else." There was an excuse for everything. He suggested that he could skip going to his house and buy new toiletries and clothes for the week. Great. I suggested he do that and get himself a hotel room or stay with a friend. How about Fireball? Besties, after all. But conveniently, FB wasn't available. Toothless' brother had a weakened immune system and couldn't take him in. He hadn't really reconnected with his old friends since he'd been back in Vermont. All of his relatives in the area were older and therefore, also compromised. I went back to the hotel suggestion, to which he claimed all the hotels were outrageously priced, if even available at all. "I thought money wasn't an issue," I asked. "Of course it's not," he explained. "But why would I spend 3-5x more than it should normally cost? That's absurd." To be clear, he didn't stay with me. He tried though, one last time, explaining that he could stay on his cousin's boat (his cousin the doctor) for a few days, however, he didn't have his medication filled and was completely out. He feared that he could have a heart attack and die while on this boat alone. If he was with me, I'd be able to spot a medical emergency and get him help before it was too late. And of course, Florida doesn't have pharmacies, doctors, or the ability to have his prescription filled here. *How dumb do you think I am, asshat?!* That was my final suggestion to him, and then I, once again, washed my hands of him. Ugh. And I really thought I had. But of course, I promised you stories of a deranged motherfucker, so buckle up. This was just the beginning.

| 4 |

The Internet Says It, So It Must Be True

Cheddar dill with cream cheese? No, maybe a turkey sandwich on an asiago bagel. I was struggling to focus on the menu, not because the bagel place was busy, but because I could feel eyes on me. Someone was staring. I ordered my lunch to go and saw him looking my way. He had a smile painted on his face, and I'm not sure he even blinked. The line was long, and clearly he wouldn't be looking away anytime soon, and I wouldn't be leaving any time soon. *Just great.* I decided to face this fool head on and walked over. "Do I know you?" I asked. I knew I didn't. I just wanted to cut right to the chase. "No, but I want to know you," he said. Smooth. We talked for a few minutes, nothing of substance, but he made it clear that I wouldn't be leaving without his number. I took it, intrigued and a little amused at his enthusiasm. He was kinda cute but in a very non-traditional way.

We had talked a bit but hadn't hung out yet. This one night, he'd ordered sushi from my favorite sushi place and was waiting for Door-Dash to deliver it. It sounded so damn good, so I decided to order two rolls for myself. I made the mistake of telling him that, and knowing where I was headed, he hopped in his car and headed there too. He told the restaurant that he was there to pick up his order, but I tried to explain that it doesn't work that way. He didn't listen, and ended up with the order he picked up plus a duplicate order, the one he'd origi-

41

nally ordered online. The fool had over $300 worth of food... just for him! I hope he was hungry!

* * *

Another night, he and his roommate were going to be grilling out, and they insisted I come by for dinner. She was a super friendly lesbian, jovial and always laughing. She made stopping by so much more comfortable. Her humor was the best and settled the bulk of my nerves. By the time I'd gotten there, they'd already made me a plate. We had a great time eating our dinner at the kitchen island and drinking wine. Lots of wine. Unfortunately, they'd plated me a little too much, and I wasn't able to finish it. Instead of discarding my scraps, he wrapped my plate and put it in the fridge for later. We're talking shrimp tails and half eaten ribs. It was very odd. I attributed this to a cultural difference or maybe a lack of concern for germs. He was persistent in wanting to show me the house and took me upstairs for a tour. His room was well-kept, but I'll be damned if I let him close the door with me inside. He told me how lucky I'd be to let him make love to me. When I declined, he tried again to change my mind. He pushed me down onto his bed rather aggressively. His door was still open, and I'm not sure if his roommate was within earshot or not, but I didn't let that stop me. I jumped to my feet and had some choice words for him. "If you ever fucking do that again, I promise you, you'll regret it." I walked past him and back to the safety of the kitchen, still angry. We talked about it for a while, and clearly, he planned to play the culture card. I gave him the benefit of the doubt. *Now, who's the idiot? Ugh.*

* * *

Who's a glutton for punishment? You know it. So, we ended up going out to dinner a few times, always to more upscale places. I have long appreciated fine dining and enjoy going to restaurants I've never been to. The experiences were new to me and most of our selections off the menu were, too. Correction—his selections. He made the decisions. He ordered what he wanted and had a really pretentious air about him. He was unbelievably rude to the servers, though I don't think that was his intention. I'm not even sure he was aware. I think it was half a cultural difference in how they speak to servers and half a means to flex. He was proud of his heritage and wanted to show off, ordering European foods and proving that he knew his stuff. I was able to overlook it for a few dinners, again, assuming he was the exuberant, fun-loving guy he'd shown himself to be. What was off putting, though, was that I'd taken the time to get dolled up, and he never seemed to care. I mean, he'd compliment me briefly, but then he was completely focused on his own appearance. He once spent forty-five minutes asking me about his new linen shirt, feeling pretty proud of it. It was white. Plain. There was nothing notable about it. "Looks great!" I said. We moved onto his Ray-Bans, his watch, and his shoes. Shit got real old real quick. In the same breath, he was also carefree, dancing down the street, skipping, his sweater tied around his shoulders. Hence, The Albanian Fairy. He gave off some serious vibes—I'll let you discover them for yourself. He was so focused on his appearance, brand names, and making sure he had the finest things. But at the same time, he was goofy. The same guy who cared about appearances was the same guy who would skip down the street. The same guy who wouldn't bring home overpriced leftovers from a fancy restaurant was the same guy who saved my scraps to be eaten later. He had even told me about his upbringing once—that his family was poor and his mother would bring scraps home from the restaurant she worked at, straight from peoples' plates. It was sad, really, how he was denying who he was to pretend to be someone he wasn't at all. Whatever charm I found him to have originally was quickly diminishing.

We hadn't had a chance to really bond, and yet he was so pushy, begging for sex. On our fourth or fifth date, he really played the culture card. He doubled down. He told me that he looked up dating in the U.S. and inquired 'what happens after four or five dates?' According to the internet, we were supposed to be exploring each other intimately by now, and he expected that. We were supposed to be fucking, and since we hadn't yet, I was letting him down. That was our last date. I've been back to my favorite of the restaurants we went to with much better company. The food tasted so much better too. Ha. I wonder why. He reached out sporadically over the next year or so, asking for another opportunity to get together, but I just couldn't shake what I'd come to know about him. And hell, if I was supposed to put out by date #3, surely I'd be expected to spread my legs for him the first time we reconnected. Math is not my forte, but he made his desires known. I blocked him on all platforms. I made mine known, too. *Please sail off in your #douchecanoe for two... all by your lonesome. Feel free to munch on my leftovers while you're at it.*

| 5 |

Clueless Knows No Bounds

So much of the trouble I get myself into is because I get bored or lonely. It's a terribly delightful problem to have. There I was, standing at the bar, solo, waiting for the bartender to get me a drink. He hadn't noticed me yet, but the gentleman just a few feet to my right had. He looked an awful lot like Guy Fieri but had salt and pepper hair instead of the frosted tips. He wore a royal blue button-up shirt and had a beer in his hand. Although he didn't make strong eye contact right away, his glances didn't go unnoticed. He seemed to be maybe a little shy, or maybe he wasn't quite sure if he wanted to approach me. When I peered over my right shoulder again, he cleared his throat, smiled at me (yup, definitely nervous) and invited me to sit next to him. I was still waiting for that drink, so sure, why not? We talked for a few minutes before Toothless showed up and arrogantly took his place beside me. Though I had made it clear on numerous occasions that we would be nothing more than friends, Toothless was quick to assert ownership over me. He put his arm around my shoulders, handed me a drink, and positioned himself between this stranger and me. His confidence was misplaced, but was still enough to do exactly what he had intended—confuse the famous chef's doppelganger. (Don't be confused here. You know who Toothless is. This new friend, we'll call him "Monotooth." Monotooth: look up Tom Cruise monotooth. Also, sorry, you can't unsee that.) So, Monotooth was confused for good reason. Here's this guy, playing like we're closer than we are, arm around me, owning the situation. I later learned that while I was in the bathroom, Toothless was busy telling Monotooth a bunch of lies about the nature of our relationship. He led MT to believe that we were more, and we were far closer than we were, saying that we'd spent the night together. The pissing match between these two would normally piss me off, but on this particular night, I was entertained, so I may have egged them on a smidge. I hadn't gotten the chance to know a ton about this guy, but he did pique my interest. Enough so that on the way out of the bar, I slipped him my business card. I wasn't sure what, if anything, would come of it, but this way I could find out. He reached out the very next day and was eager to meet up. It was harmless, though a little oppressive. He was very persistent and didn't allow for any time to pass. Within a day or two, he made sure his schedule allowed for him to meet up. When I left my office that evening, he was waiting across the street for me. Not creepy at all. We went for a short walk, and I was sure to stay on well-lit streets and not wander too far. During our conversation, I learned that he had dated a former classmate of mine. She was a respectable woman, and this leant itself a bit toward trusting him. Still, my guards were up, as they often are. The second turn off was when he was grabby and touchy way too early. Within that first 30 minutes of being around each other, he had his arm over my shoulder while we walked (do you know how physically awkward that is? It makes walking together anything but graceful and romantic).

He continued to reach out, his interest as apparent as his desperation. I mean, I'm all for knowing that someone is super into you, but not when he's showing that you're on his mind every second, as if he didn't have a life just three days ago before meeting you. He reeked of cologne and neediness, but all the same, he was also very nice, so I was game for giving him another shot.

We continued to talk a bit, mostly texting and messaging. While I was covering in another office one day, my coworkers reached out, letting me know that I'd had a visitor. They didn't catch his name, but he had come into the office and had brought me a milkshake. It was a sweet gesture, I suppose, but we hadn't even gone on a date yet. Here I was, having to explain to my staff who he was to me while trying to figure out exactly which suitor had stopped by.

* * *

We finally met up for an actual date. I pulled into the parking lot and rounded the corner of the building, eyeing a spot. As I was carefully navigating around the parked cars and aiming toward my spot, I spotted him. There he was, dressed nicely, but anxiously waiting to greet me. Honestly, he was super eager, like a puppy, and he ended up walking into my intended parking space. I backed out and looked for another spot (I should've left at this point). As I was pulling into the next spot, he walked into that spot. What the heck?! I was straight up annoyed at this point, and rolled down my window, "Hey! Do you mind if I just park real quick? Just gimme a minute and I'll come see you." He stepped up onto the sidewalk, very obviously realizing what he had done. *Poor little puppy. You're not getting any treats tonight.* I parked and took a deep breath, trying to steel myself before stepping out. He wasn't giving me any space and was already approaching my car door as I was exiting. We hugged, and before letting go, he brought his lips toward mine. You could feel the energy. He wasn't about to give me a quick peck on the cheek. He was in it to win it and was attempting to give me his DNA and a reason to skip dinner altogether. It was nearly a direct hit, but before he could sink my battleship, I dipped to the side, slow motion Matrix style, and avoided his advance. It wasn't just awkward or a misunderstanding. I had to call him on his blatant attempt to make out with me in the parking lot prior to even beginning our first date. I've never had to have such a conversation before. He admitted that since we'd talked a few times, it didn't feel like a first date to him, and therefore he saw nothing wrong with bypassing the small talk at dinner before planting one on me. Reluctantly, I followed him inside, and we ate dinner. Conversation was enjoyable enough, and I had managed to shake off the less than optimal intro.

We continued to talk over the next few weeks, and it was clear that he wanted things to become a little more physical. He bought body lotion to keep in his car and made sure I was aware that the offer for a backrub, foot rub, or full body massage, complete with a pint of Ben & Jerry's, was valid any day, any time. The offer was mentioned often and grew tiresome. *I know. Never happy. Poor me.* The offers weren't just offers. He ended up inviting me to a sneaker-centric fundraising event, and since sneakers are his thing, he purchased two pairs of Air Jordans for me. I'm not a sneaker girl, mind you, but he didn't care. He wanted me to have them. He bought me a pricey North Face winter jacket and a set of insulated Yeti tumblers as well. The gifts were practical, but I felt obligated to continue to spend time together, as if I owed him. He lived with his mother and had three jobs, and when not busy with those things, he had his beloved dog and three kids. It was kind of flattering that he was always willing to make time for me, but it was also extremely frustrating that I was expected to give up any free time I had for him, even in its tiniest increment. If I had even five minutes free, he wanted a phone call. If I had 15 minutes free, he wanted to meet up to say hi. He continually invited himself over, despite the fact that I refused to let him know where I lived. It was nothing personal. I trusted him as much as anyone I was getting to know, but in this day and age, a girl's gotta be careful. You can block a creeper on your phone, on all social media platforms and the like, but you can't keep them from coming to your house once they know where you live. I had learned this the hard way (again, see: Toothless. Not kidding. That story is gonna rock you.). The continuous need to know where I was all the time, what I was up to, and who I was with was growing very stale. It was suffocating at times, and the prospect of anything growing with him was losing its luster. *Dude, no offense. Maybe she's just not that into you.*

* * *

Monotooth continued to try, making himself available and inviting me to anything and everything. He invited me out onto his friend's boat on more than one occasion, but considering we weren't even seeing each other regularly, it didn't feel right. I worried that his friends would think we were more than we were, and perhaps he would even start to believe we were a couple. I couldn't have that. I was still seeing other people, a casual date here and there, and certainly didn't want to give this guy false hope.

My girlfriend and I made a new friend at the bar one night, and we quickly became inseparable. Every time we'd hit the town, she was with us. We would pregame and get all dolled up together. For New Year's we all donned our own version of sequined fabulousness. I soon learned that she was good friends with Monotooth, after I had just pushed away his advances for the last time. He had pursued her for quite some time, but he just wasn't the one for her. We compared notes and had experienced the same from him—the clinginess and guilt trips. He was relentless and found our newfound friendship to be beneficial to him. He was constantly asking me about her and looking for me to spill the tea. He was constantly reaching out to her and asking her about me. It was nonstop and made it hard to consider anything but friendship with him. And at that, a casual friendship at best, nothing overly intimate. I would be out for the evening, ready to enjoy some live music and tasty cocktails, and my phone would be blowing up. He was reaching out with a mission, needing to know where I was. This happened most weekends, and on more than one instance, I would be walking into a bar and see him there, very obviously trying to scout me out.

One night I had pulled into a parking spot at a local bar and decided to touch up my makeup before venturing inside. A popular band was playing and the parking lot was full, so I grabbed a spot across the street. I was touching up my mascara when I was startled by a tap tap on my driver's side window. There he was, at my window, waiting for me to get out. Not waiting, I suppose. Impatiently needing my attention so he wouldn't have to wait any longer. Turns out, he was watching me get ready. He'd been watching the whole time since I put my car in park. He had watched me add more foundation. He'd watched me apply my lipstick. Perhaps he even caught me picking a fuzzy out of my nose. Awesome. Nothing like a good 'ol invasion of privacy to start the night off right. And turns out, he had gone to that particular venue that night in hopes I'd be there. So sad. So unwanted. So creepy.

He struggled to understand that I might actually enjoy having alone time. I enjoy 'me time' as much as anyone and needed some un-interrupted time. Completely understandable, or so I thought. One evening, I respectfully declined an invitation to dinner. I wanted to stay home and read, maybe watch some trashy reality TV or waste my time on a Lifetime movie. As the night progressed, I was craving a steak and some lobster and knew just the place to get it. I headed out, grabbed some take out, and returned home to devour that juicy filet. He called three times that night (knowing I wanted my solitude, grrr). I finally answered, hoping to pacify him and get him off the phone quickly. I shared my day and what I had done, including running out to grab some grub. Can you believe he was insulted? "I can't believe you went out to grab dinner. I invited you to join me. I'm actually of-fended that you'd rather eat alone than with me," he quipped. *Another guilt trip. Fun.* Perhaps I was a little direct, but man, I was furious. I absolutely didn't owe this man any explanation. My time is my time and it's valuable AF. And guess what? I appreciate my own company and am not about to apologize for that to anyone. Another time, I told him I just wanted to lay low and have a spa night at home. He in-sisted on coming over, and I had to tell him multiple times that spa night wasn't social hour. He texted all evening. I mean all evening. When my text responses were fewer and farther between, he decided to call. Not once. Not twice. But three times. I finally answered, my teeth clenched and my heart pounding. *What gives?* I tried to be nice but struggled to hide my frustration. I tried to explain that it makes it damn near impossible to whiten your teeth, paint your toes, and put on a charcoal face mask if your hands are busy texting all night. And forget trying to watch a cheesy romcom while having to enter-tain someone on the phone. I was over it. *So over it. 'No' is a complete sentence. Period.*

* * *

We had moved past the night of his selfishness. Maybe I had been selfish for wanting my own time. *No. Absolutely not. Ladies, do not apologize for this. Ever.* I was still stuck on his selfishness, not allowing me a chance to breathe or do anything for myself. I tried once more to continue our friendship but was now positive I didn't want it to evolve into anything more. I liked him just fine as a person, but he wasn't for me. Heck, the reason I hadn't jumped into a relationship with anyone yet was to allow myself some time to heal and to grow. His suffocating demeanor wasn't conducive to that growth, and I knew what was left between us would be short-lived and platonic at best.

His birthday quickly approached, and knowing he didn't have plans with friends hit me right in the feels. After shamelessly hinting, I ended up taking him out for dinner, and surprisingly, our time together was decent. I was in a good mood and enjoying the night. He came over for the first (and only) time. I was clear that we would listen to some music or watch a movie but that there would be no funny business. No birthday head would be had. I was feeling good, lubricated by the night's libations, and found myself jamming out in my living room to some good tunes. I was playing music videos on the TV, in an effort to not make for an intimate situation. It didn't matter though. He couldn't help himself and kept joining me dancing. That would have been fine if he could've left even three inches between his hips and my ass, but apparently he was incapable of doing so. I'd push him away, and within a minute or two, he closed the gap again and was on me, hands on my hips, his mouth approaching my neck. This went on a few times before I finally hit the power button and sent him home. What a crappy ending to an enjoyable evening. I had hoped to show him a good time on his birthday as friends, but he managed to spoil the night, and I had to end it early and angrily.

* * *

In between two of his three jobs, he found himself in my neck of the woods and decided to surprise me. He grabbed me lunch from the cafe across the street and swung into my office to drop it off. Here he was again. Still not my boyfriend. Still not a date. And here I was, having to explain... again... to my staff who he was to me, or rather who he wasn't. I passed that Cajun fish sandwich off to a coworker who didn't have any food with her that day and walked him outside. I had to yet again explain that he put me in an awkward position with my staff and that they would surely all be curious as to who he was. I wasn't ready to introduce him to my kids, and I wasn't ready to introduce him to my peers. I felt bad putting him in his place, but honestly, he had put me in this place. He had caused this uncomfortable situation, and I wouldn't tolerate it again. He said he understood and for the most part backed off. His interest seemed to shift at that point. Instead of asking about me, he began asking about my other girlfriend. The third in our trio. He wanted to know how she was and would reach out every time he ran into her. "I ran into your friend." "Your friend is looking good." He even asked me for her phone number more than once. I nicely explained to him that you don't typically chase all three women in a friend group, and that if he'd struck out with two of us, surely the third would have heard all the bad and all the reasons he wasn't for us. There wouldn't be a lot of room for him to make traction with the last friend in our group. After trying to convince me that he only liked her as a friend, he asked again for her number. I told him that he was more than welcome to ask her for her number when he ran into her next. Unreal. He continued to pry with two of us, and eventually one friend spilled the tea on the other friend. This ultimately went on to destroy their friendship. Such an unnecessary bummer. I'm thinking of buying him a book on how to cultivate strong friendships and mailing it to him for Christmas. *Maybe He's Just Not That Into You*, but I'm worried I'd send the wrong message and catch his eye again. No thank you. *Sips water out of insulated tumbler. Thanks for the Yeti.*

| 6 |

He's Just a Skater Boi...

... I said "see ya later, boy!" Well clearly that's the end of the story, not the beginning. I think I met this guy on a dating website, if I remember correctly. He looked like one of the Gorillaz animated characters had walked off an album cover. But when he smiled, he made up for it. Honestly his smile was magical, and that's what kept me on the line with this one. When he wasn't smiling, his monotone demeanor was bland and plain. But when he was laughing at my jokes or talking passionately about his interests, he lit up. He had a great smile; I'll give him that. He was about seven years younger than me, which at first, didn't bother me at all. Hell, I've been married to someone 18 years my senior! What's seven years? No problemo. But the age difference quickly became apparent. He was a professional mover... who slept on an air mattress. Oh, the irony! He had never been married, had no kids and no pets. It seemed as though he was waiting to start living his life. I'm not sure why, and I didn't pry, but he didn't seem settled in life and appeared to be living in a constant state of flux. I mean, how inconvenient would it be for him to pack up his air mattress and move again? He was roommates with an older lady and had made it clear that having me over wouldn't be an option. While this should have raised a big red flag, I wrote it off as him being less established in life and trying to avoid any embarrassment. I wasn't judging, but okay, done. Mi casa is not su casa. Got it.

He was the creative type. A musical genius, if you asked him. I'll be honest, his music actually had potential. He was so focused on the image of who he was as a performer, however, and it really impeded his ability to produce good material or to promote it effectively. His graphics and images were over the top and too busy, camouflaging his actual talent. It was a shame. But again he was young and I didn't want to crush his creative spirit. Sometimes he'd come by the office to visit me. It was cute. He'd make time before or after work, always ran it by me first and met me outside under the nearby pavilion. It was the perfect amount of care and interest without being smothering. We would often 'meet for lunch,' but there was never any lunch. I think he forgot that part while planning. If you mention swinging by for lunch, I'm going to expect you to bring food or take me across the street for a sandwich. Maybe that's just me. And don't even get me started on his sleeveless shirts. He'd be wearing an oversized tee shirt with no sleeves and sometimes a red and black flannel (which by itself would have been fine). The two tops always clashed in design and color and was only made more interesting by the blood splatter print on the plaid. It was all too much and trying a little too hard to be edgy. Add in the skater shoes and the gauges in his ears—it was definitely not my style. I wouldn't say I have a type, but if I did, this was absolutely not it. But then he'd flash me that smile, and for the moment, I didn't care that his power clash lacked power and that I wouldn't be eating any lunch that day.

Our dates were casual, too, meeting at local eateries for appetizers. He had mentioned never taking the physical piece as slowly as he had with me, and there was something endearing about that. Until he mentioned sex. Again and again. He was definitely antsy and wasn't nearly as patient as he was attempting to be. At first, the mention was fine. Then it turned into him telling me about his sexual appetite and his past lovers. He had the appetite of a growing teenage boy and the discernment of one too. We hadn't become physically intimate yet and here he was, telling me all about his past sexual exploits. *Gross. Quit it. You're about to be disqualified, young man.* He seemed receptive when I told him this and backed off. He'd hold my hand, we'd go for walks down by the waterfront, and would sit and swing on the swinging benches, enjoying the view. He began writing me poems, calling me his 'White Lily,' and saying that he hadn't felt that way about anyone before. He sent me beautiful white lilies once, along with another poem. We were growing closer with our casual dinner dates and our phone calls and with less pressure to get naked. It was great.

This one Tuesday night, we met for drinks. It was beginning to pour outside, and we ducked inside the dusty old bar just before the sky really opened up. We were laughing and having a great time over cocktails, and that smile was melting me. I knew I wasn't about to take him home with me, but maybe I could give in a little. Give him a little sampling of what was to come. An appetizer, if you will. After paying the tab, we ran out into the rain and quickly took shelter in my car. I put on some music, and as if unspoken, we went right for it. I don't know what it was about this night specifically, but everything felt right, and I was ready to get close to this guy. He was eager, and his hand found my thigh almost instantly. Our kiss was electric. Maybe it was the storm brewing around us, or maybe it was the wait, but the rush was undeniable. Neither one of us stopped for air and I wanted more. In one very graceful move (if I do say so myself), I had mounted him, one leg on either side of him, facing the passenger's seat headrest. The windows were fogging and I found it increasingly difficult to stifle my moans. The tingles were moving rapidly throughout my body and I wanted more. I wanted it all. I wasn't ready to sleep with him though. Mainly because I hadn't shaved my legs. This one line from Bonnie Hunt in *Return To Me* always plays in my mind when I'm thinking of bumping uglies with someone. It's a cute scene. Minnie Driver is in the bathtub, preparing for a first date with a desirable David Duchovny. Her best friend reminds her not to shave her legs. "Sometimes hairy legs are your only link to reality," she says, a sentiment that has long since kept me from making rash decisions and therefore keeping my body count much lower than the societal norm. *Thank you, cheesy romcom. I'm only living up to half of my slut potential, thanks to you. I owe ya one.* We ended the night smiling, as he dashed out of my car into the rain, and headed to his own. After a few minutes, my windshield was defrosted, I'd had time to see straight again, and I headed home, too.

The next time we got together, I was ready. My bed was made, my living room clean, and more importantly, my legs were soft and smooth. Apollo, we are clear for liftoff! The chemistry was intense though, and we didn't even make it to my house. Like a couple of horny teenagers, we headed to a local park. It was abandoned for the night, and we were the only car in the lot. Things got hot and heavy quickly and he was on top of me in no time at all. Car sex is definitely not my usual style, but hey, we weren't hurting anybody. Why not? He started out strong, but his movements became more fumbled and spastic. I felt him grow soft against me. His body was betraying him, despite my encouragement. No shame in his game. No shame whatsoever. We ended the evening's activities early, as he was clearly embarrassed about his inability to perform. I brushed it off and figured we'd try again another time. This wasn't the first time a man has had issues on attempt #1. I gave him the pep talk he needed, several times, and thought maybe we were in the clear. The next outing, he convinced me to revisit the same ballpark. I think he needed to prove to himself that he could do it this time and wanted the same exact set up to do so. Red flag alert. Why are we parking in the same spot? *Why do we have to have car sex? We're adults. Hey, I even have a real bed.* Somehow, it didn't seem like the right moment to remind him of that.

He had pulled the hair tie off my wrist and insisted on using it on himself. He was already struggling with performance anxiety, and it showed. Poor guy. I tried to reassure him and gave him full reign. I wasn't putting any pressure on him. He finally was ready to go and seized his moment. He was on top of me, thrusting deep and intentionally. The rhythm was good, and I was relieved he was finally feeling comfortable enough to enjoy himself. My eyes were closed and I was completely lost in the moment, until... SMACK! He smacked me straight across the face with his right hand. Not a love tap. Nothing gentle about it. No testing the waters. My eyes bugged out and I looked at him with such surprise. He later explained that no one had ever looked at him with such wonder and disgust, and it pained him. To say I pushed him off me was an understatement. My full body army was enraged, and all parts came to battle, my body repelling him and pushing him out of me in mere seconds. I raced to gather all my clothing and cover up as quickly as I could. The last thing I wanted to do was stay in this moment with this guy, who just showed his true colors. *You find pleasure in hurting women, do you? Your failure to perform had you wanting to dominate me in other ways? Sick fuck.* He admitted that several women in his past had not been fans of that either. I was flabbergasted and asked why he kept trying it then. Why not have that conversation beforehand? Why not get her consent? Had he taken a minute to do so with me, he would have learned that due to my troublesome childhood, I'd made myself a promise. A promise that I would now be breaking if I gave him another chance. He couldn't possibly have known that I'd promised myself that I would never let a man hit me, but had he told me his kink, I could've bowed out and saved us both from such a horrible experience. I abruptly ended the night, kicked him out of my car, and drove away with one single tear running down the red welt of a handprint that my cheek now bore. I tried to shake off the night but was reminded the next morning when I found his underwear and my hair tie on the floor of my car. I was immediately filled with rage and decided that this boy needed a lesson in how to treat women, or rather, how to not be a total douche.

* * *

We talked about his missteps and how consent and respect are very real things. He was apologetic (I think for a second he genuinely was) and made me promise to hold him to a new standard that he was setting for himself. He agreed that we need not rush the physical aspect of our relationship, could pump the breaks, and could get back to getting to know each other a bit more. In fact, he swore that he didn't want sex and wouldn't make a move for a while and asked me to hold him to that if he should lose his way. He asked me out for a daytime beverage, and trusting that he wouldn't try anything, I agreed to meet him. Our time was awkward at best, and the cloud of regret lingered heavily. When we left the restaurant, we walked outside together. I politely hugged him and prepared to walk to my own car alone. He grabbed my hand and stopped me, asking if he could come over to my place. I quickly reminded him of our agreement and that that was a bad idea. Not lying, you guys. He put his hands in his pants pockets and jutted out his bottom lip. We're talking a full-blown four-year-old temper tantrum. I'm pretty sure I laughed audibly right then and there. Who does that? It'd be one thing if he was trying to be cute, but without a doubt, he was legitimately pouting. He admitted that it was his idea to hold off on being physical, but that he already regretted his decision and wished I would reconsider.

A few weeks went by and he was trying like hell to be on his best behavior. We hadn't gotten together again, much to his dismay, but I wasn't about to put myself in that position again. He clearly wanted sex, and we, together, weren't ready for that. He had spent the couple of months that we were talking trying to prove himself to me. Not with professional accomplishments, not having me meet his mother, but by trying to prove that he was the best lover I'd ever have. He'd made that statement many times but had yet to prove it. *Time to put your dick where your mouth is. Well, that's not exactly what I meant.* Anyhow, he begged for a chance to come over and talk. He wanted to apologize profusely and said he had given our situation a lot of thought. He wanted a chance to explain himself, express his regrets, and discuss whether or not we had even the slightest chance of a future. I'm all for making things right and reluctantly granted his wish.

He came over, and we sat and talked for a long while. He was very direct and admitted that since we hadn't successfully experienced each other physically, it was all he could think about. He was consumed by the fact that he hadn't proven himself to me and believed if given the chance, it would be so incredible that I'd never want another man in any way. He had often expressed how endowed he was, and that the women he'd had always came back for more. He was hung up on being hung and wanted—no, needed me—to tell him so. He was desperate for me to tell him he had the largest dick I'd ever seen. There was a lot of hesitation on my part. Did I hear him correctly? Again, he asked me to indulge him. "I just need to hear it. Please tell me I'm the biggest you've ever seen. I just need to hear it. Tell me you've never had a bigger dick than mine...? Please," he muttered. The hesitation continued. I swear you could hear a fly in the corner of the window, buzzing loudly, desperately trying to flee from our conversation. *Little fly, you're not going anywhere. We're in this together. Sucks to be you.*

"Do you want me to lie? Would that really make you feel better?" I replied. My delivery could have been nicer I suppose, but I was over this ping pong match and done playing this game. He jumped to his feet, defeated, exclaiming that my response clearly indicated that I had had bigger. Which meant better. Which meant that he would never be able to measure up. That he'd never be able to satisfy me. That it wasn't his fault that he had never been able to perform, but rather my fault. I was too intimidating and professional. My body was too curvaceous and sexy, and I'd been with larger-cocked men, therefore making it impossible for him to stand up to my past partners. He actually said that. It was my fault that he was sex-centric, and my fault that he never stood a chance at finding pleasure within the warmth of my legs because I was too amazing. I wasn't even mad. Just impressed. He blocked me on social media, and soon thereafter I saw he'd found a little honey—a young blonde thing in her twenties. She looked inexperienced and unexpectant, and I'm sure he was rocking her world. Good for him. I'm thrilled for them. I hope for their anniversary, she buys him a real bed and sheets with a high thread count. And all the hair ties he could ever need.

| 7 |

Dishonorable Mentions (Part 1)

DISCLAIMER: The stories you are about to read in this particular chapter, while all still true, did not necessarily occur during this open dating period in my life. I've met plenty of questionable characters over the years, and these are just a few too good not to share. A palate cleanser, if you will. Enjoy.

Playing Footsies

I met Foot Fetish Guy online. This time I was the initiator. He was cute-ish. I was single. He was receptive to meeting up. We'd talked a bunch, sometimes messaging, but lots of phone calls. It wasn't like we'd talk into the wee hours of the night or anything, but I'd chat with him when I was driving from point A to point B. He and I met up for the first time in a parking lot. He was driving by, completely unplanned, so he suggested we finally meet face-to-face. We talked for a few minutes, during which my nosy neighbor drove in. Also unplanned. He was there to pick up one of his kids, and of course, noticed me with some strange man. This married neighbor had been hitting on me, his eyes wandering, since I'd moved in next door. Foot Fetish Guy (brilliantly, might I add) suggested that we kiss. That way the neighbor would think that I had a guy, and maybe he'd move on. I had to make a split decision, and I went with it. *Nice work. Very smooth.* We ended up going on two dates. The dinners were decent enough, and we went for a walk afterward. I noticed him staring at my feet (he certainly wasn't trying to hide this), and once I called him out, all bets were off. He became obsessed, asking for foot pictures, videos, anything. *Do y'all have foot videos on your phone? I mean, I'm mighty talented when it comes to picking things up with my toes, but am I supposed to be filming these feats? Missed opportunity, I guess.* To each their own, but honestly, I'm not a fan of my feet, so if you're looking for someone who will let you suck her toes, you picked the wrong gal. *Move along. #Ikissedthatmouth #eww*

He ended up working at the bar (ya know, the one with "the" bartender), and even after I was no longer on the market, kept reaching out, begging to come over so he could massage my feet. By then, he had a girlfriend. It gets worse. After I said no, and after he surely knew I was taken, he went off the deep end, desperately asking all the servers and bartenders at the bar for pictures and videos of their feet. *I wonder if there's a support group for that. Maybe it's called "Arches." A place to meet your solemate?*

Bowtie

There's no real story here, but anyone whom my college-aged coworkers pick on me about deserves a mention. Especially if he consistently wears a bowtie. "Bowtie," as we now call him, always wore—you guessed it. A bowtie. He was always super matchy too. From his hat to his earring, his bowtie and socks. About a year and a half before, he had asked me to join him for dinner and a show. I very politely refused, citing some other (fictitious) obligation. About a year passed, relatively quickly as they do, and I hadn't heard from him. He called into the office with some sort of issue, and I handled it for him. Of course, only moments after hanging up, he called me again, thanking me profusely and asking me what my favorite colors were. He came in, again sporting a bowtie of course, and handed me an oversized vase of homegrown dahlias. They were stunning. When those died, he was back in a week later with round two. They were even more beautiful than the first. Again, his bowtie matched the arrangement he'd brought me. Again, he asked me to accompany him for drinks sometime. And by 'sometime,' he was hoping for that night. I politely declined, this time explaining that I had a fella now. He told me how stunning I was and how lucky he'd be to take me out (yada yada), but eventually he understood and backed off. Fast forward another six months. He called the office and I answered. He was tickled pink to get me on the other end of the line, and after I'd taken care of his agenda, our call ended. He'd called back within ten minutes, asking for me. "Do you remember those drinks we never got?" he asked. "I do," I replied. "Well? What do you say we get them?" Punchline: I still declined. The best part? He's 80... and married. *But thanks for the flowers. They were almost as lovely as your bowtie collection. And thanks for being half as classy.*

GI Joe

This one, a dear friend from years ago, reached out. We'd caught feelings many moons ago, but both being married, we turned it off immediately and did nothing about it. Fast forward to reconnecting while I was single. We had planned to just talk, but things happened. Before I knew it, I was straddling him in his truck (man, what is it with me in cars and trucks? #truckslut). Anyway, we were kissing, nothing more. No hands were used, but I may have begun sliding up and down on top of him. Before I knew it, our high-school makeout session resulted in just that... He returned to base from his break, still in his military uniform. His CO noticed his collar was up, but I really hope he didn't notice the wet spot on the front of his pants. *Don't worry. It happens to everybody. Now THAT'S an honorable discharge!*

The Creepiest of Patients

This 'gentleman' would come into my office. He had an appointment, during which apparently I caught his eye. He would smile at me and make small talk (honestly, my gaydar was going off). He needed some one-on-one time with me, which was normal and not suspicious. One day, he'd misplaced his phone somewhere in the office. He asked me to call it real quick, and given that I was dealing with three fires at that particular moment, I didn't truly process what he'd asked of me. With my personal cell phone in hand, he called out his number and I dialed without hesitation. He followed the ringtone and found his phone in the bathroom. I realized almost immediately what I'd done, but since we'd built a bit of a rapport, I wasn't overly worried. That is, until he said, "Great. Now you have my number" and winked at me. Eww. He started coming into the office with increased frequency, always completely unnecessarily and armed with a ridiculous excuse. He kept demanding additional classes with me, saying he needed more assistance (he didn't). I was definitely getting the feeling he was into me, especially given the fact that he'd make it a point to stop by whatever location I was in on any given day. Oh, that and the constant 'fuck me' eyes he was giving me. He would undress me with his eyes and make damn sure I knew it.

He started by texting me (now that he had my number) and ended up finding me online on various social media platforms. He was a married father of two, but that didn't stop him. Didn't even slow him down. I would get memes, GIFs, and messages at all times of day and night, and he'd invite me to events he was working. He worked at a hotel. How convenient. He was beginning to make everyone else in the office uncomfortable too. One day I was busy working and didn't notice his arrival until a coworker told me to stay in my office and close the door because he was here... again. He wasn't in the office, mind you. He was out front, pacing the front of the building as if he was on patrol, guarding our front entrance. He would do this often, hoping to catch me, and when I'd check my phone again, there'd be dozens of messages from him. I ended up telling him that if he kept messaging, I'd block him, and that if he came into any of my offices without a legitimate reason or appointment, we'd stop serving him altogether. Although the visits became more infrequent, the memes and videos were still coming in pretty regularly (a bare-chested picture of him sprinkled in the middle or a video of him wearing an open robe and pouring himself a drink). When I threatened to block him, he begged me not to and insisted he'd stop. I blocked him anyway. He texted me recently to warn me he'd be coming into the office and tried to use it as an excuse to open up a dialogue with me. I reminded him of the office phone number and told him that if he reached out to me personally, for anything, I'd be reaching out to his wife. I haven't heard from him since. *Maybe he WAS a slow learner, but damn it if he didn't learn that one real fast.*

A Part-Time Expert

My then-husband and I were in the market for a dishwasher and stove years ago, shortly before we decided to go our separate ways. We were at a big box electronics store and looking to dump money into a whole new matching kitchen. *"Assistance needed in kitchen appliances."* A pleasant gentleman approached us, ready to sell. He seemed knowledgeable, but more than anything, personable. He walked us through the ins and outs of the different appliances and mercilessly picked on my excitement over the dishwashers that were designed to hold stemmed drinkware. "Someone likes their wine," he teased. *He wasn't wrong, but hey, that wasn't the point. Also, note to self: why don't they sell wine in the kitchen section? I promise you, it would sell. Hell, I'd have bought at least two bottles (one to open right then).* Best Buy, as I call him, not only assisted us for that visit, but continued on our second and third visits to the store. We had finally decided which set we wanted and were ready to open that wallet. I'm sure he was excited for the commission, but I later learned that that wasn't all he was excited about. When we finished purchasing our new black stainless steel appliances and said our goodbyes, I didn't figure I'd be seeing that salesman again. This state is small though, and many months later, I ran into him.

At first, I couldn't place him. He definitely looked familiar, but I was still struggling to figure out how I knew him. It was only when he started teasing me about the wine-glass-holding dishwasher rack, that I figured it out. We ended up going for a walk together, and he tried for other outings after that. He was desperate to take me out on a date, but I was in my self-care phase, unwilling to commit, and he'd made it clear that he felt a certain way about me. He never knew what I saw in my ex, and like so many, promised me a rich future full of love and laughter, should I choose to date him. Another one of those men who told me I would be their queen. Another man who wasn't for me but tried to change my mind. Best Buy only worked at the store part-time, and yet he managed to find me every time I came in, which was seldom. He would reach out sporadically, keeping tabs on me, afraid of losing touch altogether. Our timing never aligned, and honestly, I have no need for a new refrigerator at the moment, so I'm not quite sure when I'll see him again.

"V-Card! Get your V-Card here!!"

I once worked with a young man who was not only immature, but clearly had been sheltered his whole life. He was still living with his parents, and at the ripe old age of 20, had to abide by their rules. They were extremely strict and sickeningly overbearing. Maybe because he was a little special. Maybe because he was their youngest and the only one still living at home. Who knows. But to make matters worse, we worked with his father. This meant that he was almost never without parental supervision. His father was his boss at home and at work.

This kid never got a nickname, but let's call him "PBR." After work on Fridays, you could find him in the warehouse, pounding PBRs, can after can. He'd be tipsy and stumbling out the door but would always get home safely, thanks to his daddy. Because his father was well-liked throughout the company, he, too, was accepted by most and grew more and more comfortable around his peers. He began over-sharing details of his life with his co-workers and wasn't shy about still being a virgin. In fact, he bravely admitted that he had yet to even experience his first kiss. Although there was some ridicule over this, it became more of a mission for his co-workers than an opportunity to harass this kid. I think they honestly felt bad for him. Hell, I felt bad for him. He'd been so sheltered for so long and didn't know the first thing about dating, much less socializing. He had no tact and no filter, and I often wondered if he was on the spectrum. He was a good kid, though, and like the rest of the crew, I'd grown a fondness for him (though unlike the rest, I wasn't on a mission to get him laid).

He'd grown more and more daring on these beer-fueled Friday evenings and would bring on the flirt (or at least try). This one particular Friday afternoon, amidst the laughter and loud end-of-week banter, we were having our own side conversation. He was telling me about an idea his dad had. "So, basically, he thinks I need to find someone 'more mature.' Someone 'seasoned' with 'plenty of experience.' An older, very experienced woman. Like you." I blinked a few times, so hard I'm pretty sure had the room been silent; everyone could have heard. I paused. Surely, I was misunderstanding what he was saying. I waited. "So, what do you think? My dad thinks that we should just go to your car and have sex. You can take my virginity, and ya know, with all of your experience... and I'm sure you have had A LOT of sex... ya know, you could teach me some things," he said. "I'd even pay you. Dad said that's the polite thing to do." I was flabbergasted. I tried to explain that he shouldn't be in a rush, and that it'd be far more special with the right woman when it did eventually happen.

Spoiler alert: I did not steal this kid's V-Card. I stopped partaking in Friday happy hour, and I no longer made conversation, let alone eye contact, with his asshole father. *Though he wasn't wrong. I'm sure I could've not only taught his kiddo a thing or two, but could have blown his mind, being the slutty vixen that I apparently am. #teacherforhire*

A Real Connection

In another life and many moons ago, I was a cub scout den leader for my sons. I helped with all the events and fundraisers, including the pinewood derby. I knew most of the parents, but not all. There was one guy who walked past me in the hall, his entire body turning my way, his eyes locking with mine. With my usual pleasant demeanor and welcoming tone, I returned a smile and kept walking. Little did I know that that one look was all it would take. He learned my first name and then found me on the email distribution list. Then, using my first and last name, he found me online. He started texting and messaging me. At first, it was relatively tame... until it wasn't. He knew I was married, but that didn't stop him from believing there was a 'real connection' between us. "You looked into my soul," he said. That one innocent smile in passing had him convinced that I was the one he'd always been missing. That we belonged together. He said no one had ever looked at him the way I had, and I could deny it if I wanted to, but that he knew the truth. Although we never got together or hung out, he became obsessed. His obsession, paired with rejection, quickly grew into harassment. He was desperate to see me, to talk to me. He wouldn't take no for an answer and the more I pushed him away and reinforced my barriers, the angrier he got. He got verbally abusive, calling me names and threatening to come find me. The graphic tee shirts he wore were disturbing enough: Ronald McDonald wanting some beaver, wording about getting pussy that left nothing to the imagination. Shirts that were as filthy as you could imagine. Nothing you wanted to be subjected to, let alone have your kids read. Really gross. No shame. No tact. His game got really old and really ugly, and despite the clear disdain I now had for him, he pressed on. He felt we had a real connection and that (ready for this?)—I owed him something. A date. A chance. Sex. A kiss at the very least. He wanted me so damn bad that I owed him a chance to experience me. To experience my body because he'd lost sleep fantasizing about what it would be like to enter me. We reached a new level of scary: absolute terror. This man had lost his connection with reality and truly felt I'd see things differently if I just gave into him. I eventually had to threaten him with the police and block him. I worried that he'd retaliate, but to my surprise, he finally disappeared from my life. Thank God he didn't know where I lived.

It had been well over ten years when I ran into him again (damn bar). His look had changed a bit, and now he gave off major Walter White vibes. His stare was just as scary and intense as ever, but after reaching out to me, he knew that nothing has changed. He did damage that he couldn't undo and I wouldn't be pulling up a seat to enjoy dinner with him anytime soon. It doesn't hurt that The Bartender is 6'5" and intimidating AF.

Two Week Notice

I was a fresh-faced 19-year-old when I met this guy, but I'd be remiss not to mention him. I was working in a retail store that attracted tourists from all over the country. He was a local DJ, onsite to broadcast live for the day. Along with his minimal radio equipment, he had a producer by his side. As a manager, I was tasked with the responsibility of tending to their every need. Get them coffee. Make sure they had what they needed. And more than anything, make sure no one else bothered them. I was the only one allowed near them, and that made many opportunities throughout the day for me to be alone with him. Just him. He was a pleasant guy and definitely knew how to play to a crowd. He was an on-air personality, after all, and it was his job to be likable and appealing to most. It didn't hurt that he didn't have the typical 'face for radio' that I would have expected. He was charming, and there was magic in his smile... and he knew it. At first, I was flattered by the attention, but as the day progressed, his comments became creepier and creepier. He liked my earrings and my top. Fine. He thought I did a great job as a manager. Thank you. But then he'd say things like, "Was that your boyfriend just now? Was he jealous seeing us together?" and "You're really beautiful. Have you thought about modeling?" What did it for me was when he told me his side hustle is photography and that he'd love to work with me... but not to call him for two weeks because he was 'working with someone' currently. When told the pair would be coming back in a few weeks, I told my supervisor that I'd prefer not to work with them. She forced me to tell her what had happened, and almost immediately an investigation sprouted. I met with the President of that (and several other) radio stations. I felt terrible for getting him fired, but honestly, if a guy ever tells you to call him but to wait a few weeks, something isn't right. I can't imagine they let him go because of that one offense. I'd like to think that this wasn't his first attempt at seducing a young woman and harassing her in the process, and that I probably spared several others from feeling accosted the way I had. *#patsherselfontheback*

The One Who Tried to Blackmail Me

I've worked with plenty of creeps throughout the years, but this one stands out more than most. He was new and cute. Ladies in the company were calling him "milk chocolate," and several wanted a taste. I was one of the "lucky" ones who caught his eye. He would walk by my desk and signal for me to meet him around the corner. He'd call the office to talk to me but never had anything of substance to say. One evening, unbeknownst to me, he had stayed after work, waiting for me to finish up. When I got outside, he asked for a ride. I'd given him a ride home once before, and with the exception of having me drop him off a block away from his apartment building (can't let the girlfriend see another woman), it wasn't anything out of the ordinary. I wasn't too pleased with his ambush method this time, but again, I agreed to take him home. Most people had gone home for the day, and we sat in an almost vacant parking lot. Before I could put the car in drive, he tried to kiss me. I stopped him well before his lips came near mine and immediately questioned him. "What the hell are you doing?" I asked. He was unfazed. He reached over and placed his hand on my right thigh, making deep eye contact. I slapped his hand and removed it in almost one motion. He was a short guy, but quite toned. He lifted his shirt with one hand and slid his other down his pants, past his waistband. He told me how hard he was for me and asked me to blow him. I was shocked and disgusted (and despite my seeming affinity for car action), refused. He tried for several minutes to convince me, telling me no one would find out about anything that happened between us. I still refused, growing increasingly angry with this young man's approach. He continued, now holding up his shirt so I could see his washboard abs, asking me to jerk him off. I was red-faced, my redness only surpassed by the red steam coming from my ears. When I screamed at him to get out of my car, he changed his request, asking me to watch him stroke his own cock. Again, I insisted he leave my car and he refused. Instead of reassuring me that no one would know, he changed his tune. "If you don't take care of me, everyone will think you did. I'll tell them you blew me. No one will believe you, so you might as well do it now. But if you do, I'll keep this between us."

I was all out screaming at this point, top of my lungs loud. I was so angry. Who did this little fucker think he was? And apparently he had no idea that he'd chosen the wrong girl. I wouldn't be forced or tricked. I jumped out of my car, phone in hand, and threatened to call the police. I meant it wholeheartedly. He knew I did too, and the look on his face changed drastically. He jumped out of my car almost as fast and begged me not to call anyone. I drove away, leaving him in the darkness alone, no ride, nobody left in the building. I didn't care. Not my problem. I went right to the COO the next day and told him everything. Needless to say, that l'il guy no longer works there. *For Christmas, I might buy him the book* The Art of Persuasion. *He definitely needs a lesson in how to get what he wants, and trying to blackmail me? Check-mate.*

Everybody Loves Jose

I worked with a really friendly El Salvadorian man years ago. He was a custodian, and since I was working in inventory control, we both found ourselves in the dark and quiet corners of the building quite often. It made for the perfect excuse for him to be where I was whenever he wanted. What he lacked in height and perfect English, he made up for in personality. He was well-known and well-liked throughout the company. I'm pretty sure it was actually impossible to dislike the guy. He'd walk through the building mop in hand with a huge smile. He'd crack jokes and tell stories. What's not to like? He was married, had children and seemed to be a real family man. That was, until he started following me around. At first, he disguised it well, but soon, it became evident that I was like Visa... everywhere he wanted to be. He started making his flirting obvious, and although it was flattering at first, it quickly became overbearing. *No way, Jose.*

His advances were unwelcomed, and I made that fact abundantly clear. I was engaged at the time, and the wedding date was quickly approaching. He was trying to convince me to spend some time with him, to give him a chance. To not go through with the nuptials. When I refused and began avoiding him, he told me he had developed a drinking problem because of me. That he drank every day and that I was the only person who could help him. That it was my responsibility to help him break free from his demons. He threatened my fiancé, claiming that he'd come to the wedding and hurt him. He said he planned to bring a baseball bat and connect with my groom's face before we could exchange vows. When this still didn't sway me, he told me he was suicidal. That he'd kill himself if I refused to give him a chance. He'd passed the point of return, and I felt backed into a corner. This guy was unhinged, and when he'd get me alone in a stairwell or hallway, the hairs on the back of my neck stood on end.

His gaze had turned from happy and lighthearted to dark and scary. He truly had me worried, not only for his safety, but also for mine. The last time he touched me, he grabbed my chin and brought his face inches from mine. When I pulled away and turned to leave, he grabbed my wrist, pulled me back, and pushed me up against the wall. He held me there in the most menacing of ways, and I got away as quickly as I could. I went to my supervisor, and together we went to HR. I hated reporting this guy, but I no longer felt safe. I was always on edge, always terrified he'd find me. Worried he'd actually show up at my wedding and hurt someone. They investigated, spoke with him, and ultimately terminated him. For the next two weeks, I had to be escorted everywhere I went. I never found out exactly what had been said, but whatever it was, they were terrified for me. I couldn't even go to the bathroom without someone walking me to and from. I never saw him again, but he's a local DJ, so I'm always afraid I'm going to see him when I'm out on the town. *He had everyone fooled with that welcoming smile and outgoing personality. If you have to paint a smile on, you can't be trusted. And that's the same reason I don't like clowns.*

"I'll Make You Squirt"

I was out with friends at the bar and this guy noticed me from across the room. He'd later go on to say that it was my eyes that got him, but he also told his friends that I had "the best boobs in the entire place." Pick your poison. Didn't matter; he was an instant fan. I ended up on the dance floor and another gent noticed me too. We were all hanging together, casually chatting and dancing (and having a decent time), until it became a pissing match between the two. They were increasing their efforts and stories, the next showing up the last. They both knew I was seeing someone and that, in fact, he was there. The Bartender. But that didn't seem to deter either of them. They started talking about squirting and their respective experiences with making women squirt on command. I was sitting in a tall boy chair at this point, and they were standing on either side of me, conversing with me between them. The one guy wouldn't let the subject change though, and continued on, bragging about his abilities. "I'm so good, man. If I bring a woman home, I even tell her, 'I'll make you squirt'" That's exactly what The Bartender heard him say to me just seconds before reaching between the two men who were making me develop a case of claustrophobia. His arm sliced through the air between this pair of fools, and his hand reached for mine, pulling me out of such an uncomfortable situation.

This guy continued coming to the bar, hoping he'd see me again, always telling me the same things. That he'd take better care of me. That I'd be his queen. All the usual lines. He started reaching out, telling me how special I was and that he felt something for me that was different. He could love me; he just knew it. He talked a big game, and even said that he could (and would) "take" my boyfriend should he try to make a scene. This so-called Squirt Expert stopped coming by the bar, knowing he wasn't going to get the ending he had hoped for. He told me he didn't want to end up hurting The Bartender, and that's why he was now staying away. *How nice of him. What a real gem.*

The Catfish

This fella reached out online, asking me for a date. His profile picture was that of Gumby, and I had no idea what he looked like at the time. I had just gotten my heart broken (see Chapter 21: Grand Finale) and had shut down my heart... and my online dating profile. He didn't seem to care and pushed for a date. Thinking it best to strike when the iron is hot, he was really pushing not only for a date, but to meet up that very night. It didn't work for me, and after telling him that a few times, he finally relented and decided the next day would suffice. He wanted a date even though I told him I wasn't ready to date. We finally agreed to meet up, though I made it abundantly clear that it was NOT a date. I asked him how old he was, and when he refused to tell me until I met up with him, I told him to forget our reservation altogether. He told me he was sixty but then showed me a few pictures of himself looking decent for his age. We were back on for drinks, but still, not a date. I had such a nagging feeling that something wasn't right and tried to cancel, but he managed to make me feel bad for him. He said he was recently widowed and was just looking for some company, 'no pressure.' Against my better judgment, we agreed to meet.

I had parked across the street from the restaurant and was crossing the street when he saw me. "Scarlett?! Is that you?" he asked. I turned and waved to him but continued to cross the street. I waited for him to take care of his parking meter and join me. He was very obviously frustrated with me, though, asking why I didn't come right to him. I hadn't even met the man and wasn't about to run to his side. If that didn't already leave a bad taste in my mouth, when he came into the light, I got a better look at him. He might be sixty, but if you told me he was seventy, I'd believe it. The pictures he'd shown me had to have been taken at least 15-20 years ago. He was gray-haired and cross-eyed. He was definitely not the guy he had pretended to be. We sat at the bar and ordered apps and a round of drinks. He did the thing (ladies, you know what I'm talking about) where he turns in his stool toward you and puts one foot on the rung of your stool and the other on the rung of the bar. I was basically between his legs. Super gross. He spent the entire time telling me what a catch he was and how lucky I would be to give him a chance. I couldn't look him in the eye though (mostly because I wasn't sure which one was looking at me—I'm an asshole, I know). I respectfully reached out later that night, telling him I wasn't interested, and he did his best to convince me to reconsider. It was like a weird real estate negotiation. Zero interest. When I turned him down for months in a row, he asked about my sister and my friends. What a creep! *Pretty sure they wouldn't be able to keep their eyes off him. Mainly because it's hard not to stare. Well, it might actually be hard for him to stare. You laughed too. Don't worry—I'll save you a seat in Hell.*

| 8 |

The Vegan Saga Continued (Part 2)

We're back to The Vegan. He was an ongoing and recurring part of my life during this open season of mine, dating and trying to rediscover myself. But not dating him. But kinda? So, I'm sorry and you're welcome. I hope you have your popcorn ready.

The Vegan and I were hanging out more frequently. He introduced me to some new music, and it was one of the only things we had in common. We found one TV series to watch as well. It may not seem worth mentioning, but it was extremely hard to pin him down for anything as mindless as watching TV. He only wanted to do things that 'fed into him' or were an investment into himself. He would cook food to eat food. He would work out or work on maintaining his work out equipment. He would practice playing the guitar but he wouldn't perform on the guitar. A performance "wasn't practice" and therefore was a "waste of time." He would practice yoga or tend to his garden, all things that would directly benefit him. But watching a movie or going somewhere? Forget it. Unless it was mountain biking or grocery shopping, it didn't benefit him, and he wasn't about to waste his time on such foolish things. *What the hell was he doing spending any time with me then?*

Our schedules were opposite, and he was always gearing up to start his work day when I was wrapping up mine. This meant that to see him, I would often try to meet up with him for a few minutes in between. Sometimes, I'd miss him altogether. Some days, I'd meet him in the parking lot while he finished shopping for overpriced natural foods at the co-op. Having a conversation wasn't really a good investment of his time, so naturally we'd pull into a secluded spot and get sweaty in the back seat of his truck. Just like planning well-balanced meals and scheduling his time as efficiently as possible, he'd made provisions for our short time together, pulling out a blanket, a gym mat, wipes, etc. He was ready for the 20 or so minutes we'd have together before he headed out on his busy night of work. And forget trying to connect at all while he was working. On more than one occasion, he was quick to snap at me for calling him while his focus needed to be 100% on the road. But then, when I didn't call or text him, I was accused of not caring enough to reach out and ask him how the roads were. I just couldn't win. He even went so far as to say that he wanted to continue to see me, but to do so he'd have to ignore the things he didn't like about me and pretend they didn't exist. Read that again. I should have told him to fuck off right then, but I attributed it to his inability to filter anything or be tactful. From the start I had the feeling that he fell somewhere on the spectrum, and quite often his actions reaffirmed that.

* * *

One night, he came over to my place. He was all wound up from the activities he'd gotten into at home. He had recently found a rodent in the basement wall and had finally eradicated the problem. This didn't come without a massive clean up though, and he didn't hesitate to tell me all about it. Apparently, it was a North American shrew. He didn't know much about them prior to discovering this trespasser in his home, and now that he knew all about these little suckers, I was about to also. *Did you know that the North American shrew has a gnarly set of 32 teeth built for seizing, grasping, tearing, crushing, and chewing? It has claws ideal for digging and can use echolocation to find its way through the darkness. Scariest of all? It's venomous, but thankfully it lacks the fangs to directly inject its venom into you.* Point being, I learned so much more about this little rascal than I wanted to, and now you have too. You're welcome. In addition to the removal of this vermin, the sheetrock needed replacing, to be mudded, taped, sanded, painted, etc. I heard every last detail of the project. He'd recently finished up a project concerning his furnace as well and gave me a solid education on SharkBites and O-Rings too. *Plenty of O-Rings but no cock rings—we were definitely focused on a category I cared far less about. But how to redirect...?* I'm not kidding. He sat on the floor of my living room, discussing ad nauseam the process of making these repairs and was talking a mile a minute. He wasn't pausing to take a breath and would pause only to take a sip of beer. He must've crushed three IPAs, and surely he'd had a few before he left his house. He was a whirlwind that night, an unstoppable force. At one point, I suggested we put on a show or a movie. He didn't skip a beat and responded with, "No thanks" before launching right into the next set of facts about plumbing and the like. I was trapped. *No thanks, man. If I'd wanted to learn all this, I would've gone into the trades.*

Then I had a brilliant idea. Boobs. The best distraction I've ever found. Let me tell you—I feel truly blessed to carry a set with me at all times. I lured this drunk schmuck into the bedroom, and he took it from there. Do you remember me telling you that he went down on me once? Just once? This was that one time. Up until this moment, I just assumed it was the vegan in him, afraid that I'd taste like fish. Or not be organic enough? If it's true what they say (you are what you eat), he was probably afraid of my affinity for salmon and beef. Or that the foods I ingested were not always organic. He chose a plant-based diet for physical and economical reasons and had given me a hard time for not choosing a plant based lifestyle as well. He insisted that had I chosen that path years ago, perhaps I wouldn't have a bad back or suffer from migraines now. That had I consumed only organic vegetables and foregone the dairy, I'd be a much healthier, happier version of myself. *No cheese? No ice cream? What's the point in living?* He'd gone so far as to say that his friends (the few that he had) were in their 20s (he was in his 40s, mind you) and were a better match for him than my 30-something-year-old self. *Fuck off.* But here he was, chin deep, exploring me more thoroughly than he ever had before. Honestly, I was a little off my game because I was in awe that he actually knew what he was doing. He was going strong for a few minutes, moving his tongue fast and in a repeating pattern, until I felt the weight of his head pressing hard against my pubic bone. He had fallen asleep during his spelunking expedition, confirmed by the soft snoring that soon followed. I pushed him off of me and rolled over to go to sleep. Waking up several times during the night, I saw him in rare form, sprawled out on his back, limbs stretched out, as naked as the day he was born. I hopped up and turned on the heat—clearly he needed it. After a good night's slumber, we started our day. He had no recollection of pleasuring me whatsoever. He didn't remember our time in the bedroom, or the two-and-a-half-hour lecture on hardware and its installation process. So for those of you doing the math, he traveled south once. And didn't remember it. Did it even happen? *Local IPA—1, Scarlett—0*

* * *

We were spending time together when we could, but there were no dates to be had. I'd visit him for all of 10 minutes while he was chaotically running around his house, putting on socks and warming up his truck. Or he'd come by at night and grab my hide-a-key, unlocking my door and letting himself in. We always agreed to this beforehand, as some nights were better than others, or if I'd had a long day I might not be as welcoming of the 2:00am wake up call. I was dating other men, of course, but when we were hooking up, he was the only one I was active with. He was definitely the only one spending the night from time to time. We had talked earlier in the day and The Vegan had wanted to come by after work to slip his chilled body into my bed and enjoy my warmth before drifting off to sleep. This only worked out some nights and was dependent on so many variables. How was the weather? Had he gotten a chance to eat dinner? Later though, he had called me, explaining that it was going to be a later night than usual and he didn't expect to be done until maybe 4:00am. He was bailing on coming over and wanted to give me a heads up. I appreciated the warning and wasn't heartbroken anyhow. It was kind of nice to know that I would have some semblance of a chance to get a good night's sleep, uninterrupted for a booty call. He would always fall asleep right after, and I'd be staring blindly at the ceiling while the clock continued careening forward toward 5:00am.

It was early enough in the afternoon when The Vegan had told me he wouldn't be coming by, and another lad had reached out hoping to come by for dinner or a movie (see Chapter 12: Plow Guy). He'd been over before, and although down for whatever I'd be down for, he was respectful and never pushed for more than I was willing to do. He was an avid pot smoker but never pushed it on me or even suggested smoking at my house. He had been celibate for quite some time (since his last relationship ended), but respected my timeline and lack of desire to jump right into bed with someone new. He came over with his tiny dog in tow, and we proceeded to curl up with a blanket and watch a movie. We had a good time and enjoyed the flick and each other's company, like usual. Noticing the stiffness in my neck, he began rubbing my neck with one hand, then repositioned himself behind me and started using two. He was looking to me for physical cues to stop, and I wasn't about to give him any. My muscles were sore and his touch was so appreciated, kneading the knots and navigating through my tight shoulder blades. At some point, he suggested adding some lotion into the mix. I took my shirt off but was quick to use it to cover my front side in its entirety. He wasn't trying to make this sexual, or if he was, he was not being overly obvious about it. And hell, I could use the massage. Eventually, he suggested I lay face down so he could continue the massage and I could get more comfortable. I was a bit hesitant but had no reason not to trust him. He'd been fully respectful so far and we'd hung out several times.

We resumed the movie on my bedroom TV and I slipped under the blanket, remaining covered at all times. I was naked down to my waist, but never once did I catch him trying to catch a glimpse of more. The comforter stopped on my hips, keeping my back exposed, all the way to the small of my back. Plow Guy was putting in maximum effort, working out knots, methodically working his hands down my spine and constantly reapplying lotion. I had grown so relaxed and was succumbing to my fatigue. He suggested exactly what I was hoping he would and told me to stay in bed. He would let himself out and lock the door behind him. I could indulge in this zenlike state and drift off, no need to shut down the house or see him out. What I didn't know was that this guy, who did leave the house (or so I thought), came back. He had made it to my front yard with his pup, and after she'd relieved herself, noticed the time. Realizing how late it was, he decided to come back in. He hadn't locked the door upon exiting and made the executive decision that surely I wouldn't mind if he stayed over. Of course I would understand, as it was nearly 2:00am and his drive home would be at least 30 minutes. He held up to part of his agreement, though, and turned off the lights and locked the door before removing his clothing and slipping into my bed. Unbeknownst to me, he was laying beside me in nothing but underwear while I slept in nothing but pajama pants. Imagine the look on The Vegan's face when he had changed his mind and decided to stay over after all? He had swiped my spare key and let himself in, not wanting to wake me after his change of heart. He saw the random truck in my driveway but apparently had dismissed it as perhaps belonging to my sister. Even so, why let yourself in in the middle of the night if you think my sister is over? Why come over without warning a bitch? He didn't ask himself these questions though, and stood at the foot of my bed, watching the two of us sleep, naked, as it would appear. He apparently stood there in silence, unmoving, for several minutes. He was in disbelief and eventually left as stealthlike as he arrived, locking the door behind him. *Maybe you should've called first? If I knew you were coming, I'd have baked a cake—vegan and non-GMO. At the very least, I wouldn't have had another man in my bed. My bad. Next time, call first.*

I awoke the next morning, and like I always do, reached for my nightstand to check my phone. I hadn't yet put on my glasses, so like usual, I held the phone mere inches from my face to be able to read the screen. I'm virtually blind without my contacts in and can't see more than a foot away. I had text messages. Many text messages. And a few missed calls. All from The Vegan. They were increasing in anger as I read through them. And there it was. "WHO THE HELL IS IN YOUR BED?" I turned to my left, and to my horror, I could faintly make out a figure laying beside me. The Plow Guy. I was stunned. And seeing red. I was confused but so fucking angry. I threw on my glasses and he woke up as if right on cue, flashing me a sleepy smile. "Get out. GET OUT," I managed to get out between clenched teeth. "I mean it. Get the fuck out!" He looked confused, too, but quickly got to his feet, pulling his shirt over his head. I beat him to the hallway and threw his boots to the landing at the bottom of the stairs. He tried to explain himself, or maybe ask for clarification, but I wasn't showing him that grace. He and his dog hadn't even cleared the front steps before the door slammed behind them. *If you have to get a woman undressed by the pretense of a therapeutic massage and get into her bed when she's unconscious, you're doing it wrong. Nice try, asshole. Try talking yourself out of that one.*

And how am I gonna talk myself out of this one? Fuck. Me.

| 9 |

He Wrote a Book But Can't
Read the Room

The Author was another failed attempt at meeting a man through online dating. I guess it wasn't a total failure—we did become friends, but the dating thing just wasn't for us. Our first date was extremely sweet and thoughtful. He lived a small jaunt away and decided he'd spare me the drive and come to my neck of the woods. He had sourced an entire picnic basket of charcuterie, complete with candles and a small bud vase with flowers. He brought the meat and cheese. I brought the wine. Priorities. When I pulled into the parking lot of the park we were meeting at, I pounded the one shot of bourbon that I had brought with me before leaving the car. I had Wells with me (but thankfully he didn't seem to judge me). I guess that shot was fast-acting, because I remember giggling when I reached the picnic table. My opening line? "Ha ha, I just did a shot. I'm wicked nervous. Sorry." He was amused and loved my honesty. He never forgot that line or let me forget it either. The whole setup was very charming, including how nervous he was. Not long into our conversation, he clumsily reached over and spilled water all over the table. It got on my white shorts but luckily wasn't a huge spill. He was attentive. This fella was a bit awkward at first, but thankfully Wells came in clutch, providing the perfect distraction. The Author (turns out he wrote a fiction novel), seemed to love my little pooch, and once we finished snacking and packed up the fixin's, we decided to take him for a walk. We were in a park after all. Leading up to this date, when we'd talked more intimately, he'd mentioned not wanting to kiss on a first date. It was cute, but naturally I took that as a challenge. In an attempt to be playful, I pushed him to the ground and climbed on top of him on the ground. He was so shy, and you could tell this was a first for him. I got really close... but didn't kiss him. I teased a few times, bringing my face close to his, but still didn't kiss him. I dismounted him, smiling, knowing I'd just blown his mind by doing nothing at all. More than a kiss without kissing at all. Not gonna lie. I was pretty proud of myself for the game I had just played... and won.

* * *

The next day, I received a bouquet of flowers at work. They were beautiful. Bigger than the flowers from the day before, but nothing over the top. Perfect. The card though? The card read, "I had a great time. I can't wait to make you wet again." I know he was trying to be funny, but that man almost didn't get a second date. So cringey. Ugh.

I was dealing with some family issues (see Chapter 11: First Call) almost immediately after meeting The Author, which made finding time for a second date a bit challenging. I had a lot on my mind, and while my family was breaking, so was I. He was so understanding and offered to meet me at another park, no pressure. We played bocce, and minus some healthy trash talk, he was supportive and a good friend when I needed one. *You could've let me win, though. Maybe. Just sayin'.* It was a huge turn-on that he understood that life happens and was willing to let me get through my family crisis before pushing for another date (or the pressure that comes with it).

* * *

Then I had an event to coordinate, and in light of the family situation, I needed to call in some extra help. The Author came to my rescue, no questions asked. He brought energy drinks, chocolate and lunch. He came early to help me prepare. He arrived in leather loafers

(I warned him) and schlepped folding chairs through tall wet grass and up a hill. When we were done setting up 200 chairs, he stayed. He didn't have to, but to ease my anxiety and make sure I was in a good spot, he helped set out lanterns, candles, and the like. He helped pull together twenty or so tablescapes before taking off and even offered to stay longer to lend a hand. Although it was a lot of work, we laughed along the way. I found a blue Sorry game piece in his truck, and the 'sorry' puns didn't stop the entire time. I remember finding his humor silly but endearing all at the same time. My kind of humor. His favorite word might be 'indeed.' Honestly, if I hadn't met him in person, I'd still be picturing a Ned Flanders sort of guy. *Hidee ho, neighbor. Okalee dokalee!* Seriously though. One time when we finished talking, he thought he had hung up the phone. I most definitely heard him say to his dog, "What a hottie. O. M. G. Wowzers!!" You bet your ass I made sure he knew I heard every word.

At the same time that I was dealing with my family situation, he had a family situation of his own. His parents, older and one now completely blind, sadly needed to be moved out of their home and into assisted living. It was a tough decision but a necessary one. He and his sister had a lot on their plate, and The Author started pulling away. Our last 'date' was an invite to his parents' anniversary dinner. This was our third date if you count bocce, second if not. He and his sister sourced the requested dinner foods and hosted us all at their parents' house. It was an honor to be included but also incredibly anxiety provoking to be included in such an important occasion. All said and done, I'm glad I went. I think it was the right call. Unfortunately, he got a little overwhelmed with what he was dealing with and assumed I probably also needed space during mine, and slowly jellyfished his way out of my life. I know he had a lot going on: partial custody of his kids, an important job that kept him busy and sometimes traveling, and a homestead of his own.

* * *

We hung out one more time, but I was no longer in a place where I was open to dating him. And honestly, the get-together was really for the dogs. He had since gotten a beagle (I like to tell myself it's because he was such a fan of Wells), and we really wanted to get these boys together. They hit it off beautifully. He made us a lovely salmon and couscous dinner and was a wonderful host. We took the dogs for a walk and not once did he try to push the boundaries I'd put in place. He gave me a signed copy of his book. He put on some Stevie Wonder and made the whole experience a great one. He could be a great friend. *The only thing I'm sure about? I don't plan on him getting me wet again. One and done. I'm all set. Sorry!*

| 10 |

Still a Liar...

DISCLAIMER: I just want to take a second to remind you all that **I DID NOT DATE THIS MAN**, which is kind of a bummer, because it would've felt really fucking good to dump his sorry ass!

* * *

So we're back to Toothless, who at this point, was still toothless, btw. This guy was your classic narcissist. He knew the game and how to play it well. He'd build these elaborate stories with a foundation of guilt and layer reasonable doubt between each and every brick, adding in more guilt here and there just for good measure. Guilt trips galore. He continued to beg for a chance to see me again, explaining that it was all a misunderstanding and maintaining his innocence in the matter of Toothless vs. The Mispriced Whiskey. Against my better judgment, I started letting my guard down a little at a time. He was harmless, wasn't he? He was lonely and appreciated my company. That's all. And he respected my need and my want to date other men. And to not date him. He was okay being a friend (albeit a friend who is constantly professing his undying love for you, telling you how beautiful you are and how no one will ever love you the way he does). But still, a friend nonetheless. It was easy to fall for the support and friendship he offered and to feel guilty about pushing someone away who was only trying to help. It was easy to fall for his BS, so naturally I did just that.

* * *

He'd gotten tickets to see an adult magic show, one that he knew I wanted to see. Truth be told, I wonder if he even bought these tickets. They probably fell off the back of a truck or were part of a drug exchange. It wasn't until much later that I learned he was selling his suboxone to the highest bidder. Well actually, to anyone who wanted it. He had plenty of buyers and made the rounds monthly. Who knows? I was hesitant to spend any length of time with him, but eventually he wore me down, and I decided that it really wouldn't be a big deal if I went. I arrived at the theater and when I reached the row that he was seated in, I quickly realized that the seat left open for me was directly between him and a man doused in Eau De Marlboro. Fucking Fireball. I did my best to remain civil and appear unbothered, though internally I was fuming. I took my seat, both men inhabiting their own respective seats and a good portion of mine as well. I was instantly wedged in, their bellies literally resting on my love handles, and clearly wouldn't be going anywhere until the show was over. Eww. Eww, eww, eww, eww, eww.

Fireball had friends next to and in front of him. Exes, to be more specific. He clearly had been drinking with the blonde lady and must've started long before the show began. Together, they were howling with laughter and obnoxiously commenting without any attempt to lower their voices. It was so embarrassing. The woman was wearing the shortest shorts I'd ever seen in real life. She had beautiful legs, which would have been better showcased in tastefully short shorts. This was a very obvious and pathetic attempt at getting the attention of everyone who saw her. Including me. It wasn't long before I realized he'd known I was coming, and this blonde bimbo at his side had already been turned against me. I don't know if he encouraged her to try to make me jealous or if that was of her own doing, but she quite clearly wanted nothing to do with me and everything to do with pissing me off any which way she could. And at first I stayed strong and didn't let her get to me. The show went on, and nip after nip of booze, they got increasingly more rambunctious. Without fail, they'd end up dropping an empty plastic bottle every single time the theater got quiet. Everyone would turn to look. I was mortified to be with the whole lot of them.

Directly in front of Fireball was another ex. She was a brunette, and from what I could tell, sweet as pie. I'd heard of this one before. Sometimes you get stuck in the loop that two interconnected circles can make, and I think that was her remaining connection to these two winners. She'd known them for years and had no reason to be anything but her genuinely nice self. If the over-the-top flirting with Legs on his left wasn't enough, he kept reaching over the seat in front of him, playing with the brunette's hair and shoulders. He was more than a little drunk and had a lot of revenge to serve up. Although he had nothing to get back at me for, he was still salty that I'd refused to continue seeing him. He'd lied about so many things and was very self destructive. I wasn't about to let him take me down with him. Honestly, he'd made my choice for me. And he'd made it an easy one. #fuckingcrazypants

When the show was over and folks began exiting the venue, filling the street outside, we did the same. The brunette had made a smart decision and had taken off while the rest of the crew had decided to make a night of it, even though it was a school night, so-to-speak. Fireball wasn't hiding the fact that he smoked now, proudly lighting up just feet from me. And Toothless was busy trying to convince me to stay a little longer, let him buy me one drink. "Just one," he begged. "Please. No pressure. It's just good to see you. Ya know what I mean?" Ugh. I hated that line. He'd say it all the time. "Ya know what I mean?" I can still hear that stupid phrase when I close my eyes at night. Matthew McConaughey can get away with his, 'Alright, alright, alright." He's got the conviction and southern drawl to pull it off, but Toothless had anything but. It gave me bad, cold chills every time he uttered those words.

The bitchy blonde's tone had continued to become increasingly agitated, her words penetrating any thoughts I was having and interrupting any conversation I tried to partake in. She was talking shit about someone loudly enough to hear, and it didn't take long for me to realize that I was the object of her scrutiny. I could only assume that she was on Team Fireball and held a grudge alongside him. In thinking I was dating Toothless, I'd heard that she'd referred to me as a 'homie hopper.' I wasn't, but even if I was, what a shitty thing to say about someone you'd never met, who had never done a thing to you. I'd caught several of the backhanded things she'd been muttering all night and was done. So fucking over it. Before heading out, I made it a point to say goodbye to my new friend. "Hey, it was nice meeting you. Yeah, that was me. I said that. The homie hopper." She was not impressed. Apparently, when you're a certain breed, it takes almost nothing to convince your always angry, always defensive, inner ego to make an appearance. She did not disappoint. She was scrappy and mean, immediately turning my way and lashing out at me, continuing to pile on the unwarranted insults. I laughed, making sure she saw my utter lack of concern and abundance of confidence before turning away and walking down the street to my car. *What a nasty little thing. Someone needs to get laid. Or maybe tested. Who knows what crawled up her shorts. Maybe she's just cold. Someone get that ho a pair of pants!* (I later learned that this woman had committed check fraud to multiple previous employers. Good company keeps good company. That checks out (pun intended). *I'll talk to you again when you stop being the queen of Whore Island.*

* * *

Toothless had convinced me that he meant no harm and had talked me into a few more hangouts. I was sure to make it clear to him that these were not dates. In no way, shape, or form was this becoming anything of a romantic nature. Friends and nothing more. If that. I don't know what he told his friends and his family, but despite supposedly knowing we were platonic, they all acted as though we were more. Maybe they were just following his lead. When his mother was in town, I had joined his family for dinner. It was a surprisingly casual meal at a less-than-fancy chain restaurant. For a family so well off, I was always surprised by their restaurants and retailers of choice. I also found it odd that she'd put together a gift for me (just because) and flew with it in hand all the way from Florida. Having never met me. She was only in town for a quick stint, so her phone was blowing up as local family members were reaching out, one after the next, to solidify plans with her. At one point, she referred to me as his 'friend.' In the next phone call, I was his 'girlfriend.' I'm pretty sure he had told his mother and his brother that we were more, but to play it cool.

* * *

In addition to the charges (that I'm sure are still pending) in Florida, I'm convinced he was running from a court-ordered paternity test or two. There were at least two women from his past who claimed he'd fathered their children. These boys were now full-fledged teenagers. The mothers were looking for support and had been trying for some time to reach him. *I wonder if he had still had teeth when they conceived. Hmm. Hard to say.* He was also trying to cover up his past mistakes in other ways. He'd finally reached a point where he wanted to cover up the many tattoos that paid tribute to his old flames. He had their names displayed on his chest and two others on his forearms. They were prominent in size, detail, and placement, and that would take some seriously impressive design work to cover.

He consulted with me several times on this, determined to choose something I liked and wanted since I'd be the one looking at it most of the time. *Like hell I would! Grrr.* He ended up choosing some Japanese styled piece that would span across his chest and down both arms, heavily shadowed with flowers and eventually would be complete with a detailed, pink koi fish. He was there to cover these women's names, convinced I cared either way. I wasn't jealous, nor did I care if when I looked at him I saw their names staring back at me. Honestly. Did. Not. Care. Couldn't care less, in fact. He wasn't one to learn from his mistakes though, and while having these drawn over, he was adamant that he wanted to add my name to his body in some way.

He had tried to convince the tattoo artist that we were together, and when I refused to let him add my name to his flesh, that helped settle any argument. Apparently, he settled on an 'S', somewhere hidden in the mix of magenta flowers and ebony swirls. The tattoo artist eyed me, and I him, both trying to figure out if this guy was batshit or what. And secretly, I wondered if he'd had any real relationship with the other women, or if they, too, were paying tribute on his body without their consent. He certainly didn't have the koi fish's consent. I saw the beginning of this process (and vacuumed up many ink black, dried flakes of skin) but never saw the finished product, no longer speaking with Toothless when it was presumably completed. In the midst of this several-months-long tattoo journey, I was told that Toothless was in talks with the owner of a local barbershop. He planned to buy it and lease it to the owner of the tattoo shop so the tattoo artist could have a more affordable option and Toothless could seize an opportunity to make some easy money. Ultimately, he planned on reselling the newly acquired space. And of course, he'd get free tattoos for life—a bonus that would be extended to me as well. Gosh, I had it made for a second there.

I had made the mistake of sharing a children's book I'd written but had never done anything with. Toothless, whether truly impressed or not, claimed to be a big fan and thought that it had legs. On his own, without my consent (turns out he wasn't big on consent in any avenue of his life), allegedly provided a copy of my book to this tattooist so he could illustrate it. He planned to pay him thousands of dollars to do this and then would invest whatever was necessary to get my book published. He had done all of this without my knowledge as a surprise to me. A favor. Whatever happened to men buying you flowers?! After everything shook down, I reached out to this artist, begging him to delete the short story he'd been sent and forget the whole thing. Turns out, Toothless had never shared it with him at all. Or offered to pay him. He'd merely mentioned the idea once in passing and surprise surprise, never followed up. Another shocker? He'd never broached the subject of buying that building or rehoming the tattoo parlor at all. And yet, he'd told me about many meetings he'd had with the bank, the building's owner, and others who would be involved in the transaction. *What a fraud.* I was sick to my stomach to learn this asshat's true colors. I wasn't surprised though. Not one bit.

Toothless was working hard at alienating me from everyone I was close to while worming his way into my inner circle. Correction: he wanted to BE my inner circle. Just him. He tried to become the middleman between my landlord and me, offering to be there when maintenance needed to be done or hand deliver my rent check. There was always some mishap or miscommunication when he was involved, and when I'd try to recover the fumble myself, he'd insist on handling it. I bought a new bed when I moved, and once it was unwrapped, I'd discovered a small tear on the top of the mattress. He insisted he'd handle it and at least get a partial refund. I followed up with him on this for months, and no check ever came, despite saying that it'd been dealt with and I should receive the money any time. He had taken Wells to the vet that one time—I had no idea what he was doing. But he did. (Let that sink in for a moment. Everything this creep did was meticulous and calculated. And oh so creepy.) He'd show up often to places without being invited, or he'd invite himself. I was too nice to say no, and so he'd find himself at the table alongside my sister, my children, etc. He would steal private moments with them, promising them their own treasures and gifts. To appeal to them each in their own way. My son was in the process of collecting the parts needed to build his own super computer, and this creep promised him parts beyond what his father and I were prepared to provide him for his birthday. My other son was obsessed with Pokemon at the time, and Toothless had gone out and bought a ton of trading cards to disperse when it suited him best.

He had managed to get himself invited to my son's birthday party and had spent weeks trying to be their cool friend who was essentially trying to buy them, well, basically anything they ever wanted, and thus they had quickly consumed copious amounts of the KoolAid. At some point (which was never really clear to me), he'd lost his job at the towing company. He'd been let go due to downsizing (they were now down a truck and only had so much administrative work for him to do), so he had plenty of free time on his hands. This simply meant that he had all the time in the world to formulate his stories and lies. To tell friends of his that we were together. He'd printed photos of me or selfies he had taken of us together and had many of them framed. He put them all over his bedroom and even kept one of the more vulnerable shots clipped to the visor of his truck. Every single person who got in or out of his truck saw that damn picture, and no matter how many times I asked him to take it down, he had refused. He had made me both the wallpaper on his phone and the lock screen. Anyone who ever saw his phone saw me. If they didn't assume we were together, he made it clear that we were (don't forget—we weren't!). This piece of work continued mastering his craft and would even fabricate entire stories and alibis. He declined one dinner invite, saying that he and I were going to dinner that night, and he'd be staying over at my place afterward. At this point, he and I weren't even speaking, and I had him blocked on almost every platform. I'm jumping ahead though. Let's rewind a bit.

This guy had hours upon hours to himself. To eat, to sleep, to lie. I didn't yet know the depths of his deceit or how far he was willing to go to get the life he'd painted for himself. The life he'd led everyone else to believe he already had. With me. With my kids. With my dog. A future we'd never have. A future he could only dream of having.

One night, my son began having an allergic reaction. It was relatively mild, and we decided to let him sleep on it. We'd go to the ER in the morning if it had worsened or if it wasn't better. He woke up with Kardashian lips, a swollen nose and ear, and was covered head to toe in hives. My sons and I headed straight for urgent care and let their father know so he could join us when he was finished work. It wasn't an emergency, but still, he planned to come by once he could. They put my kiddo on an IV concoction to help with any discomfort and to lessen the reaction he was having. The most difficult part would prove to be the wait. They wanted to observe him for at least four hours, so we knew we'd be there for a while. I had stepped into the hall-way bathroom, and when I was returning to my son's room, I was approached by a nurse. "Your husband is here in the waiting room," she said. "Oh, I'm not married. You must be mistaken," I replied. "Oh, I'm sorry. Your son's father, I guess. He's here," she stated. I was confused. I had just spoken with him, and it'd be at least another two hours before he'd be nearby. "It can't be him. He's a few towns away working," I explained. She looked very confused at this point but calmly said, "Well, I don't know then. They just told me that your husband is here to see you and your son." At this point, I was not only confused, but was becoming a little irritated at the mix-up. I checked my phone. There it was. Toothless had texted me several times. He was on his way. He was almost there. And then, he was there. He was in the lobby. He wanted to see my son. He brought him Pokemon cards to cheer him up. Without telling my boys anything they didn't need to know, I excused myself and headed for the lobby. There he was, in all his busted-up, stretched out glory, eager to see me.

"What are you doing here?" I asked. I was clearly agitated by his unwelcome presence. This was a family matter, nothing for him to feel the need to be a part of. "I brought him some cards," he said. It was admittedly a nice gesture, but the fact that he kept a supply of these cards in his house and his truck (almost like dog treats) was already an issue in and of itself. "Only family is allowed in the room," I said, "and only two visitors at a time. I'm not going to make his brother leave the room." He said he understood and pretended to be okay with that answer. I know it must've killed him to hand over this little gift and not have the ability to take full credit or hand them to my son personally. I thanked him and tried my best to focus on my son and his needs. I started to walk away and then stopped dead in my tracks. He wasn't going to walk away without giving me some sort of explanation. "Hey, the nurse thought you were my husband. Why's that?" I asked through gritted teeth. "Oh, well, they must've just assumed, I guess. Ya know what I mean?" I knew exactly what he meant, but I also knew he was full of shit. "Really? I don't think they'd draw that conclusion without some sort of verbiage or suggestion from you." I was pissed. He could tell. "Well, I mean... I did say I was your 'better half.' I figured it would simplify things and get me into the room with you guys faster." Another lie. "Well, you're not," I said, as cold as I'd intended. "You're not my boyfriend. We're not together. We're not even dating. Hell, I'm seeing other men. I'd really appreciate it if going forward, you'd respect that instead of telling people I'm yours. 'Cause I'm not." Mic dropped. I walked away down the corridor, around the corner, and never looked back. *Who the hell did he think he was?*

* * *

He still kept in touch, trying to weasel his way further and further into my life, but I was on high alert. I'd refused to let him be involved with my kids any longer but agreed to keep in touch. Just us. Just as friends. But he wasn't to reach out to my sons for anything. Honestly, he had no reason to. He had gotten tickets to a Dave Matthews Band concert a few hours away. I'd never seen DMB perform, and I'd never been to Saratoga, so I decided it was worth at least considering. It wasn't too far away in the grand scheme of things, but just far away enough that we'd have to get a place to stay for the night. He secured an Airbnb for us—this attached apartment only had one bed, but it was king-sized, and he agreed to be a gentleman and stay on his side. It was pet friendly, so I wouldn't have to leave Wells behind. That was the point that finally tipped the scale and convinced me to go. He'd alluded several times to what a big night it was going to be and joked about proposing to me, suggesting that he'd made contact with the band's manager and had made arrangements. A huge public spectacle was the last thing I wanted. Correction. Being proposed to by a man I wasn't even dating? That was the last thing I wanted. Although I was sure he was only joking, I reiterated that if he did propose to me, he'd be finding his own way home and that our friendship would cease to exist. His jokes around the subject slowed down and eventually stopped altogether. He purchased items for our one night trip—a picnic blanket, some snacks, etc. Nothing too extravagant to have me concerned that he may be planning a night to remember (I snooped for chocolate covered strawberries or rose petals). We drove to NY, Wells in tow, tickets in hand. We checked into our home for the night, made sure Wells was situated and fed, and took a cab to the venue. We wandered for a bit while I took in the sights. I'd never been there before and was tickled by the carnival-esque feel of the place. We eventually settled on a spot on the grass, far removed from any seats or structures. We laid the blanket down, claiming our spot for the evening, then strolled to grab some greasy carnival eats. The show was enjoyable, even though as a less-than-avid DMB fan, I only recognized a few of the more popular songs. There was no announcement from Dave, no grand gesture or proposal that would mortify me publicly. Phew. I was sort of waiting for it all night, holding my breath, never fully being able to enjoy myself. (Update: he has since shown me a picture of the vintage engagement ring he supposedly purchased for me and had in his pocket that night.) Who knows?

We hailed a 'cab' from two strangers who were headed the same direction we needed to go. We paid them in pizza, as the wife refused to accept any money from us. They ended up being my favorite 'cabbies' of all time, and I've even kept in touch with the missus. I let my guard down a bit, as Toothless had stayed true to his word and hadn't popped the question. Yeah, I hear it now. Hindsight, I tell you. Anyway, there was a small, pristine yard behind the house we were staying in. The lawn was neatly mowed, the gardens were small but plentiful, their flowers in full bloom. The *piece de resistance* (and probably the reason he'd chosen this particular spot) was the outdoor hot tub in the middle of the yard. He promised, again, to be a gentleman, so bathing suits on, we hopped in for a soak. The night sky was clear and filled with stars. Too many to count. The temperature outside was perfect, and he'd even put some music on. Clearly he had a plan, but still, I chose to believe his words, hoping he wouldn't turn a decent night into another regret. Just as he had supposedly paid the band manager to have Dave propose on the big screen, surely he had paid God to adorn the sky with stars as far as the eye could see. Or maybe he was just a lucky bastard and things always seemed to work out in his favor. He snapped one pic of us in the hot tub, friendly for sure, but definitely not a lovey dovey pic by any means. I didn't love the idea of taking such an intimate photo together, but I obliged and posed for the shot. (I'd come to regret this the next day, when I discovered that he'd posted this on Instagram.) The optics were that of two people who were together, maybe even in love. Not to mention that it showed more of my body than I'd ever willingly post myself. *Grrr.*

We'd gone into the room, changed (I feel the need to clarify, separately) into dry pajamas, and were in for the night. I figured we'd watch part of a show at most and then turn in, on our own edges of the bed, respectively. Toothless had other plans and struck up a conversation. No small talk. He talked about life in general, love. A future with hopes and dreams that had yet to come to fruition. My attention was on Wells, petting him with my right hand, barely listening to what this guy was droning on about. He was a droner. A talker. I'm convinced no one has ever enjoyed hearing his own voice more than this fella. I was busy playing with Wells' ear when Toothless grabbed my left and quickly slid a ring onto my finger. I was startled by this and jerked my hand away. The ring, made of a collection of smaller diamonds, had stopped at my knuckle and just needed a smidge of effort to slide fully into place. I looked up at him, bewildered, and honestly, frustrated AF. "What are you doing?!" I snapped. "Calm your tits, sweetheart. This isn't an engagement ring. You made it clear that you weren't ready for that tonight. I'll save that for another time," he said. "This? This is just a—ya know, a gift. It's me showing you that I care about you. That I'm not going anywhere. Ya know what I mean?" Ugh. That fucking phrase again.

"How many of the guys you're seeing would give you a diamond ring so early?" he asked. "Or at all?" We argued, politely back and forth for a bit, him explaining that he understood my situation, but that he truly wanted me to have this ring. Me explaining that I didn't want a commitment or the strings that surely would come with it. "There are no strings," he repeated. While we talked, he managed to push the ring into place with ease. It had been a long night, and I just wanted sleep (his voice was getting under my skin and I just wanted him quiet). Since defense attorneys are expensive, I put the pillow back down and let him win this argument for the time being. When silence once again returned, he looked at me and smiled, proud of his victory. "And all I ask is that you stop seeing other men by the end of the month. That gives you two weeks," he added. And there it was. He was absolutely serious, not a hint of joke in his tone whatsoever. "There it is! The strings!" I snapped. The ring was off and in his hand in record time. I turned the lights off and turned away from him, Wells curled up, entangled in my legs. I said nothing else to him all night, despite his efforts to resurrect the conversation. The next day, we drove home in silence. The comment was a joke, he'd said, but the ring wasn't, and he really wanted me to take it. He wasn't going anywhere, he reassured me. This was the point where I realized he really wasn't. He would never leave me. No matter my wishes. He'd always be there. Always waiting for more. Always planning. Always three steps ahead of me, scheming on how to make me his wife. How to make my family his. How to make this happen. *Buying me that house would've gone a long way, dude. Just sayin'.*

| 11 |

Just a Phone Call Away

O ne unusually warm night in September, my sister had a rough go of it. I answered the phone late at night, and it was her. Tears flowing and her voice trembling, she was clearly upset and needed her sister. Without hesitation, I drove to where she was. Luckily, she was nearby and I was there within a few minutes. Chaos ensued, and I managed to get her into my car, and we drove away from the situation. I carried her drunk body up the stairs, dropped her onto my bed, and dosed her with a muscle relaxer for good measure. As I gathered more information, it was clear that I needed some help with the situation. In the morning, I reached out to a local resource who sent out a representative to chat with us. He was very flexible and willing to meet us wherever we'd feel most comfortable. My sister, still grateful for someone else to take the lead, asked that we meet at my place. The gentleman they sent out was great. He was dressed professionally, arrived promptly, and seemed to really care about the situation and about my sister. I took the lead, my sister and mother interjecting here and there. He asked plenty of questions and took notes. When he was done with his intake, I walked him out. Our conversation continued at his car, and he seemed to realize the severity of the situation. Something changed when we were outside. We connected on a more personal level; he shared his own story, that he'd been in trouble before and was in recovery. His situation was very different than ours, mind you, but it was nice to know that he understood how hard it was to ask for help and how badly we needed it.

Over the next week, I remained in touch with this gent. Let's call him "First Call." He was working hard to facilitate things on his end and coordinate the help my sister needed. I was in contact with him every day. Several times a day. At first, I didn't know a crush was developing, but as soon as I recognized it for what it was, I went directly to my sister. She was in better spirits and when I asked if she'd be comfortable with me pursuing him, she said she was. "Well, I don't blame you. He's cute. And he's already met Mom, so he knows she's crazy," she joked. "And if you guys get married, I'll be able to tell everyone at the wedding that I introduced you." This was a funny thought (mostly because I'd already decided never to get married again). He was only involved in the start of her journey and wouldn't be connected after that, so given that he wouldn't be involved, I decided it'd be okay to see if anything was there. He had worked very diligently to help our family, and in addition to this work, he worked at another do-gooder clinic as well. He seemed to have a good head on his shoulders and was putting his degree to good use. For every compliment I'd pay him, he'd give one back in return. I was impressed by all he did, and he felt the same about me. He viewed me as the glue that was holding my family together in that season of our lives and gave me credit for being the successful single mother that I was. Plus, there was a mutual attraction, so that didn't hurt either.

* * *

He admitted that he wanted to keep in touch, too. It wasn't one-sided, and that was a pleasant surprise. I thought that perhaps he was just doing his job and remaining polite while this crazy lady's daughter hit on him. He didn't want to waste any time, and with our schedules being as busy as they were, we agreed on a mid-week meet-up for drinks. I took my lunch break and joined him at a tavern nearby. We hit perfectly between the lunch and dinner rushes, so it was quiet and relatively private. He ordered a rum and coke, and I, being the square that I sometimes am, made sure to keep mine non-alcoholic. I would be heading back to work after and wanted to keep everything kosher. We chatted for a bit, smiles contagious. Our time together was enjoyable, and his honesty refreshing. I liked everything I was learning about him. He was great. He almost seemed too good to be true though, and that feeling didn't last long before he solidified what I was feeling. "Scarlett, I'd love to date you. I've got to be honest, though. I may have misled you a little when I told you I was divorced," he said. Turns out, he was married previously and divorced, yes. They shared a son together. He'd since remarried and they, too, were having marital troubles. They also shared a son together. When he'd indicated that he was 'going through a divorce,' what he meant was that his marriage was in shambles and he'd filed for separation. They weren't divorced, they hadn't filed for divorce, and they still lived together. Very different. He badly wanted to explore things with me, but knew it wasn't in the cards at this point in his life. I was disappointed, of course, but appreciated his honesty. He could have led me on and used me, but he didn't. He admitted that it'd been hard to focus when he first met me. He was supposed to be completely focused on the one needing help, but when we'd make eye contact, he'd lose his train of thought. This guy was killing me. *Tell me how much you want to date me but that you can't. Awesome. Why don't you offer me a sandwich and then tell me you'd already promised it to someone else? Lame. I decided I'd be gluten-free in that moment and didn't want his sandwich anyway. So there.*

We left the tavern, a smile still on my face, albeit a little smaller than when I walked in. I was bummed but I understood. We walked to the end of the street, and then he'd be heading east and I'd be heading west. We said our goodbyes, and he leaned down for a hug. When he was pulling away, he stopped. He leaned back down and kissed me. Not a gentle thing, laced with hesitation. An intentional, deep kiss. It wasn't long, but he made sure I could feel his regret in one swift motion. And I could. He pulled away, my hand falling out of his as he walked away. He looked back at me one last time and said, "I had to kiss you. Even if only one time. I just had to know what it'd be like."

He flashed me a huge grin, crossed the street, and headed on his way. I didn't think I'd hear from him again, and I had made my peace with that. But I was wrong.

* * *

He would reach out sporadically. His text messages were always at random times, but I continually made excuses for him. He worked late. He worked two jobs. He had two kids. He was married. There it was. *He was married.* Of course his messages were sporadic. He couldn't be openly texting me while sitting down to dinner next to her or while bathing their son. Oh, and turns out, they even worked together. His desire for me won out, and he began retracting his previous sentiment. They were married, yes, but they were separated. They still lived in the same house, but that was simply due to logistics. It was easier to co-parent their young son and it wasn't financially feasible for either of them to move out just yet. But they were absolutely done. He made sure I understood this. I so badly wanted to believe him... so badly that I did. I chose to. We weren't having official dates or anything, but when he could find five or ten minutes during the day, he'd swing by my office and pick me up. We'd drive around the block or park somewhere and talk for a few minutes. Nothing earth-shattering, but still, a nice break to my day. I always loved seeing him, even in such short increments. He was a smoker, which is a huge turn-off for me, but he always masked the taste and smell by chewing gum. Cinnamon gum. Another negative for me. Somehow, the two were a magical combination and canceled each other out almost completely. And he never smoked in front of me, which I appreciated.

* * *

He'd start offering to come over late at night when he got off work. *When a guy wants to come to your place at 2am, remind yourself that he's fucking married!!* He was adamant that they were done and that they were on the same page about it. He'd come in, smelling good, looking good, and our conversations were always deep. He'd talk about his former sports career, the one that led him to opiates in the first place. Had he not taken the missteps that he did, he wouldn't be in the line of work that he now was. He was changing lives and saving lives, and it was easy to get lost in that. He'd hold my hand, his thumb rubbing gently across the top of mine. He'd stare intently into my eyes, and I'd fall a little bit more for his charade. At some point, conversation would lull and give way to me straddling him or him laying me down and climbing on top of me. We'd make out for a good stretch of time, but I was careful to not let things get too hot too fast. I really liked him and it was easy to push the wife into the back of my mind. He had maintained that it was over and that they were taking steps to dissolve their marriage. One night, he pulled my pants off so quickly I didn't even see it coming. It was like the culmination of ten years of practicing the tablecloth trick—he'd mastered it and applied it to getting a woman naked in a flash. I had to admire his ingenuity. He was using his powers for good. *Give that man a standing ovation! But first, let him finish giving me an o...* It was a really fun night and I was bummed to see it end. He couldn't stay over. Right. Because he's married. A fact I'd almost forgotten. He reached out the next day. When he'd arrived home at 3am, his wife was drunk and bawling her eyes out. She had apparently locked his bedroom door so that he'd be forced to join her in hers. She cried, "I don't care where you've been or who you've been with. Please don't leave me! We can make this work! Please!!!" He'd told me this for a reason, even if he didn't realize it. He felt bad that she wasn't ready to throw in the towel, but he swore that he was... and had.

* * *

Another morning, after a long shift at work, he wanted to come over. He wanted to decompress and snuggle. I understood (and saw through) his suggestion. He came by and joined me in bed. We laid on top of the covers. I had no intention of sleeping with him, but that didn't mean I couldn't make him feel good... Holy dicksplosion! When he finished, we laid together. I was in his arms and he seemed peaceful. Relaxed. His life was so chaotic and busy, and he was always stressed to the max. You could tell he needed some quiet in his life. A safe space and some solitude. I was happy to give him that. He brought up his son again, and his wife. His damn wife. Although he referred to her as his "ex-wife," the validity of their marriage wasn't lost on me. He couldn't commit to a date with me; he couldn't even make plans a few days out. And although he couldn't see it, I could. He was still in love with his wife. The realization hit me hard. A solid gut punch worthy of a heavyweight title. He wanted it to work out. He was just hurt and masking that by walking away and blaming her. Truth is, he needed that safe space, but he already had it. He just had to make his way back there. A tear formed at the corner of my eye when I told him he should leave. "You're still in love with her. You realize that, right?" He remained silent for a few seconds, just blinking at me, words escaping him. "I know," he finally whispered. I truly don't think he was being malicious, and I do believe they'd made an agreement to move on from their marriage, but I also believe that neither husband nor wife was truly ready to walk away from the life they shared. It needed work, and after giving him a much needed pep talk, and a motherly nudge from the nest, we agreed this would be the last time we'd hang out. I knew I'd miss him, but I also knew that I didn't want to be the reason that a little boy grew up in two separate homes. And I also knew that I wouldn't want to wonder where First Call was while I was at home, lying in bed, waiting for him to come home.

* * *

He still reaches out from time to time, asking how my sister is doing, how my kids are, and telling me he misses me. He would write suggestively, hoping we could connect. He'd compliment me, saying he missed everything about me from my eyes to the curves of my hips. I'd bluntly ask about his wife and how they're doing. He'd immediately apologize for suggesting we hook up, stating that he thinks he's a sex addict. I stayed single for quite a while after our encounter, and he'd contact me saying how shocked he was that I hadn't found someone yet. That he couldn't believe that someone hadn't snatched me up. I wasn't looking for a bookmark; I wanted the real thing. I was holding out for someone who I deserved and who deserved me. Nothing less. *I wasn't about to settle for cinnamon gum and cigarettes. Champagne wishes and caviar dreams? That's more like it. But I've never been a fan of either, so maybe tacos and some margaritas? Who's with me?!*

| 12 |

The Best of Intentions

I remember our first date. I'd met The Plow Guy on a dating site, and after chatting a bit, decided to meet up IRL. He suggested a local Italian restaurant, one where the owner/cook would serenade his guests from the kitchen. It wasn't anything overly fancy, but the suggestion was a refreshing one. Albeit, a closed one. We met in the parking lot, and seeing that it was dark, we opted for the restaurant next door—an Irish pub, known for its mug club and pool table more than its food. It was fine. Still a first. We chatted—he ordered the first of many margaritas that I'd watch him order over the next few months. The date itself wasn't notable, good or bad. When we finished and walked outside, he opened his car door to allow his dog to exit. She was clearly obedient, as she strayed only far enough to relieve herself and didn't attempt to run off. I was distracted though—the strong stench of pot wafting out into the cold night air. We continued to talk, ignoring the chill in the air that hovered around us and the steamy breath that escaped both of us. I couldn't tell you the subject matter but I can absolutely tell you what interrupted our pleasant conversation. "You're not inviting me over?" he questioned. I was shocked that he was so forward but managed to shake my head. "I've never had a girl not invite me over after a first date. Ever. Like every time, for sex." It was so gross and such a turn off. *Should I ask your middle name, your favorite color, your favorite movie, or just skip to what venereal diseases you have?* Ultimately, I wrote this off, foolishly, giving him the benefit of doubt. Maybe his mouth moved faster than his brain.

We hung out again, and he redeemed himself. It wasn't an amazing time, but he stopped talking out of his ass, and our time together was mostly enjoyable. He was predictable, always ordering fried pickles and a margarita or two. Sometimes three. And that damn— I mean, sweet dog, went everywhere he went. He lived with his parents and his brother. It would seem that maybe once in a while his pooch could stay home, but no, every time. Everywhere we went. And that little bitch didn't like me. He, on the other hand, grew attached pretty quickly. He brought me flowers once. Turns out his mother had arranged them for him while he showered for our date. It's a sweet sentiment, I suppose, but I wasn't sure if I was dating him or his family.

I had never met his parents, but damn it, I heard about them all the time. He was clearly bitter toward his life, not loving his living situation or his career. They had a family-owned landscaping business, owned at this point by his brother, and he'd become the unsung hero. He orchestrated the jobs they had, curated the relationships they had with their customers, hired and fired when needed, and would even forgo a paycheck when the funds were tight. His brother, who no longer held an active position within the company, collected his take (and then some) without fail. The Plow Guy was overworked, underpaid, undervalued—and he'd done it to himself. On more than one occasion, he told me how he would walk around a corner or into a room only to hear his mother putting him down. She'd be running her mouth to the other members of the family, complaining about how fat and lazy he was. It kind of broke my heart, actually. His version painted a very different picture. He would often shoulder the responsibility of the family, cooking for everyone, and was the only one working full time. His parents were retired, his father was ill and continuously declining, and his brother didn't 'work' these days. PG's work ethic and his commitment to his family was unmatched. It was time for that all to change. He needed to fight for himself and make the changes he needed to see. To start living for himself and to start putting himself first. Our conversations were often overshadowed by his Eyeore personality, lamenting about how awfully his family treated him or how, yet again, he was breaking his back for a company his brother benefitted from—but he didn't.

The Plow Guy was handsy at first, but after I stated that I really wanted to take things slow, he was respectful and backed off a bit. Not in trying to see me, not in expressing himself, but in trying to explore a physical relationship with me. He knew I was dating other men, and although I'm sure he didn't love that I wasn't always available, he wasn't overly pushy about it. He was easy going and easy to talk to, and that made it really easy to drink too much around him. Not because he over served me or pressured me but because I trusted him. I had no reason not to. If we went too long without hanging out, or if something happened at home, he'd call me angrily, clearly intoxicated. He'd take it out on me not acknowledging until the next day, what a jerk he'd been. *2/10 would not recommend.*

* * *

Every time snow fell, even in its tiniest increment, he stopped by. I'd come home after work to find not only my driveway plowed, but a path to my front door and back deck shoveled as well. It wasn't lost on me what extra effort that took. On those snowy days, he'd been up since 2:00am. He'd worked all day, plowing, shoveling, unburying walkways and stairways. A very laborious job, and yet, before heading home and hanging up his hat (it was cute, fuzzy with the ear flaps), he'd drive out of his way to my place to make sure this damsel wasn't in distress. He wouldn't knock. He wouldn't let me know he was on his way. He just made sure I came home to a place to park and that Wells had a clear path to use the bathroom. His thoughtfulness was never in question, and our time together was usually fun. Sometimes though, after an evening where drinks were involved, he would make our next interaction unnecessarily awkward. And so serious. He'd insist on revisiting what was said the night before, knowing that often

I couldn't recall what he was alluding to. This got real old real quick. Apparently, when drinking, I'd return his words of affection. He'd tell me how amazing I was or how he felt about me, and I would return the kindness in true reciprocal fashion. And then he was angry, of course, because I wouldn't allow my guard to be that low in my sobriety. I was so afraid of falling for someone, becoming vulnerable and getting hurt. Instead of navigating the roadmap I'd laid out for him, he would take advantage of my weakened security system when whiskey came to visit and would throw our lavish parties back in my face the next day. *You need to wait until I'm drinking to get me to share words of affirmation? Or to hold your hand? To allow you to get close to me? So sad. Not saying you're doing it wrong. But, you're doing it wrong. No need for me to say it.*

When Valentine's Day came, I started my day like any other. I showered, got dressed, and dried my hair as normal. I wore red with the holiday of lovers in mind. I had no plans, no date, and no promising suitors on the horizon, though. But I still had a festive heart and a really cute crimson top suitable for work. After letting Wells out the back door to use the bathroom, he circled the house and met me at the front door. While letting him back in, I noticed the gift that had been left for me. There was a box and a card on the front step. I brought them inside, and despite needing to get to work, took the time to open the card. It was from him. It was no ordinary card though. The Plow Guy had typed up (in six point font) four pages of the reasons he loved me. Yes. Four pages. You read that correctly. Six point font. He made sure to include my weird affinity for scents like Pine Sol, rubbing alcohol, and hand sanitizer. He included my dislike of my feet, and that in addition to being self conscious about them, I obsessively needed to wash them. *Y'all don't need to judge. We've all got our weird quirks. My feet are always clean. You could do worse. Let's move on, shall we? And no matter how good Pine Sol smells, don't taste it. Just don't. Speaking for a friend.* He had typed up four pages of reasons I was the one for him, the queen to his king, and that someday I'd realize it. And when I did, he'd be there, waiting for me, ready to give me the world I deserved.

The gift was logical and thoughtful—a migraine cap to help alleviate the painful migraines I often deal with. Although it was incredibly sweet, I was extremely bothered by the delivery. Picture this. I'm a single woman living alone with my dog. My sons are only with me part time and I'm basically blind every night, all night. I'd lie in bed, glasses on the nightstand, my pup as my only active alarm. If he was on alert and began barking, I'd struggle to make out who the dark figure was on my doorstep at 2:00am. It's an awful feeling, and yet, that's when he dropped off this gift. He thought of me, yes, but why couldn't he have stopped by later in the day? He told me I was unreasonable for questioning his method and that he'd simply wanted me to wake up to this gesture of his. He promised that he'd been careful, doing his best to not raise alarm for Wells or for me. At the end of the day though, I don't need strange men leaving gifts at my door in the middle of the night. There's nothing about this that felt okay, and after expressing my frustration and disappointment, I reluctantly moved on.

* * *

We'd had to take a few steps back every time he was handsy or grew impatient with my lack of commitment, but then he'd claw his way back, hoping to continue building something with me. One night, The Plow Guy came over to my place and we put on a movie. Knowing my back was bothering me, he quickly suggested he rub it. Yes. That massage. That night. When I was relaxed and drifting off to sleep, he said he'd turn off lights and lock the door on his way out. *Thanks, man. You're a fucking hero. Honestly, someone give this man a medal!*

* * *

I woke to bright sunshine seeping into my bedroom through the blinds. Blind as usual, I grabbed my phone. I had so many texts from The Vegan. I was so confused. "WHO THE HELL IS IN YOUR BED?" Instant cold chills. I've never reached for my glasses faster. Yup. There he was. The Plow Guy. He was softly snoring and... naked? I couldn't believe it. *What the hell are you doing in my bed?? What the fuck is wrong with you?? You left last night! How the fuck does The Vegan know you're here?!!!* Ugh. Unbelievable.

* * *

For a few weeks, I barely spoke to him. He had taken full advantage of my trust. We had never spent the night together and I was not comfortable with him sleeping in my bed. Had he approached it differently, I would have considered letting him sleep on my couch. He hadn't been drinking, mind you. It wasn't an issue of safety. Apparently, he got outside with his dog, and realizing the late hour, simply decided he'd rather stay. A choice, not a necessity. His choice. And the fact that he made this choice after leaving my house only pointed out the fact that when he went outside, he intentionally left my front door unlocked. He had absolutely planned to come back inside. I'm sure of it. Surely, he waited long enough to make sure I had fallen asleep before letting himself back in, stripping down to his boxers, and sliding into bed beside me. Of course, he remembered to lock the door that time. A locked door is no deterrent for someone who knows where the spare key is hidden, however. *Enter Stage Left, The Vegan. #regrets*

The Plow Guy would text me often, begging for a chance to make things right and claiming that his intentions were innocent. He admitted that he shouldn't have assumed I'd be okay with it, but that he really thought I wouldn't mind. That I'd understand it was late and not blame him one bit. That it scared him when I'd looked at him with that look on my face that morning. A look that he'd never seen before. He, too, was shocked and disappointed. He didn't understand where my frustration was coming from. My anger. My hurt. He was surprised to learn that The Vegan had found us in bed together, and that seemed to be the only thing that changed his tune. He was truly apologetic after that, asking for a chance to prove himself again. He couldn't have known that we'd have a visitor any more than I did. It took me a while to consider seeing him again, but eventually he wore me down, and I stopped listing reasons to deny him a dinner.

* * *

The Plow Guy had a few splashes of culinary experience on his resume. He'd worked in commercial kitchens throughout his years and had learned a good bit along the way. He was especially proud of his baked scallops, and knowing that I was a scallop fan too, wanted to show off his favorite dish. He came over, and although my guard was up more than the last time we'd hung out, I was doing my best to be chill and give him a chance. He insisted on making dinner, and with the exception of allowing me to play sous chef once or twice, he made the dinner almost completely by himself. As I sipped on my wine and he continued to prepare the meal, it was evident that he was distracted. He'd been on his phone quite a bit. This wouldn't normally bother me, but it was very unlike him. I called him on it once, and he casually blew it off. My concern grew when he continued to miss my jokes and stopped interacting with me. Dinner was admittedly delicious, as I had expected it to be. The aroma in my kitchen was amazing and was filling my entire house. He continued to text, even as we ate. I grew frustrated and asked him once more what was going on.

He finally admitted that he was messaging someone back and forth. He didn't want to show me but I insisted, giving him an ultimatum. If he refused to tell me what was going on, I wanted him to leave. He was texting Toothless. For many reasons, I had removed this man from my life. I had blocked him on social media, blocked his number in my phone, and refused to engage when he'd find yet another avenue by which to reach me. And yet The Plow Guy was in a texting war with him? In my kitchen?! He was wasting his chance at redemption. He was giving me even more reason to not trust him. Apparently, Toothless had sent him a friend request on Facebook a while before, and The Plow Guy, being the friendly and outgoing guy that he was, didn't give it a second thought. He'd probably forgotten that they were even connected on there. What he didn't forget was that I had this guy blocked. That I'd grown frustrated of Toothless' bullshit and had decided to remove him from my life altogether. Imagine my frustration to find out that this guy, who stood here before me in the safety of my kitchen, was engaging in a virtual pissing match with a guy from my past. The man was a pathological liar and a shitty excuse for a son and a friend. He certainly wasn't a friend of mine, and yet, here was The Plow Guy, messaging him about how great I am. Toothless was quick to say that I was out for money, and in an attempt to disprove that, PG was quick to say that I always paid when we went out—making him look like less of a man than he was. He was quick to make up lies about me, and PG was typing fast and furiously back, arguing every point, oftentimes making me look worse in the process. We cleaned up from dinner and I promptly asked him to leave. I was very clear about what he'd done wrong and that, yet again, he'd given me even more reason to distrust him. Although I was sure there was no malicious intent, I had grown skeptical that we could even remain friends at this point. According to his words and his four page card, he was completely in love with me—a feeling that wasn't mutual. Perhaps we had a shot at friendship, but he was blowing that in spectacular fashion every time I tried to let him in again.

* * *

Our relationship had turned into one of infrequent phone calls and no face-to-face time. I missed our conversation and laughter, sure, but I didn't miss having to keep my guard up and my wits about me at all times. I couldn't drink around him anymore because I didn't trust him. Not that he'd physically do anything to me, but I worried he'd end up in my bed, innocently. That he'd throw in my face the next day the nice things I'd said when enjoying myself and letting my hair down. That perhaps, he'd be a moronic knight in shining armor, spilling the details of my life to the one person I chose to not have in it. He didn't do any of this maliciously or intentionally, mind you. He just couldn't help himself. He always thought he was being my biggest supporter and standing steadfastly behind me. If I'd had a security code for my life, I'm pretty sure he would have handed it over to TL without even

realizing he did, while patting himself on the back for being my sav-
ior. *A for effort. Two steps forward, six steps back.*

Christmas was nearing, and he'd made mention of buying gifts
for my sons and me. He had proudly boasted about the custom neon
signs he'd had made for them. Their names, respectively, in their favorite color. It was a sweet gesture—one that resonated with me. My
mother had always said to give gifts to others by giving them something you'd love to receive yourself. As a child, he'd always wanted his
name hanging on his wall in neon lights, and it had sadly never happened. He'd made mention of other gifts he had for me as well, keeping them a surprise. I'd later learn that while I was all in my feels and
sharing on social media that I wanted nothing more than to find my
other half, he'd been busy wrapping the gifts he'd hand-curated for
my family. He was excited and eager to see the look on my face when
opening what he'd selected for me. He finished, completing them with
gift tags, labeling me his queen or his baby. *Definitely not your baby.*
Moreover, most definitely not YOURS. That post wasn't about or for him.
If he wanted to take it personally, that was certainly his prerogative. If
he'd been my better half, I wouldn't have posted that. If he had come
into my life and proven himself to be the missing piece, I'd have had
no need to write what I did. So naturally, it broke his heart to read
such a public declaration that I had been, and was still, searching for
my soulmate. Call me callous, but the thought that he'd even seen that
post didn't register for me. The next few months passed, and although
we talked some, he never gave me those Christmas gifts. Honestly, I'd
forgotten all about them.

* * *

He had asked for one last chance to see me, explaining that if it
wasn't meant to be, he'd understand, but that he truly believed he'd
fallen in love with me for a reason. He wanted one dinner. One night
out to show me that he could be thoughtful and not a creep. That he
could respect my boundaries and wants. He wanted one last chance
to show me how special he thought I was. I was hesitant, but he

promised a good time and that he'd take care of everything. It can be very tiresome to have to be the one to plan everything, and it was refreshing to know I could just sit back on this. I was very reluctant, to be honest, but looked at this as one last opportunity for him to fuck up. If he did, I could walk away with a clear conscience. I'd given it ample tries. If he surprised me and pulled off a nice date without stepping on his own foot, maybe there'd be a chance for another. He'd already begun making changes in his life. He'd respectfully left his job, demanding better pay and to be finally valued by an employer the way he deserved. He began looking for a new place to live, out of the shadow of his family. He was holding himself hostage in his childhood bedroom and needed freedom to blossom, to grow, and to become his own man. He certainly didn't stand a chance of being someone else's man when he wasn't even the puppeteer of his own life. I had so many reservations, but he pulled out all the stops. Two song lyrics later, and I agreed to dinner. He was beside himself and promised me I wouldn't regret it. He told me to bring Wells with me, explaining that it'd be a bit of a drive and that he should come with us.

The day before, I was growing anxious, not being privy to the details. Don't get me wrong, I love a good surprise. No one ever surprises me, actually, and I'd love more of that kind of thing. But in this case, I didn't know how far away our drive would be, where we were going, when we'd be back, etc. He'd taken me to New York once before, to his favorite brewery for dinner. I thought maybe he was doing the same. His excitement was different this time though, and I wanted a little more information. I finally asked point blank if we'd be gone overnight, to which he responded that we would. Frustration set in. He'd asked for an evening out, not an overnight, and I still lacked information. We weren't sleeping together, and he knew how upset I'd been when he joined me in my bed that one regretful night. He'd have to be the world's biggest idiot to set up the same scenario again. Sigh. I could handle an overnight, knowing he was aware of my boundaries and that he'd made provisions for my dog.

When he arrived to pick me up on that Friday night, he had a blanket, a dog bed, dog food, dog treats, and a water dish ready to go. He wasn't kidding. I had packed treats, but even those weren't necessary. The little part deep inside every person that makes the internal joke to self about someone drugging them and stealing their kidney started vocalizing concern. Not about losing my spleen though, about waking up in an ice bath with my dog nowhere to be found. Maybe he was in love with Wells, not me. After we'd hit the road, The Plow Guy admitted that his plan was to take me to see the ice castles in Lake George, although, due to weather, they'd been canceled. Instead of telling me this and making other plans, he decided he'd still take me all that way for dinner at a place he'd never been to. Just because. It gave him my undivided attention for far longer than he would have had at a local eatery, and it also was a great way for him to keep me captive, having driven all that way in one car. Turns out, he'd had no plan for an overnight stay at all until I mentioned it. He assumed that by me asking, it meant that I'd be okay with it, so he jumped at the chance. Originally, his plan included dinner and ice castles and a very late drive home. We would have been back the same night. Sigh.

I walked Wells while he got us checked into the hotel. We made it down the hallway to our room (one room? Perhaps a suite with two separate bedrooms?). He granted access with one swipe of the room key, and I followed him inside. One room. One bed. I quickly glanced around, wanting to ensure I wasn't missing a second bed before confronting him on his grave mistake. He seemed to anticipate my question and beat me to it. "I tried to get a room with two beds, I did. But it was too last minute and this is all they had left," he nervously explained. It was clear that he knew I'd be upset but tried to remain confident in appearance, "Honestly, I didn't really think you'd mind. We've already slept in the same bed. It shouldn't be a big deal. It's not like I'm going to try anything... unless you're okay with it." I shook my head in disbelief. Did he notice my disappointment? How could he not? I wasn't trying to hide it in the slightest. I'd developed a nice migraine on the drive there, though, and dinner and rest was needed. It wasn't going to be an option to head back that night, a two and a half hour drive ahead of us. I'd have to make the best of it, him sleeping on one edge of the bed, myself on the far other. Wells between us. Thank goodness it was at least a king bed.

He'd made reservations for dinner at a charming little place only a few minutes away. He'd never been there, but he'd done his research and the reviews were good. I'll admit, I wasn't disappointed. The place was classy, yet clearly a favorite of the locals. It was dark and sophisticated inside, sconces lined the walls and the dimly lit room was elegant without being pretentious. It was a nice choice, especially having had nothing but reviews to go by. He'd done good with that part. I still maintain that this shouldn't have been planned as an overnight trip, and once the main event had been canceled due to weather, he should've scrapped it altogether. But here we were, sipping on some cleverly named signature cocktails and enjoying some even more unique appetizers. Dinner was scrumptious, and between the complex flavors of the food and the very strong spirits, I had almost forgotten about this guy's big mistake.

After dinner, and with no other activity planned, we headed to the club next door. The place was huge, and from across the parking lot, we could hear the music bumping and feel the bass. It was a chilly night and that made the allure of the nightclub all the more appealing. The dance floor was empty and the DJ was getting set up. Clearly, the party had not yet begun. That didn't stop us, though. We ordered a round of drinks, followed soon after by another. We met this lovely couple, and of course I needed to try what the missus was drinking too. A few times that night, I was reminded that he and I would be going back to the hotel together, sharing one room, sharing one bed. The drinks kept me happy though, and I was able to keep that thought from consuming my night. When we finally did retire, he slept on his side; I slept on mine. I was too drunk to give him hell. I just wanted sleep. Clothes remained on, and he didn't try to cross any lines. The next day, getting up and getting ready to leave was awkward. Our drive home seemed to take much longer than it had to get there. I

stared out the window while he stared straight ahead, paying attention to the road and the traffic. He eventually broke the silence, asking about the night before. He insisted that I had yet again said sweet
things to him and returned his affectionate words. This was becoming a pattern. I remembered the night. It wasn't like I had blacked out
or anything, but apparently I couldn't remember this part of the night
that only he could. How convenient. He complained for all but a few
minutes of the drive, that he wanted to hear those things when I was
sober. Yet, I didn't know what I'd supposedly said, nor did I remember
having any conversation like the one he was recounting. I was so over
it. I tried to explain that maybe we shouldn't see each other again.
That again, he put me in a situation he knew I wasn't comfortable
with. That if I was going to feel the way about him that he'd hoped,
I would have gotten there by now. Reciprocity wasn't coming, sadly.
I could see the disappointment on his face. I'm pretty sure I could actually hear his heart breaking. I felt terrible, but it needed to be said.
Maybe I could've saved us both so much time and energy if I'd said it
sooner. He was a nice guy; that wasn't the issue. He just wasn't the guy
for me. I didn't drag him along. He kept insisting I be open minded
and give him a shot. I should have listened to my gut, though, and
ended our friendship far sooner. We weren't going to be more than
friends and he didn't want me if I was going to be anything less than
his queen, even though he tried to put on the facade that he did.

* * *

We had a snowstorm the next week. By 'storm,' I mean, we got a
few inches, nothing crazy. It was the perfect excuse for him to come
by and plow my driveway. He no longer worked for his brother and
therefore no longer had 24/7 access to a truck with a plow. But still,
I came home from work to a plowed driveway, clear from snow, including freshly shoveled paths to my front and back doors. I questioned if it was his doing, but knew it must be. He was the only
one who had made it a point to come take care of snow removal
for me, and he'd proven this time and time again. I reached out to

thank him and politely relieve him from doing this going forward. It wasn't his responsibility, and since he wouldn't take money for it, I had often repaid him with dinner. This wasn't something I was willing to do any longer. It's part of the reason we spent time together for as long as we did. I felt somewhat obligated to him, and I needed to cut that tie now. He denied plowing my driveway, which left me scratching my head. *Who else would have plowed my driveway? Toothless?! He'd had my lawn mowed several times for me. Was it Fireball? Maybe The Vegan?* There was a whole slew of men I could think of, several of whom I'd removed from my life on less than ideal terms. I asked again, thinking that perhaps The Plow Guy was just trying to be funny. Again, he maintained that it wasn't him that had taken care of my driveway. I was really starting to get freaked out now, not knowing who it could've been. I was actively avoiding a few men who'd proven themselves to ignore boundaries and who lacked respect for my wishes. *Who was stopping by my house when I wasn't home? Were they also stopping by when I WAS home?!* The possibilities my mind came up with were horrifying, and I was truly getting scared down to my core. When I admitted to Mr. Plow that I was freaked out and wished it had just been him, he began laughing in my face. He admitted that he had been the culprit. "Of course it was me, Scarlett! How many people do you know who have a plow and would do that for you?" Tears welled up in my eyes. I'm not sure if it was the way he was cruelly amused by my fear or the fact that he had no idea how scary it can be to live alone. I've had several men stalk me through the years, and during this time of being single and dating... at least a couple more. To allow me to think for a second that some strange man had been coming by my place when I wasn't home? That was pretty shitty of him.

We talked later that week, and without waffling, I made my intentions clear. The trip to New York was the final straw. He made assumptions, yet again, on what I would be comfortable with. He put me in an uncomfortable position again. And although he tried to do something sweet and thoughtful by plowing my driveway, he missed the mark and it left me terrified. And then laughed at my fear. Clearly, he'd been giving the whole situation some thought, and that night, after I'd already gone to bed for the night, he reached out. It was very late. The next day, he sent me another message. It was at four something in the morning. I hadn't seen it, of course, and then he sent another before 7:00am. I saw these messages upon waking up, but getting ready for work didn't leave time to respond. His messages were increasingly nasty. No doubt he'd been drinking when he wrote them. The first was passive but tolerable. The second was snarky, and the last basically told me to fuck off since I hadn't responded to him in a timely fashion. I was wrong. THAT was the final straw. I had given him so many chances. Too many. I was willing to remain in a place where we could still reach out and say hi from time to time as long as he was clear that we had no future as a couple. We had it out on the phone. He was defeated and was taking it out on me. He was angry and sad. You could hear it in his voice. He had wanted so badly for this to work out, but I think he'd grown tired, too, and had finally stopped fighting for it. We talked several times that day, and I remained adamant. "I don't want to see you again," I said. It wasn't easy to say but had to be said.

When I arrived home from work, there, on my steps, were four nicely wrapped packages. There were two for my sons and two with my name on them. I brought them inside for safe keeping, but had no intention of keeping them. I didn't even open them. I reached out to The Plow Guy, who admitted to leaving them. He had stopped by while I was at work. He'd purchased these gifts months earlier (for Christmas), but now that I wanted nothing to do with him, he wanted closure. Which meant giving me the gifts he'd gotten for me. I didn't want them. That's not closure in the slightest. I tried to give them back, but he refused to take them. I even suggested leaving them at his house, outside, and that we wouldn't have to see each other. It was impossible to have a conversation with this man. He was so hurt, and it was spewing out of him in hatred-filled beams of anger. I felt bad. A necessary evil. We needed to be done. I couldn't do it anymore. Just trying to keep a friendship going with him was exhausting. I knew I'd miss him, but I knew it was for the best.

* * *

Time had passed. Weeks. Then a few more. I had finally met someone (that damn Bartender, Chapter 25) and wanted to close anything that hadn't officially been closed. He was patient with me while I 'tied up loose ends' before we made anything official between us. I'd been a patron at his establishment a bit more as of late, so it wasn't out of sorts to meet my sister there for a drink after work. The Plow Guy was reaching out again. He really wanted to talk. We'd tried this several times and all that would happen is that we'd meet up for a drink, our time together didn't involve any talking through our past issues, and once we'd reach the parking lot, that's when he'd try to open the dialogue. He'd wait until we were outside, standing in the cold, before he wanted clarity and resolution. So we never got any. He'd talked through his feelings more than a few times, and it always ended the same. I didn't want to pursue anything with him, and he wanted me to give him another chance. On this particular evening, he wanted to meet up face to face to talk. My sister and I were finishing our margaritas when he arrived. Two birds, one stone. I had alluded to having met someone, and when he saw The Bartender approach our table, he must've seen it on his face. He was unimpressed that I'd meet him at the bar where my new love interest worked. I'm all about efficiency, what can I say?

I stepped away just long enough to use the restroom. Just long enough for pleasantries to be misunderstood. When I joined them both back at the table, he was upset. He kindly waited for my sister to leave before addressing what was bothering him. In an attempt to make polite conversation, she had asked him how he knew me. He was unbelievably offended at the notion that she didn't know who he was or anything about him, especially since his family and friends had heard about me on numerous occasions. *Of course she knows who you are! You don't think she knew why you were meeting me here or what I was about to say to you? She may have forgotten your name though, since I only ever used your nickname. That's my bad. Sorry.*

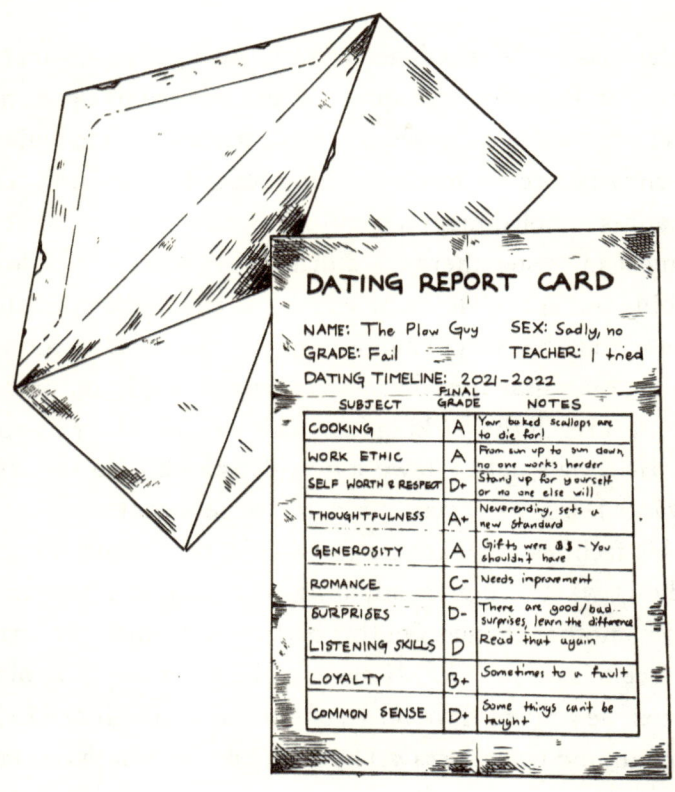

With just the two of us still seated at the small bistro table, the server took his drink order and grabbed me another. I gave him a chance to speak his mind and relay what he so badly needed to say. He pulled up the final letter he'd written to me. I'd read it just days before, but he'd put a lot of time into it and wanted me to absorb his words in front of him. Honestly, I thought he was going to ask me to read it aloud right there. *Um, no.* This went on for four hours, tears coming to the surface, his voice shaky. I honestly felt bad at first, but when we neared the two hour mark, I was becoming frustrated. By hour three I was annoyed, and as hour number four drew near, I'd become more direct and harsh than I'd ever intended to. The dinner he'd ordered himself (clearly underestimating what this meet up was for) remained untouched, and at some point, had been boxed up for him to bring home. The servers had exchanged glances with each other and with me, clearly feeling my pain as well. The one server made sure my drink made it onto his bill. We bitches have got to stick together. Thanks, lady. If he was going to get four hours of my time and make me watch him cry, the least the man could do was buy me a drink. One of his last complaints was that while he pined over me for the better part of a year, he waited for me. He didn't date anyone else, had no hookups, and kept hoping that at any given moment, I'd come around. I was horrible for denying him physical affection. *Ironic, huh? The Plow Guy never plowed me. Shucks.*

| 13 |

A King Without His Queen

L et me start by saying that I affectionately refer to this bloke as "Jiffy Lube." Not for any reason other than the fact that he graciously changed the oil in my car one time. That was pretty much a first, so it stuck with me. I met Jiffy Lube online. He had come across my profile and decided to reach out. This, however, was definitely not a first. Usually, when these strangers reach out, I play the game. "Do I know you?" "How do I know you?" "Have we met before?" This time, I wasted no time. With his directness and our flirtatious personalities, we had a breakfast date scheduled for the very next day. I eagerly began rummaging through my closet to find the perfect outfit. I picked out my best ass-hugging jeans, cute brown booties, and a cream sweater to match. Ya know, the kind of sweater that's just thick enough to look 'cozy' but thin enough to not add bulk and falls perfectly to accentuate your breasts and your hips. C'mon guys, not my first rodeo. I knew what I was doing.

We met at one of my favorite diners—a favorite among many locals, in fact. I expected the wait to be painfully long and awkward, but we were ushered into a booth in no time at all. He led me through the restaurant, his right arm extended behind him as he held my hand gently but firmly enough at the same time. Firmly enough to show me he was in charge, but gently enough to let me know he would go at my pace. *Fucking hot.*

He was wearing a red ribbed sweater and dark rimmed glasses. Very scholarly. I had picked up on a military vibe while creeping on-line—he was shirtless in some pics, covered in mud in some, and racing on his crotch-rocket in others. I had gotten the impression that this man wasn't afraid to play rough and get dirty. *Deep breath.* And here he sat, looking suave and studious. These were two very different versions of him, and I wondered if there were any more. The conversation was seamless, despite my hidden nervousness. I'm sure he noticed but I was thankful that he didn't call me out on it. He ordered a meat-filled omelet and made easy conversation while drinking his orange juice. Not a coffee drinker. Noted. Most definitely a meat eater, not a vegan. *Phew.* I asked questions and answered his. I didn't learn his mother's maiden name or his astrological sign, but I did get to know a little more about his time in service, his kids, and his job. He offered up a bit about his most recent ex-girlfriend, but I wrote it off (red flag #1). It sounded like she'd done a number on him and was continuing to do damage since they still worked together. Maybe he was oversharing because he was nervous too? One could hope. We finished (mhmm, at the same time) and he walked me to my car. Neither of us wanted the date to be over, so we ended up taking a stroll down the nearby side streets. He was the utmost gentleman and would reposition himself every time we crossed a street, so he was between me and any potential traffic. (It was sweet, but ladies, don't give 'em too many points for this.)

Things progressed very quickly after this, and that very night, I found myself at his place. It was an innocent hang out and he delivered the dinner he had promised—pork chops. Just pork chops. No side, no condiments, nada (red flag #2). He didn't even serve it with a fork. I think maybe he just wanted to see how I'd handle his meat. (Eww. I know. But you know I had to say it. My apologies.) We started spending more time together. Sometimes I was with the Army vet, sometimes the worn out, tired, sad father of two. I never knew which version was going to greet me when I got there. His playfulness turned into friskiness. His confidence into cockiness. His meal making into laziness (but hey, he was cooking for me, so I wasn't about to complain). One night, he surprised me and made me chili, remembering I had mentioned liking it but that I never make it myself. This chili though. I've never had anything like it. It had pepperoni but lacked veggies and beans. I'm pretty sure it was actually some kind of pizza soup, though I never said anything other than how delicious it was (pro tip, ladies: just smile and say "thank you"). He introduced me to music that I had never heard, and with the distance between our homes, we'd stay over at each others' place once or twice a week. While snuggling and watching TV, or chatting while he worked on the doggie door he was building, our nights were usually lowkey and we were in bed by 7:00pm. He was a tinkerer and very handsy—handy, I meant 'handy'. Ahem. He enjoyed a good bourbon as much as I did. What wasn't to like? The man not only changed my oil but purchased the oil and filter as well. I was all but drooling that day, watching his muscles flex while he was half-hidden beneath my car. He moved about his garage with ease, and I was soaking up every minute, watching this man do manly things. Yes, please. I briefly considered smashing a taillight while he was down there so I could watch him fix that too. Mmm.

* * *

My girlfriend had reached out and invited me to join her and her boyfriend for a local charity event. This gala was the perfect opportunity to dress to the nines while contributing to a good cause. I was stoked at the thought of a fun night out with her and had wanted to go to this for years. With the roster of lame exes I had collected, I'd never had anyone to go with. This was my chance! Without hesitation, I purchased tickets and immediately pulled out the asymmetrical gown that had hung in my closet for years. I'd only worn it once and feared that the beautiful red and burgundy sequins would soon be covered in dust if I didn't take it out for a night on the town. Jiffy Lube agreed to go and almost seemed excited. I had noticed his collection of expensive watches, and he'd mentioned his custom tailored suits (plural) with pride. In his defense, the invite was pretty last minute, but in my favor, he didn't have to commit to go. The days passed quickly, and the evening before he reached out to tell me he might not make it after all. He'd been in communication (in hindsight, that's rich) with the owner of an overpriced truck in Virginia, and he might need to go make the transaction the next day. He had the whole weekend free, mind you, and more vacation time then he'd ever be able to use, but was considering bailing on me to hit the road earlier. In true asshole fashion, he went quiet on me the day of the dance. I called him and texted more times than I'd like to admit, trying to solidify our plans for the evening. Mere hours before (we're talking 3 hours before), he finally texted me back, confirming what I'd been dreading... he wasn't coming. No real explanation. No 'I'm sorry.' Nothing. I was standing in the middle of the intimates with an arm full of strapless bras to try on, and the disappointment was palpable. I was crushed and began altering plans and trying to salvage the night. (The Vegan had learned that I was going to this and had spent the week hinting, hoping I'd invite him as my date. Needless to say, with three hours to spare, I reached out and asked if he was busy. You'll read about that disastrous night in The Vegan Saga.)

*** *** ***

He wasn't ghosting me, per se, but his reach-outs were becoming fewer and farther between. (I guess you could say he was Casper-ing me, a friendlier ghosting.) Sometimes he'd send me video clips, responding to me while he was driving. These weren't unlike the super arrogant videos he was posting on TikTok. At first, I didn't hate the thought of being the woman he was into until I realized that he was making these videos *while* seeing me, and they were intended for all the thirsty women out there, not for me (red flag #3). I ignored this as much as I could, but often found myself revisiting his profile, wondering if he had posted anything that would give me a clue as to where we stood. We didn't go out often and when we did, he'd lead me through the restaurant by hand. I loved that. There were a few redeeming qualities like that that kept me on the line. But then he'd order for us both without a discussion—oftentimes a basket of fries and an order of fried pickles. I like pickles as much as the next girl (maybe more), but what the heck? *If you want me naked, let me eat a salad once in a while. Geez!* Our conversations had grown choppy, and when he did share, it was usually about the ex-girlfriend and the drama she was causing at work. It seemed to me that he fed into it and perpetuated the mess. I got the feeling that he wasn't over her in the slightest, and that I was a failed attempt for him to distract himself. And I got the feeling that I wasn't the only one he was distracting himself with.

The day I came over and found various empty (or mostly empty) bottles of booze, his explanation was weak. He'd said that he had 'a drink of this' and 'a sip of that' and neglected to clean up his mess from the night before. When I questioned the lube next to his bathroom sink, he simply said that he'd moved it off his shelf while cleaning. Simple as that. And when I found the discarded wrapper of a feminine hygiene wipe in his bathroom garbage, he tried to convince me it was mine. (Oh my goodness! So many red flags!) He began sending me videos he was taking each morning, standing in the shower, completely nude, shaking what he had. I'd be mortified to share a video like this (there was nothing deserving of a <u>standing</u> ovation, if you get my drift), let alone send them intentionally! He'd send me videos with his tongue out and explained that that was basically him sending me a kiss. Seven-year-olds send pics with their tongue out. He began sending me the same videos again and again, forgetting I'm sure who he'd sent them to already. Gross.

Some weeks I wouldn't hear from him for days, and then he'd reach out, take me out for fried pickles and a beer, and then take me home. When things were a little more solid, he'd want the domestic piece, asking me to make treats for his office holiday party. Then, when I'd try to connect with him, he'd disappear again. I'm guessing some other ho ended up Ho Ho Ho-ing for his holiday party when he stopped reaching out to me for it. Thank goodness I didn't waste my time or cover my favorite apron in flour for that loser. He'd go into work early and stay late, and there was always a 'reasonable' excuse for why he was so elusive... again.

As Christmas neared, he'd head into the office on the weekends to decorate, and then wander the office that week in a full Grinch getup. From the stories he told, they seemed to love him at work, yet he was more despondent and distant all the time. He would compliment me and make his interest known, and in the next breath, text me that he wasn't feeling it. In one text message, he blatantly admitted to having absolutely no draw to me whatsoever. Naturally, this hurt, but more than anything, I was angry that he'd been saying the exact opposite, keeping me on the hook and keeping me in his bed. I honestly don't know why I had put up with so much for so long. Oh wait. I remember. #fourgasms. I guess I had clung to the hope that he'd come around and give me a chance to be the one he'd never had in his life. The queen to his king (I know, cheesy, but he had the tattoo and story to match this sentiment). "I've never found my queen," he'd say, pointing to the ink on his bicep. Gimme a break. Maybe I kept coming back for the party tricks I was learning. The night of 29 orgasms was definitely a night for the books (see what I did there?). I remember climbing off his face, completely struggling for breath. "I can't breathe!" I gasped. He responded with, "And you think I can?!" and went back for more. What 30-something woman in her prime years could say no to that? Don't worry, eventually I did.

* * *

Weeks went by and I heard he moved out of state. He unfriended me on Facebook and stopped reaching out. I had mostly forgotten about him (but man, how I missed that pizza soup) when he reached out on a random Tuesday morning. He started by feigning concern for me and the idea that he missed me. I could see right through his bullshit this time and called him on it with zero fucks given. He wanted sex, but I had reached a point in my dating career where I was ready for more. I was finally open to the possibility of a relationship, and he clearly wasn't going to be the one. *You ARE the weakest link. Good-*

bye! He said he respected where I stood and wouldn't reach out anymore. More bullshit. Fast forward a few weeks. He reached out again, this time explaining that he actually did want to explore a relationship with me. He said it came to him suddenly, an epiphany. He had apparently not only been pushing me away, but everyone. He blamed his being distant on PTSD and entertained me with this story about how he had brain damage and couldn't remember things. He didn't remember telling me that he felt nothing for me. He said he had once lost an entire vacation he had taken and felt like an amnesia victim while later looking at the photographic proof. And in this case, he didn't give me a fair chance because he had never given himself a fair chance. *Poor guy.* I had nothing better to do that night, and he was so damn apologetic. He promised to cook for me and wanted to show me how he'd changed.

He just wanted one more chance. He showed up to my place without groceries. Not a good start. He suggested we grab take-out and come back to watch a movie. His acting was terrible and unconvincing at best, and I wasn't falling for it. He had brought two small gifts for me: a cheap stocking dress and a tee shirt (size medium. I haven't fit into a size medium since I was wearing scrunchies and listening to my Walkman). He said he'd purchased both for me but unknowingly showed his hand when showing me the link he'd ordered it from. His realization of his feelings for me had only occurred two days before, yet he'd ordered these items at least a week ago... and not in my size. I've never been good at math, but c'mon. And that sexy barely-there dress? He wasn't intending for me to wear it that night, of course, but for a future night, since now we had another shot at love. Surely there would be plenty more opportunities to wear this $9.99 lycra dress for his pleasure. The night was fine, and we did a lot of talking. We filled each other in on the time that had gone by, and I mentioned meeting someone who actually knew him (someone who wasn't a fan and had told me all about the previous domestic violence charges that JL had). Our night was surprisingly enjoyable, but I remained skeptical of this newest version of him.

The next morning, his messages were few and cold. *Jiffy Lube Version #27: Hi. Nice to meet you.* When I asked him directly, he didn't sugar coat anything. He said he had changed his mind and realized that yet again, he had no feelings for me and no interest in pursuing anything with me. He also notified me that his house was under contract, and he'd be moving out of state soon (for real this time). And the fact that I'd spent time with someone he knew? Well, that was just the icing on the cake. He wanted nothing to do with me if I'd been with this other guy (see Chapter 21: "Grand Finale").

Months went by, as they often did with him, and guess who reached out again. Any guesses?! I'll give you three, and the first two don't count. He had nothing to lose and went right for it. He apparently missed my body and wanted to revisit the fun we used to have, but not date. We were at an undeniable impasse. Though I tried to express this numerous times, he'd reach out randomly and threaten to pay me a visit. He wanted to come warm up my bed, knowing damn well I had no interest. He began asking to stay over and eventually asked to park his RV in my driveway. He had sold his house and was living in his camper full time.

The last time he reached out, I was still far too nice and humored him with small talk. I explained the mystery illness I was dealing with, and after sharing that I most likely would need a blood transfusion or iron infusion, he saw his opportunity to shine. He offered me his blood. HIS blood. They have blood donors and blood banks for this very need, and

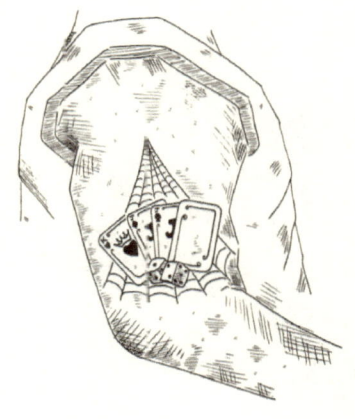

yet he was adamant. He wanted to help me out. He was willing to donate, come to the hospital with me. Whatever was needed. Cringe warning: he insisted one last time, really wanting me to take him up on his offer. When I declined for the final time, he left me with these words: "Please let me give you my blood. I want to be inside you forever." Deleted. Blocked. No, thank you. I'm good.

| 14 |

The Hockey Dad Who Wanted a Trophy... Wife

Online dating was still new for me, and I honestly didn't know where to begin. I just knew I didn't want to sign up for anything that I'd have to pay for. One lesser-known site proved itself to be scammy right away. I'd had a dating profile for all of a week and had almost three hundred messages. Although there were some legitimate messages, many were very clearly some bots as well. It was absolutely overwhelming, and I stopped looking at it altogether. I signed up for a few others, but in the same fashion, I was a bit overwhelmed, and after connecting with a few guys, stopped logging in to those as well. After another failed attempt with someone I thought there might be a future with, I was crushed. He broke me. I was so distraught that I decided I'd rather be single. I signed onto my two remaining online dating profiles that I had, with plans to shut them down for good. When I signed onto the one, I received a message almost immediately. This man was currently active and sent me several messages in rapid succession. He was desperate to get my attention. I responded and let him know that although I appreciated his interest, I was only online to delete my profile and I was no longer interested in dating. He quickly explained that this felt like kismet to him. He'd seen me on the first dating site and after he'd messaged me, I never logged back on. He had come across my profile on this site and couldn't believe he'd 'found me' again. He admitted to checking back on both sites often, hoping I had responded to his messages or at least logged on. The creepiness level was set to a solid 8, and I should have stuck to my guns. While I did shut down my profile, he convinced me to connect on another app so we could stay in touch. He was mostly harmless, albeit showing signs of obsession-like behavior. I knew I wouldn't get attached and therefore didn't mind humoring him. Our conversations were fine. Nothing notable but nothing awful either. He seemed nice enough and eventually talked me into meeting up. He wanted a date, just one. Just one chance to meet me in person. One chance to prove that there was a reason he had been so hung up on my picture for so long and a reason he was able to get ahold of me before I took down my profile for good. That it was meant to be.

Even though I had agreed to go on one date with him, the jackass couldn't get out of his own way. He even decided that instead of being a gentleman and inviting me to dinner, we'd go out for a drink. Not drinks, just one. And I was to pay for my own; he'd pay for his. He was laying out all the rules and informing me he only wanted to commit to one drink in case he didn't enjoy my company. I mean, how dare he be subjected to spending a full hour and a half with me if we didn't hit it off? I stopped him in his tracks and told him that if I wasn't worth investing ninety minutes of his time into, he could forget about it altogether. I wasn't about to dedicate my evening to a man who wouldn't even buy me a drink. Get real. He quickly changed his tune and asked for a second chance. This ended up being his theme, always asking for yet another chance.

About a week prior to our date, he was in town for his son's hockey game. I decided to surprise him and stop by the rink. Best case? I scope him out, he seems like a good dude and I go introduce myself. Worst case? I scope him out and sneak out before he knows I was ever there. That was the plan anyway. I stayed on the top of the bleachers and watched him for a minute. He was standing alone and intently watching the game. He was a very enthusiastic spectator, and I appreciated the supportive father that he seemed to be. I made my way over and made sure he saw me before I got too close. He was thrilled to see me, which was a relief. He asked for a hug and I obliged, although it felt a little forced since I barely knew him. Within the fifteen or so minutes I was there, it quickly became apparent that he was losing interest in the game and became more interested in the folks around him. I don't mean me necessarily, but rather that he was preoccupied with the other parents in the stands. He had moved closer and closer to me, a little at a time. It was obvious that he wanted to make sure the other parents, especially the dads, saw that I was there with him. I told myself I was imagining this and, noticing the time on the scoreboard, tried to excuse myself and head out. The game was almost over, and the last thing I wanted to do was still be there when the crowd began to disperse. He leaned in for another hug. Super awkward. As he was sniffing my hair (I heard the sniff y'all), I pulled away from the hug just as the clock buzzed. The game was over and folks cheered and jumped to their feet. My exit was blocked and so were the stairs. He continued talking, and I realized I'd have to keep watching for an opening in the crowd so I could make my escape. His daughter appeared by his side, and I was stuck. I didn't want to walk away right when she approached, so I stayed and said hi. His son might be the fastest to change out of his equipment ever, because he too, was approaching his father in record time. I ended up walking out to the parking lot alongside all three of them. Exactly what I was trying to avoid. Awesome. He reached out later that day to tell me what a 'smoke show' his twelve-year-old son thought I was. It didn't seem to be a compliment for me, but rather a flex on his part. Like he'd nabbed some hot piece of ass and everyone would soon know it, starting with his son. So fucking weird. *I'm not an accessory. I'm not a fucking Michael Kors handbag. And I'm not yours. At this rate, you're destined to have a clearance Route 66 purse on LayAway. And if you keep this up, you're not even gonna get that first date.*

We continued to talk but our phone calls were short and I was more than okay with that. He wanted that first date, and I agreed, deciding that maybe I had caught him in a weird moment by surprising him at the game. With time to prepare, maybe he'd surprise me on this date. We agreed on dinner, and he insisted on coming to town, saving me the drive. I wasn't comfortable with him knowing where I lived (I'd grown accustomed to this practice and it was working for me), so we met right at the restaurant. He was dressed nicely and dinner was tasty. The conversation, however, left something to be desired. He spent entirely too long telling me about how he wasn't the best husband and lost his wife to divorce. How she was a trophy wife and he hoped he'd find someone else like that. When he wasn't talking about her, he was busy talking about how successful and accomplished he was. It was leaving a bad taste in my mouth, and I had no desire for dessert. He didn't want the date to be over, and since he'd driven all that way, I decided we could make one more stop.

I took him to my favorite whiskey den. I had taken many a first date here, but never a second, knowing that if I ever did, he'd surely be special. While this guy (let's call him "Dream Girl," since that's what he called me) stayed at our table, I went to the bar to grab us each a drink. While waiting for the bartender to pour, I glanced back and noticed he was on his phone. Not like he was checking his email or playing a game. He was very clearly texting a friend, and he had a huge smile on his face. He wasn't checking me out or nervously wiping his brow. He was definitely enjoying whatever was going on on his phone, and it clearly didn't involve me. When I returned to the table, he volunteered that he had been texting his friend, telling him what a great time he was having. That I was so beautiful and that he couldn't wait for his friends to meet me and see how lucky he was to have me on his arm. And there it was. He thought he had found the replacement to his trophy wife: his trophy girlfriend. The man knew nothing about me but was in love with the idea of me. He called me his dream girl. Even the whiskey wasn't strong enough to continue this date. I paid the tab, and we headed back down the street toward our cars.

It was winter and the trees that lined Church Street were aglow with white lights. It was always so warm and romantic, no matter the temperature outside. Dream Girl hit 'play' on his phone, tucked it in his breast pocket, and stopped me from walking. He grabbed my hand and asked for a dance. And because I'm too nice (and didn't want to embarrass him in front of strangers), I humored him again. We danced right there in the middle of the street. There was nothing organic about it. It all felt so forced and so unnatural, and as soon as the song was done, I tried to get us moving again. He asked for a picture and had his arm extended in front of us before I had a chance to say no. He took a selfie or three and promised me he wouldn't post anything anywhere. I wasn't impressed. I was doing my best to end this date as quickly as possible. I just wanted to go home. This wasn't what I had signed up for. He didn't ask me any real questions or try to get to know me. It wouldn't have mattered. He was so superficial and shallow, and I knew there was no way I'd be able to stomach a second date with him.

We reached the parking lot of the restaurant, and before I could head toward my own car, he stopped me to say goodnight. We were talking and I was doing my best to remain polite. I didn't have to let him down here. I figured I'd wait until I was safely and comfortably home before sending him the rejection text. As I was wishing him a good night, he leaned in and kissed me without so much as a warning. I'm usually pretty good at seeing the signs and knowing it's coming, but again, nothing about this kiss was organic. I abruptly pulled away, determined to not let this go on for even a second longer. He was aiming to make us a full-fledged couple by the end of the night, and there was nothing I wanted less. I had to get out of there and fast. I made it into my car and locking the door, breathed a sigh of relief.

* * *

Despite my directness, he kept reaching out, hoping for another chance. He didn't realize how pushy he'd been and justified his actions by telling me that from the moment he saw my picture online, he knew I was the one. His 'be all, end all.' Sometimes his messages were laced with arrogance and cockiness, other times nothing but that. He was very full of himself, and even though I never asked for pictures of him, he would send me selfies. All. The. Time. He'd even send me terrible selfies and preface them by saying, "terrible pic, I know." *Why are you sending a terrible picture of yourself? Can you not take ONE good one? I thought you were Mr. Amazing. He had this Tony the Tiger look going for him but still managed to take pictures from the one angle that showcased his triple chin and not his prominent jawline. And he lacked the sense to not send them. I'm not saying you need a life coach, but...*

He wanted a chance to reconnect and promised it'd be as friends and nothing more. He had asked this many times, and finally I told him I'd consider it. I know. Don't do as I do. We made plans to tentatively connect for a drink after work one night. We didn't have anything solidified, and my day got away from me. When I was finally out of the office, I called him to check in. Instead of reaching out during the day, or even sending a text message, he'd driven the hour home. And instead of having a reasonable conversation with me about it, he blew up. He was so upset. He acted as if I'd stood him up.

Every time he reached out after that, he begged for another chance with me. He claimed he was new to dating and hated how he blew his chance with me. *Was he new to interacting with people altogether? Apparently, forty-something years on this earth, and he views people as prizes and takes what he wants. No fucks given. If it hadn't worked out for him yet, what made him think he was doing it right?*

The last time he contacted me, he was telling me about his son's recent hockey game. He had encouraged his son to suggest to the coach that they give this one player a chance to get in the game. This kid had some developmental delays, and since they were ahead by such a large lead, it'd be the ideal time for him to get some ice time. In Dream Girl's retelling of this story, he told me how this boy's parents were thrilled to see their son playing, and he was quick to tell them that it was his idea. The idea was a great one, sure, but why couldn't he just let his son take the credit? He was so defensive when I explained this to him, and I realized that there's just no getting through to him. Hell, I wouldn't be surprised if he hopped up on stage to accept his kids' diploma some day. #kanyemuch? *Dream Girl, you have a lot of growing to do or the only girl you're going to get will be just that—in your dreams. See ya.*

| 15 |

The Vegan Saga (Part 3)

The first time I went over and visited after that episode, things were awkward AF. He was slow to roll and kept asking questions. Same thing the next time. After that, I basically said that he had to move on or we had to move on. He quickly changed his tune and got a little warmer towards me. I think some part of him felt a little guilty when I called him out on the fact that he had never once told me I was pretty or made reference to us dating. That he often told me he only wanted the 'abridged version.' That he had once told me he'd 'ignore the things about me that he didn't like.' Maybe I finally got through to him, and he realized he'd been a shitty friend and definitely hadn't stepped up to the plate in a boyfriend capacity whatsoever.

I wasn't about to introduce him to my children, but unfortunately, two of our sons had gone to school together and were familiar with each other. My son, really admiring his son, wanted to swing by and play some Xbox with him. We did this once or twice, but I was very hesitant to get them together more often. If The Vegan was awkward and unfiltered with me, I feared that he'd end up saying something off the cuff to one of my boys as well. I did my best to make sure any time together was scripted and limited. One time he joined us at an arcade and bowling alley. He made snide remarks all night about how the money I'd spent in the arcade was a waste, his time playing in the arcade was a waste (but then smiled like a school girl while playing laser tag). Ya don't say. We grabbed some dinner afterward, and while we waited for our food, my son asked him a 'would you rather' question. Nothing crazy. Something about world domination, to which this personality-less man responded, "Well, that's not a possibility, so I won't waste my time answering such a foolish question. Frankly, why waste yours?" His answer shocked me and pissed me off. Had he never had fun? Never played a game? Was he born this snarky? I may have taken a little pleasure in hearing the waitress say that they were out of falafel. He proceeded to order a hummus plate and complain about it the rest of the meal while he pushed other veggies around with a carrot for a solid twenty minutes. He eyed all of our meals sideways and made comments about how we all had made unhealthy choices. You better believe I made sure to enjoy every bite of that cheeseburger in front of him, savoring each morsel as the melted cheese lingered on my lip and the grease ran down my chin. I'm usually more lady-like than that, but damn, I wanted to drive my point home. Fuck him. And honestly? If it wasn't the meat, but rather the caloric intake, have at it, man. *I promise you your fridge full of beer is anything but low on the calorie chart. And your beer belly will back me up on that.*

Another time, we played Cards Against Humanity, a game he'd heard of but had never played before. He was upset by the rules: if it's your turn to judge the cards, you don't get to play one also. He was instantly in a foul mood because of it. And if you've ever played this game, you know it can get pretty crude depending on the cards you draw. There is one card (one card only) that I always discard upon drawing. Not much offends me, but this card does, and without any argument from other players, I always swap it out. No biggie. Of course, The Vegan had to challenge me on this, telling me that I was breaking the rules, that swapping out a card isn't allowed, and that if I couldn't play by the rules, maybe I shouldn't be playing. *Well, I guess he sure told me.*

Our hangouts were more frequent again, but still not often enough for his liking. I was never invited for mountain biking because I wasn't a vegan. Kid. You. Not. He'd reference that if I didn't eat meat, I'd have a stronger spine and would be in better health, therefore have the potential to ride the rough terrain on a fatboy. Forget the fact that I'd been in several horrific car accidents. Does that mean that removing dairy would have prevented those car accidents? *Shit. Someone should tell the insurance companies STAT!* The one invitation I did receive was to go visit his friends for the day. His friend's girlfriend had a beautiful lakeside property and we were invited to join them for the day, followed by dinner on their balcony. I had the good sense to ask him which friend we were visiting, and my intuition was right. *Hi, Dr. C! It's been a while. How are you? My vagina's doing great, thanks for asking!* They were surprisingly great hosts and made pleasant conversation all afternoon. The Vegan, however, was off doing his own thing. He insisted I let Wells stay off leash and promised he'd be on duty. This meant that anytime Wells disappeared from view, so did The Vegan. He kept tabs on my dog all day, wandering around their property, and when the wind was more subdued, even found time to try paddle boarding for a quick stint. In my mind, this further solidified that we weren't anything more than friends. Friends with benefits, I guess. But even at that, the sex was so vanilla. So bland. But I guess he's a vegan—bland is what they do best? Kidding, kidding. Looking back, I really don't know what I was in it for. And on this particular day, I was flooded with the same sentiment.

I was conversing with his friends—the good doctors—and he wasn't seated beside me. He wasn't holding my hand or providing support while I was getting to know them. But he had invited me to spend the day with him and his friends. I never could figure him or his intentions out. When the doc poured bourbon for folks to sip, he poured only three, not four. Apparently, The Vegan had mentioned that I was currently on antibiotics... to my former doctor. "I can't pour you any, Scarlett. You'll be sick as a dog if you drink this while you're taking the medication that you're on. Sorry." Not embarrassing at all. Our meal was so fucking good, despite the awkwardness and undefinedness of it all. It was my first time hearing about how you have to abuse the kale to make it taste so good. I have always 'abused the kale' since, and I've always thought about how it's too bad we didn't have a future because I really liked the docs. They could have been good friends. The Vegan? Yeah, I'm good. Despite this being the only time we had hung out with other people, he invited himself to join my family for Thanksgiving. Having never met them, and not being a man I was pursuing a future with, I checked with my sister and my mother first, expecting them to say no. I'd be okay with it. After all the hoopla and telling him he was welcome to join us, he changed his mind and decided not to come. *Thanks, pal. Was that just to stick it to me?* I'm just glad I didn't run out and buy a $25 organic apple pie and dairy-free vanilla ice cream that no one else would've eaten.

When we did hang out, he was always the same. Every time. No change in mood or tone. Oftentimes, he was annoyed and would vent about his roommate taking advantage of him or imposing on his lifestyle. The friend worked days, and with The Vegan working nights, heaven forbid he had to flush the toilet or take a shower in the morning. Every last thing he did was problematic for The Vegan, and it made me feel like I must be an inconvenience too. That summer, I had purchased a vintage road bike for a camping trip. Without asking, he loaded the box into his truck and brought it home to assemble. When I picked it up a few days later and thanked him profusely, he explained that while I didn't mean to be an imposition, I was. *Are you kidding me?! He took the bike without asking! He assembled it without asking! But I'm an imposition and impacted his day negatively? I'll keep that in mind. Next time I have to sneeze, I'll run outside and down the street. I wouldn't want to bother you. I'll forgo the orgasms too. Don't want to be a bother, sir.*

* * *

One of my girlfriends had invited me to a charity event. (Remember? The one I went to with The Vegan.) I was stoked about going and had invited Jiffy Lube. In his usual form, JL had let me down in spectacular fashion, with only a few hours till showtime. Meanwhile, The Vegan knew I planned on going and about a week prior started subtly hinting that if I had an extra ticket, maybe he could make the time to go with me. I suppose I didn't take him seriously. I wasn't sure the man was capable of having fun. In fact, I thought perhaps he was allergic to fun. Like full-on anaphylactic allergic. I mean, he avoided it like the plague. It was a dance, after all, and I could not picture that man dancing for the life of me. His hinting turned more aggressive, and he started insinuating that maybe I already had a date and that maybe he could at least watch my dog while I was at the event... with another man. *Ladies and Gentleman, it is my pleasure to introduce you to the Master of Guilt Trips. Ooh! Maybe we should have The Vegan and Toothless enter the ring and battle it out for that title. Now that's a match I'd love to watch!* Eventually, he came out and asked if my extra ticket was claimed because he would, in fact, like to go with me. My plus one. When I told him that I didn't think it was his cup of tea, he was rather insulted and somehow managed to turn that on me too. He never took me on regular run of the mill dates. Why on earth would I think he'd want to take me on a date supreme? Besides, I was still holding out hope that JL would accompany me. Four hours before kickoff, The Vegan reached out yet again, asking if I needed a date. With three hours to go, Jiffy Lube bailed. With two hours and forty-seven minutes to go, I admitted defeat and invited The Vegan to be my plus one. I had a pit in my stomach but ignored it and headed home to begin getting ready.

In his defense, The Vegan didn't have time to get a haircut or pick out anything new for the bash. He had a decent suit hanging in his closet and wore it well. He definitely could have used that haircut, though. He called while I was getting ready (keep in mind, we're at about 2 hours until go time here) and decided to launch into some conversation about his time spent in India, best yoga practices, and shishito and poblano peppers. I was most definitely tuning him out as I was doing my best to get ready in a hurry. I had to politely ask him if we could resume the (oh-so-riveting) conversation later in the evening. My group had already made reservations for dinner, and upon hearing where we were going, he was disappointed. Not because he'd been there, mind you, but because he hadn't. Even though this particular restaurant is award-winning and has been around longer than I've been alive, he feared the unknown and worried that they wouldn't have a lot to offer in the way of his restricted diet. I offered several times to go elsewhere with him and just meet them at the venue, but he declined and reluctantly agreed to go with the original plan.

I had asked him to come by about a half hour before we absolutely needed to leave to make it to dinner on time. Naturally, he showed up about an hour early, let himself in (clearly hadn't learned his lesson), and followed my voice down the hallway. He planted himself in the doorway to my bedroom, leaning on the door casing and being difficult right from the get go. He wore *difficult* more often than he wore cologne. I mean, it suited him well, but still. He harassed me for not being ready to go, knowing we had an hour before we'd need to leave. I was standing in my gown, my hair curled but my makeup not yet done. The more I rushed, the more nervous I got. The sweatier I got, the more I messed up my eyeliner. This guy was killing me, staring at me and critiquing everything I was doing. When he turned and squatted down to greet Wells, I gently pushed my door shut. Obviously irritated, he questioned me immediately. "I just get nervous doing my makeup in front of people. Please don't take it personally," I answered. He stomped down the hallway toward the kitchen, suggesting that maybe he just wait in his truck since I'm so uncomfortable around him. I didn't stop him. No. He was bluffing. He went into the kitchen and made sure he was loud enough for me to hear while he was talking to my dog. "Poor boy. You're almost out of water. I can't believe your mom didn't fill your bowl. Poor thing." Now I was red. Almost out of water, meaning he still had water in his dish. He moved onto dissecting my messy kitchen and commenting on everything in sight. I had tried and failed to drink the colonoscopy prep the pharmacy gave me weeks before, and the jug of solution was still on top of my refrigerator. "You didn't drink your colonoscopy prep. Well THAT'S why you weren't able to have it done!" No shit. Literally. I couldn't drink it. *What else do you want to point out?* The insults kept coming faster than I could take them. In record time I was ready. Ready to go? Maybe not. Ready to end this onslaught? You bet. I threw on a jacket, grabbed my clutch, and threw a shoe box under my arm (Thanks, Monotooth. The sneakers will be a delightful change later in the evening). We joined my friends at dinner and took our seats.

The atmosphere was fun, and the patrons were all so complimentary. My one-shouldered sequined gown and my girlfriend's show-stopping red dress were out of place for sure, but even more so appreciated by the men and women around us. So many compliments. For a brief second, I thought the night was looking up. I was so wrong. The Vegan glanced at the menu, but only briefly. There are only so many vegan options after all. They were out of falafel too! (Internally, I was laughing so hard I was crying!) He ordered a meatless burger with fries and made the best of it. It wouldn't have been my first choice either, but it looked decent. Ya know, for a lover of veggies, he doesn't even like the good veggies. He's not even a good vegan.

We made it through dinner and off to the main event. I pulled up the tickets so we'd have accurate directions and know where to park. When we arrived, we saw the long line of people wrapped around the building. I pointed out the parking lot that the email suggested, but he ignored me and continued driving past the hoard of people. He rounded the building and took a parking spot near the back door, completely unmarked and unattended. When I insisted that the instructions indicated that we'd have to enter the building through the main entrance, he laughed at me and said that a door is a door and surely someone would take our tickets there. We were, of course, turned away and told exactly that. Instead of moving his truck, we then walked around the entire perimeter of the building and past the ever growing line of ticket-holders to the very back. In the drizzling rain. There goes my hair. And all that walking? There goes the equivalent of 36 minutes of dancing in those strappy heels. And here comes the embarrassment that being the only assholes to ignore directions comes with. Awesome. We're off to a great start.

He didn't dance. He didn't want his picture taken for the photo-booth. Everything was very bougie and glamorous and definitely... wasn't his cup of tea. Go figure. He didn't complain about the pricey drinks, thank goodness and he didn't mind holding my drink while I danced with the ladies (and their fun-loving dates). When I would go to the bathroom, I'd tell him as a courtesy. He was annoyed and told me not to bother. When I didn't tell him, he later grew frustrated, not knowing where I had gone. Ugh. Can't win. He joined me for the silent disco party though, I think because it was unique and he wanted to see what it was all about. Even then, he bopped a bit, but I was pulling my dress out of my way and shaking my tail feathers like nobody's business. Clearly we weren't a match for that, either. I kept leaving the dance floor to stand with him and even walked the length of the building with him several times in an attempt to not make him feel left out. I wanted nothing more than to be getting down with my friends on the dance floor, but I'm not about to leave my date hanging, even if he wasn't my first choice. Hell, he wouldn't have even been my second choice. Despite the night not going the way I had anticipated, it wasn't a total suckfest, and my friends and I made the best of it.

I'd made friends with another Scarlett (you can't ignore a budding friendship with someone of the same name). When the night was wrapping up, she insisted that my date and I join her for a bit at a hole-in-the-wall bar downtown. He was less than thrilled, but given the hour, we wouldn't be stuck there long before they closed as well. The two venues were only a few minutes apart, and just as we pulled up to the bar, I realized I had forgotten my jacket at coat check. He was thankful to have something else to do and dropped me at the door while he headed back to get my coat. Scarlett and I met out front and tried to enter the bar. Well, she did, but without my ID, they wouldn't let me in. I tried to explain that my ID was in my jacket, which was on its way, but the bouncer clearly was in a mood and made me wait outside. It was chilly, and there I was, bare-shouldered in a floor length gown. I don't know about you, but I don't know of many gals dressing up to the nines and trying to get into bars underage. I waited for a solid 15 minutes outside alone in a very sketchy part of town. Just waiting. A guy I knew exited the bar and was delighted to see me. We chatted for a minute, and after explaining my predicament, he vouched for me with the bouncer, who was still having no part of it. We continued to catch up, and mid-sentence he interrupted to say, "Damn you look so good in that dress. Absolutely stunning. I just want to run my tongue down your neck, down your shoulder..." To my horror, I spotted The Vegan just behind him, rapidly approaching. I quickly grabbed my jacket and thanked the friend while wishing him well. He said goodbye and continued on his way. The Vegan looked upset, so I quickly explained what happened. It hadn't been a long conversation, nor had it been sexual in nature. He just happened to walk in on that particular line. Before I could finish, he angrily said, "Should I go chase him down? Should I punch him?" I talked him down quickly (and apparently he hadn't heard a word the guy said, so I should've kept my damn mouth shut). His resting bitch face had fooled me again. Ugh.

Finally, we made it inside and grabbed a beer. Scarlett was busy continuing some drama with the DJ from the event. Apparently, when she invited me to join her, she knew he'd be there and just wanted a friend to tag along. I also knew the DJ and before leaving, stopped by his barstool to say hi. I paid him a compliment about the night's tunes, we briefly caught up about our own lives, and then we dove into the mess that she had made of the night. We shared some laughs and warned each other that she might be trouble. I wasn't talking to the DJ for more than five minutes when I looked over my shoulder and saw that my date was no longer at our table. Another minute passed while exchanging yada yadas, and still, he didn't reappear. My hope that he was in the bathroom was quickly diminishing, so I said goodnight and headed outside. I was checking my phone to see if he had texted just as he was driving by. His text message suggested that I continue to enjoy my company and then grab an Uber home. He stopped at the stop sign, which gave me just enough time to pound on his back window. He drove off but did answer my call.

I demanded that he not leave me downtown in a bad neighborhood without my purse or keys to my house. He met me around the corner and decided he'd be kind enough to bring me home, albeit screaming at me the entire time. The ride home seemed twice as long as normal, and he didn't stop belittling me and tearing me down. The two men at the bar were enough to push him over the edge, and he'd finally lost it. He went up one side of me and down the other. It was awful. When I had a chance to talk, I had nothing left. He had made me feel so small. Jiffy Lube had already crushed me earlier. Now him. A girl can only take so much rejection in one night. When we pulled into my driveway, he jumped out, threw the shoebox and my purse on the ground, and screamed at me some more. I asked him to calm down and have a conversation, but he wouldn't listen. His final point of contention was that he was really hungry and had he known that his only option for dinner was going to be a Beyond Burger, he would've eaten a real dinner first. The best example of hanger that I've ever seen. Definitely the most extreme. *Someone get that man a Snickers! Wait, are Snickers vegan?!*

* * *

Despite saying he wanted nothing to do with me and never wanted to see me again, he kept reaching out. Not enough to move past what had transpired, but just enough to keep a connection. But then something changed in him and he decided to go for broke. Maybe he was soul searching. Maybe he realized if he continued this way, he'd never find a partner. Whatever it was, HE changed. The Steve Urkel-like man that I'd gone to the dance with showed up at my office a few weeks later, but now he more closely resembled Stefan Urkell (if you don't know this reference, Google it. You're welcome). He asked me to meet him across the street from my office. He was still in his work uniform, which made me think that he'd been thinking of this for hours and had neglected going to bed just so he could meet up with me. He told me I looked beautiful and that he missed me. A first. I was flabbergasted. He told me that I looked better than ever, and he was regretful for not having said it more often. He was complimentary and affectionate, hugging me repeatedly and giving gentle kisses. He knew my time was limited, so he wrapped things up with a gift. He handed me a chocolate bar. It was one of those big, gourmet ones from a local company. It wasn't the chocolate bar that sent me though. It was the handwritten stack of post-it notes on top. There's no way to really explain what was written without simply showing you. This might ruin chocolate for you forever. So on that note, I'll leave you with this. You've been warned.

| 16 |

Steak for Two

I t was foolish of me to have even given this guy another chance. The first few dates with him were duds, but he did send me flowers early on. And I had known him for years. And he was a good dad. On one date that was actually rather pleasant, he had worn me down. We'd spent hours together that night, and when he wanted more, I finally gave in. A girl has needs. THIS girl had needs. Don't judge. Anyway, I had one condom on hand (and surprisingly, for a man who wanted it so badly, he didn't have anything with him). There was no foreplay, no lead up. He was ready to go and unwrapped that little sucker like a kid opening his first present on Christmas morning. I was still dressed but that didn't phase him. He was just so damn eager. There was no grace with which he opened that wrapper but such hustle and determination, that he not only opened its packaging, but destroyed the condom in the process. The look on his face was priceless. He looked as if he'd just been turned down by his middle school crush or that he'd learned there was no Santa. He glanced up from the carnage in his hands, looked up at me, back to his hands and once more, back into my eyes. "Do... do you have another?" he stuttered. He already knew the answer. "Can we still—" he gulped sadly. "Can we please still?" I shook my head slowly and did my best to hide my amusement. *#neverbeensothankfulforabrokencondom #divineintervention But I still gave him another chance. What a fucking pushover.*

152

* * *

Another date over, and I laid there, aimlessly scrolling through Netflix. I'm not sure I was even reading the titles. I just so badly wanted to wash away the evening. Maybe I was just clinging to the hope that he could still turn it around and surprise me. Or maybe I was just lonely. Was it crazy for me to assume he planned on paying for dinner after choosing the restaurant and very clearly saying he "couldn't wait to take me out to a special dinner for my birthday?" I don't mind paying, mind you—It was 2021 after all, but it was my birthday. Seriously. I don't know what shocked me the most. The fact that he made multiple jokes about how "if I was a good girl" I could keep some of the leftovers, the part where the check remained on the table for a solid five minutes (and I most definitely saw him glance down at it), or the part where he waited until I had given my card to the server and she left the table with it before blurting out, "Are they ever going to bring us the check?!" Ridiculous. I think my favorite part, however, was early on in the night, walking up to his beat-up, rusty ol' sports car while trying to figure out if I was on a hidden camera reality show. Much like him, that car had seen better days, and when he opened the door, a waft of stale air smacked me in the face. No exaggeration. The skunky aroma of cannabis and musk (note to self: Cannabis and Musk—could be the name of a candle fragrance, most likely Vegan, made with soy, a good market for it here) was so thick that it immediately turned my stomach. I should have faked an illness right then and headed back inside, but alas, I'm too nice. And the Picanha for two is to die for. Honestly, maybe that was my driving force in going. I was practically salivating at the thought of that delicious Brazilian style steak when I climbed into his car, knowing full well that no steak would be worth what might come. Even with the house-made black garlic sauce and fresh horseradish. Not. Worth. It.

It wasn't until we were crossing the parking lot toward the restaurant that I even realized what he was wearing. I had hoped that the lighting was just too dim and that maybe he was more appropriately dressed than I thought. Nope. My eyes, sadly, were not deceiving me. Inside the restaurant, it was clear as day. There he stood, a full-grown man in his 40s wearing sneakers, jeans, a hoodie, a puffer vest, and a baseball cap... to a restaurant that had roasted oysters and steak tartare on the menu. *You're killin' me, Smalls.* At one point he began taking his long sleeved shirt off, but the graphic tee underneath bore a lively scene with Michael Myers from Halloween, and I quickly distracted him. Holy hell. Not sure how much more of this I can take.

* * *

I was derailed from my train of thought as Wells nudged my leg and returned me to the task at hand. The main menu was shuffling on repeat, and I still hadn't selected anything to watch. What was that noise? I looked at my phone and saw that it was almost midnight. What kind of jackass would be revving their engine so late? Couldn't be my amazing date—he had left nearly a half hour before. His pathetic ploy to come inside was far too obvious, and after letting him use the bathroom (I'm not a monster), I promptly sent him on his way, sans cuddles. Before I could climb out of my warm bed and peer through the blinds, there was a knock at the door. Wells barked, clearly not any more a fan of this late night intrusion than I was. There he was, the best date ever, standing on my front steps, out of breath, explaining that his car was stuck in my driveway and it might be best if he spend the night. *Spend the night?! Move aside, sir!*

I slipped past him in only a hoodie and pajama shorts (the short kind you would never wear in front of anyone). He turned around in the doorway, his eyes following me down the steps, clearly shocked that I'd embark into the snow in only slippers. The sheer amount of determination that I was flooded with in that moment was incredible. Maybe only topped when birthing my sons. I had never wanted anything more than to get this man's car out of my driveway and on its way. He showed me where the back tires were slightly elevated off the ground after slowly trying to leave the driveway. The berm of snow left by the plow (thanks, Plow Guy) was there for sure, but nothing a true Vermonter couldn't handle with ease. Maybe he was worried about damaging his rusty excuse for a car. Seriously, the man was so proud of this damn car but it didn't show. If he hadn't driven like a pansy, he would've cleared that snow without any issue. But here I was, bare-legged, snow falling into my shearling-lined moccasins, my breath escaping all around me into the cold night air. Looking back, maybe it was emasculating of me, but at the time I was seeing red. He'd wasted so much of my night with his absurd behavior, and I just wanted to reclaim what I could of it. I grabbed my shovel and went to work on the front tires. They were freed in mere seconds and then I turned my attention to the rear of the car (the only rear that would be getting any attention that night, much to this guy's dismay). I've never been the best at math, but it was incredibly obvious that we just needed a little weight on the trunk of his car. I made him hop his cute little denim'd ass up there, and promptly took the driver's seat. True, it was stuck, but with a little will power and some muscle, I nudged that car forward and backward as many times as it took. After all of ninety seconds, the front tires broke through the wall of snow triumphantly, and came to a stop in the middle of the street. I threw the car into park and hopped to my feet. Without so much as a second thought, I wished him a great night and walked swiftly out of his night and back into the warmth of my house. I never even looked back at the poor guy. He reached out the next day with a bizarre request—a picture of our meal. And another date. I'm sure the taste of rejection was far worse than the delicious leftovers. And man, were they delicious.

| 17 |

Dishonorable Mentions (Part 2)

DISCLAIMER: Second verse, same as the first. More creeps. More failed encounters for your reading pleasure. Cleanse that palate. After this, shit gets real.

It's All Greek to Me

I love a good whiskey as much as the next guy, probably more. And so did this guy. I met him online (I know, shhhh! I get it, I get it!) and we talked a bit. A few times we planned to share some scotch around a fire, but it hadn't happened. Life kept getting in the way. Apparently, he felt disrespected or blown off, and the world being as small as it is, word got to one of my best girlfriends. She encouraged me to give him a chance, saying that she'd only met him once but that he was a great guy. He had hooked her up with all kinds of meat when Covid times made provisions scarce. *I get it. There's a lot I'd do for some free bacon.* I felt kinda bad for my lack of effort and agreed to try again. We met up for a nice dinner at one of my favorite places. It's not super fancy or anything, but he showed up in his work sweatshirt—a black hoodie that was definitely due for a wash. Dinner was okay but I quickly learned that his style of engagement was to jokingly repeat what you said. It was a bit obnoxious but tolerable, and potentially, I could get used to it with time. He had worked for years at the local drive-in movie theater and suggested putting on a movie (any movie I wanted) during the winter. We'd have the place to ourselves. It was a really sweet thought and most definitely appealed to my nostalgic side, having always gone there as a child and now bringing my own kids. And in conversing, he learned that Greece holds the top spot on my travel my bucket list. Being Greek himself, he didn't hesitate to tell me he travels there often and even suggested we visit together sometime. Although a little forward of him, it was a sweet gesture and I thought nothing more of it. With no glaring red flags, we decided to go out again. Same black hoodie. Still unwashed. Still badly in need of a haircut and a fresh shave. I'm not just being a bitch here—his hair was rat fucked, and he looked like he'd just gotten out of bed after a 48-hour bender. His nails were jagged and his conversation, again, was repetitive at best. He was a nice enough guy, but I don't think he was feeling it any more than I was.

Two months later, a mutual friend of ours reached out saying that they'd just gone to a college basketball game together. Apparently this guy was telling the whole group about how he'd gone on a few dates with me. I'd get it, I suppose, if he and I bumped uglies and he wanted to brag (still not cool, but I can almost understand that flex). We didn't though. We didn't even kiss. And yet, here he was, months later, bragging about having gone on two dates with me that amounted to nothing. I definitely don't see what that accomplishes for him. In fact, another guy in attendance at the game was bragging that we were "talking." Once. Only once on the phone, and we'd never met in person. I had no plans to. During our one very short phone call, he not only invited me to come meet him at the campground he was currently living in, but invited me to move in with him. Into his camper. Having never met me. You read that correctly. He wasn't harassing, just an idiot. Very sporadically, he'd message me and ask me how I was doing. He had reached out on the day of the game, and I responded twice with the shortest of answers, so clearly, we were "talking." *Pathetic on both of them. I thought the Meat Guy and I had let things end as bluntly as they'd started, but what do I know? It's all Greek to me. All I know is that I didn't get any meat, and this time, I wouldn't have complained about getting meat on a first or second date.*

The One Who Didn't Understand Sarcasm

I worked with this guy years ago. He was younger than me but nice enough (they all start out that way). I wasn't single though, and made sure to let him know at the first sign of his affection. He didn't like that answer, but it was his friends (other coworkers of ours) who really disliked my situation. They invited me out to join the three of them. It would surely have proven to be a night of shenanigans (riddled with drugs, alcohol, and adultery) if I had let it. I knew better and politely refused. His buddies had it out for me after that, sending me dirty looks in the hallways. They were trying to be the best wingmen, and my lack of interest foiled their plans. Despite their aggression, this young man and I forged an unlikely friendship. He was actually pretty funny, and he had an unassuming disposition. He loved Disney movies and had lines from several of his favorites memorized. Folks often said he resembled Luke Combs and he was quick to tell you that he sounded like him too. I never heard him sing, but he convinced me to sing for him once. I'm pretty sure that was my mistake. *Who knew I had the voice of an angel?* He fell for me right then and there. I quickly realized that I'd have to pull away from our work-ship. He was getting smitten, and I didn't want to lead the poor guy on. There was zero chance of us ever dating, and meanwhile, I'm convinced he was naming our future children (Esmerelda, Gaston, and Jasmine, no doubt). While I slowly backed away from the friendship we'd begun to form, he tightened his grip and did his damndest to hold on.

We both ended up in different jobs at different places, but he'd made it a point to stay connected. He'd reach out every once in a while, even long after he'd entered into a committed relationship. This girl was beautiful—a cute brunette, curvy with a pretty face. He had it good and was lucky to have her by his side. They even moved in together. It didn't matter. Queue the 2:00am dick pics and Snaps.

It was neverending. It started with a blurry TV in the background and his boxers standing at attention. Sometimes, he'd be suggestively stroking atop the thin fabric. And then the nudes started coming. He begged me to come over, to see him. To give him a chance. I'm sure he would have made good on his promise to 'rock my world,' had he been given the chance. At first, I countered his Snaps with witty comebacks, but that didn't phase him. Then I turned to sarcasm. "OMG, yes! Are you free right now? I can't wait to fuck you!" And that poor fella, he thought I was serious. Every. Damn. Time. Without fail. At what point would he learn that I was obviously kidding and had no plans to cheat or to help him cheat. Nor did his unsolicited bulging boxers do it for me. He was relentless, so I ended up blocking him on most platforms, forgetting one. When he became single, he reached out again, drunk. Not a little buzzed, but shitfaced. He threw himself at me again, and when I rejected him for the last time, he told me he was going to kill himself. That he had nothing to live for. I sent him the link for a suicide hotline and wished him well. Then promptly blocked him. Imagine my surprise when I ran into him just a few weeks later at the bowling alley. *Hopefully he bowled a better game than he had with me.*

Get That Man a Snickers!

A few weeks after my friend died, a man reached out to me online, claiming that our loss was mutual. Even though we had stopped dating quite a while before he passed, his death was still really hard for me, and this guy knew it. He had heard about me and sought me out. He was at the funeral and had figured out who I was but never said hi until after. "He spoke very highly of you," he said. "I know he was upset that it didn't work out. He thought you were really special." It was nice to hear that I'd meant something to him and that part of him regretted ending our time together. My new friend and I bonded over stories about our late friend, commiserating about our loss. Our conversation remained platonic on my end, but he'd insert phrases and questions that made me begin to wonder where he stood. He suggested we get together and meet, so we did. We hung out a few times, and I quickly realized that he'd used this loss as nothing more than an excuse to talk to me. He worked with laser cutters and made me a gag gift: an anklet adorned with a cat-etched charm. He joked that he wanted to bend down and put that on my ankle... and visit my other cat while he was down there. *Ewww. Stop talking.* When a last minute plan to grab dinner got derailed and we met up almost two hours later than planned, he yelled at me. I don't mean a little. His voice reached a supersonic, high-pitched level and he whined. Boy did he whine. Like a spoiled little brat. He was so hangry that I didn't even recognize him. Maybe he was having a Snickers moment. Or maybe he shouldn't wait so late to eat. Two bites in, he calmed down. It was really off-putting, though, and made me not want to see him again. Definitely not in any dating capacity. The conversation turned to our late friend, and without hesitation he said, "Yeah. He said you were a good fuck." *So that was the real reason he reached out. He couldn't even find a date on his own. He had to prey on the sad women his friend left behind. Ya know what? I was damn good, and he wasn't about to find out.* At one point when we were still in touch, he began telling me how he had a different woman lined up every day that week. He had two on Twosday. It was so gross, and I didn't hesitate to tell him what I thought. He was looking for sex and only sex, and it showed. *Anyone want a cat anklet? Anyone? Free to a good home.*

A Storebrand Saltine

One thing my staff at work knows is how I rank my interviewees. It's become measurable lingo in the office, and no one questions its validity. Sometimes there are Saltines (boring and bland). If they're really not knocking my socks off, they're storebrand Saltines. I only hire Ritz. This date, however, was a storebrand Saltine on a good day. He was very persistent in asking for a date, and after he groaned on about what a loser he was, I felt bad and reluctantly agreed. *Ladies, if a man tells you who he is, believe him!* I was sure to make it a lunch date though, and knew it would be our one and only. More than three times, he made it clear that he'd be treating me to the meal. This was planned at one of the least expensive, most casual places around. The fact that this was a big deal to him made me realize that he probably didn't get out much, let alone on dates.

Over my bed of lettuce, I learned that he lived with his parents and his sister. He had a dead end job that he hated but no motivation to make a change. When he wasn't busy playing video games, he made plenty of time for self-loathing. Just like in an interview, I knew 60 seconds in that he wasn't getting a second interview—I mean, date. How could I be expected to love him when he didn't love himself? When we finished our lunch, he walked me to a nearby gazebo. *Dude, my car's that way.* He sat down on the wooden bench inside, and I took a seat beside him. In an effort to let him down easy, surely I could tolerate another five minutes. It was only five minutes. Easy enough. He told me I was beautiful and that he wanted to kiss me. I politely declined. Three more times he tried to convince me to let him kiss me. It was a non-starter.

A week went by and I had stopped reaching out. I didn't ghost him per se—he had stopped reaching out to me too. He was making it really easy for me to walk away guilt-free. He had a lot of growing up to do, and I wasn't signing up to be his nanny. A bouquet of sterling roses arrived at my office followed by a call. He wanted to make sure I hadn't forgotten about him. *But honestly, how could I? You never forget the one that got away. Sigh.*

"Yo, What's your credit score?"

I had rushed across the street to grab a quick lunch at the market like I often do. A gentleman who was standing outside grabbed the door for me. When I went to exit the store, he was still there, holding the door again. *I sure hope they were paying him.* I recognized him, but he didn't seem to remember having met me before. Actually, we'd met on more than one occasion, but no skin off my back. I thanked him again but didn't slow my roll on my way back to work. He stopped me, stuttering. "I, uh, I don't know how to do this," he stammered. In hindsight, he knew exactly what he was doing. He's an actor and a comedian. He's a storyteller, and in his other life, he fundraises for a private school. Everything about this man screams manipulation and bullshit. He knew how to talk his way out of the best situations, and as I've learned, also the worst. He feigned a nervousness to ask me out, but ultimately, it was all an act. He played his cards right, though, and asked me to take his number instead of asking for mine. Smart move. His references checked out, and a few days later, I texted him.

Turns out, he wasn't exactly divorced. He still shared his house with his wife and their two kids. He explained that although they were in the process of getting divorced, since it wasn't final, his lawyer suggested that should he date, he should keep it on the down-low for now. She worried that he'd have a much weaker case if he was already seeing someone romantically. So in other words, dates were out. No going out. No hanging out unless I went to his place or he came to mine. I tried visiting him at his place a few times. He was very specific on where to park and when to approach his house. He'd sneak me into the garage and in whispered tones, he'd try to connect. He would wrap his arms around me and try to make our short time together more intimate than it deserved to be. *I'm not about to be somebody's dirty little secret. No thank you.*

He began telling me tall tales about his soon-to-be-ex-wife, saying that she was crazy and accusing him of all this really absurd stuff, like -setting up surveillance to spy on her and spending her money on random things just to spite her. She was the breadwinner of the family, and apparently she was using this against him during their separation. Honestly, it was too much drama, and I wanted no part of it. We never went on a date. One night, he was in the area when I was out with friends, and I decided that was a safe enough group setting, so he joined us for a little while. He was there for less than an hour and somehow convinced my girlfriend to donate to his passion project.

She sent him $200 right then. I was flabbergasted. I'm not sure which one knew how to schmooze and play the game better. *Impressive.*

He started taking the liberty to call me whenever he felt like it. I'll be the first to admit that I'm not a morning person, a fact he chose to disregard when it didn't suit him. With no coffee in my system, he'd call at the ass-crack of dawn, asking my stance on things like abortion and gun control. His sons weren't even allowed to watch cartoons that had mention of lasers or nerf guns, and I'd have to get rid of mine if we decided to give this a real shot. The man was demanding to know my credit score and my religious beliefs. It was bizarrely forward of him and left such a bad taste in my mouth. He ended up dating some-one else (apparently, he got over the optics of dating publicly pretty quickly this time around). This only helped to heighten their court drama. His wife came into my office and (having no idea who I was or that I knew who her husband was) demanded records and receipts. Of course, I was unable to provide these to her without a court order, but I knew who she was before she said anything about him. And I got to hear her side of how everything had gone down in their marriage. He seemed to be crazier and scarier than I'd even realized. *My credit score could be better and I have no problem with guns. I'm thankful, though, because I definitely dodged a bullet with this one.*

The Groom

I've helped to plan and coordinate hundreds of weddings and events over the years. I always refer to my couples as my 'brides' and 'grooms.' This particular couple was a lot of fun, and I really enjoyed the family traditions they incorporated into their celebration. Their friends were a blast too. Four years have passed, and with that, they've had their ups and downs. I see The Groom often at a bar I frequent. He's usually there with his guys and often hits on me. According to him, his marriage lacks the physical intimacy it once had, and I'd be a suitable replacement for the night. Or several nights. Apparently, he's wanted me since his wife hired me to coordinate their wedding. Sure, it was flattering at first, I suppose. But then, one night he was direct AF. I was able to keep it innocent, and he respected that for the most part. In an effort to walk away from his burning gaze, I played it off by suggesting that I'd see him later on the dance floor. He grabbed my hand, pulled me back toward him, leaned in close, and in my ear said, "I can't wait to fuck you later." Oh. My. Goodness. I turned fifty shades of red, and my jaw hit my tits. I quickly slipped out of his view before telling my sister. I shook it off. No literally, I shook those tail feathers and moved on with my night, my friends and I laughing at the sheer audacity. Every time I see him now, he licks his lips and stares intently from across the bar, making his intentions known. I make sure to keep my distance. *A happy ending is his responsibility in the marriage, not mine. That was definitely not included in our contract.*

Love Thy Neighbor

It's no wonder the woman next door didn't like me. I figured she was just bitchy, overworked, underpaid, tired. Ya know. Turns out her husband was a total creep and had been drooling over me from the second I moved in. I'd be in the kitchen doing dishes, and he'd look up and see me in the window. Every. Single. Time. If I was walking to or from my car, he'd find me. His timing was uncanny, and pretty quickly, I learned that it was intentional. He kept finding excuses to talk, signaling me to come outside for the simplest of things. And naturally, when Wells would break free and I was in risque pajamas or a bathing suit, he'd catch me mid bend, wrapping my hand around Wells' collar. He'd keep me talking for several minutes, and all the while I'd be mortified at my current wardrobe choice. As always, I'm too nice and would stay in a compromising position much longer than I should have. He pulled me aside once and told me how attractive he found me, citing that his marriage wasn't what it once was. That he'd probably be getting separated soon. Of course, he said all this from the privacy of his shed where no one would spot us. After telling me how great I was, he point blank asked me what I thought of him. I took a step toward him and, finger in his face, said, "I think you're married. And I don't think you're being a good husband right now." His advances stopped almost immediately, and later, he even apologized for his approach.

He did have a rough relationship with his wife and it made sense, if for no other reason than being busy hitting on the single mothers of the neighborhood. I'm sure I wasn't the only one. You could often hear yelling coming from his house. And if it wasn't his wife, it was one of his four children. Someone was always fighting with someone. One day, he apologized for the noise. "Things have been really rough lately. We might actually be getting a divorce," he explained. "If you hear screaming coming from my house, it's just us." I didn't miss a beat. "I totally get it. If you hear screaming coming from my house, it's because I'm single." I was pretty proud of how quickly I'd come up with that one. *Drops mic.*

"I Could Eat a Peach for Hours"

Years ago, I was in the market for a game console for my sons and a friend suggested a little store that sold devices and games—both retro and new. I had contacted the owner beforehand to discuss availability and pricing, and he was super helpful. I was running late and hoped he'd stay open just a few minutes longer. At the door's jingle, he looked up from the counter, and his whole demeanor changed. Any annoyance that he might have felt immediately dissipated and was replaced with, I don't know. Hope? Excitement? He eagerly assisted this single mother and took his time. He knocked even more off the price, clearly not wanting me to leave his store any time soon. I appreciated his help and made it a point to thank him one last time. He kept the messages going, albeit platonic. Everything he said was laced with flirtation, but he maintained a certain level of professionalism. I had ended up in a relationship before he had mustered up the courage to ask me out. After that, he was sure to keep in touch but also sure to keep his distance. He'd taken a liking to me but didn't want to cross any lines. I respected that about him. An avid sports fan, he had season's tickets for the Red Sox every year, and I managed to buy a pair off him. Our friendship came close to blossoming several times, but he was adamant that we couldn't spend any time together due to his feelings for me. Mad respect.

* * *

He was a big fan of Tim Tebow and a steadfast supporter of his Night to Shine—an event that supports young men and women with developmental delays who might not otherwise get to go to a prom. Just one more reason to respect the hell outta this guy. I decided to volunteer as well. The evening was so rewarding, and although you could see the way he looked at me, he still managed to stay in his lane, and me in the friend zone. I admired him, of course, but since I wasn't single, I didn't entertain the thought for even a second.

When I first met him, he was living in the back room of his store. At some point, he made some life changes and began working full time at a gym. It seemed promising. It was only a brief stint though, and he went back to running the store full-time. It was a one man show, and his lack of commute made life easy. He started sleeping at the store again. When I'd come in to visit and pick up a few things for the kids, he would wait until they were out of ear shot and suggest we fool around in his 'room.' This is the same man who refused to grab a drink with me because his feelings were too strong and he didn't want to cross any lines. I was still in a relationship, but he seemed to no longer care, telling me how I was the only one he wanted and he'd do anything to be with me. He crossed that line full throttle. He was especially hung up on wanting to taste me, saying there was nothing that he loved more than 'eating a peach for hours.' He desperately wanted to show me that he meant it. His newest play was that he had made a commitment to his parents. He planned to transition his store to online-only and close the brick and mortar. At some point in the coming years, he'd move into their home and live out the rest of their days with them as their caregiver. This wouldn't give him the bandwidth to date, he explained. He could have hookups, sure, and plenty of 'em. He made that abundantly clear. What he wouldn't have time for, however, was a relationship. But if he ever did, I would have been the one. The lucky one to have his time and attention. The only one who would be able to tie him down. I was 'special.' My goodness, how many times he told me I was special.

His approach changed. He was reaching out sporadically and began guilting me for not inviting him over to my place to hang out. Knowing it would just be for a booty call, I had zero interest in doing so. Then he started getting mean about it, placing blame and telling me how it obviously would have not included any funny business and how dare I assume that's all he wanted? Ugh. Everything he said and did only made me want to see him less and less. His last few messages were sweet, as he was very clearly trying to get back in my good graces, but he still maintained that it broke his heart to not be able to date me at this point in his life. Fast forward to him actually moving in with his parents, meeting a neighbor, spending all of his free time with her (for a mere three days), and then making it not only official, but Facebook official. Confused (and perhaps a little butt hurt), I reached out and wished him nothing but happiness in his new life and new relationship. He abruptly unfriended me and reached out saying that he'd had me in his phone as "Princess Scarlett," which popped up in front of the new girlfriend when I'd messaged. With the nickname and my looks combined, she was instantly jealous and had a lot of questions. In an effort to make this new love of his work out, he unfriended me—the only person he'd ever considered dating, had his life turned out differently. What a crock. Fast forward again, two months. I wanted to give you all an accurate update, so I looked into it. They're engaged. 60 days in. *Must be true love. I should probably recommend an oral surgeon or TMJ doctor. His poor jaw. #millionsofpeaches*

Twisted Tea

"Don't look now, but do you see that guy over there?" my sister asked. "Twisted Tea is looking at you." She gave him his nickname (I've never been prouder). He was a bigger guy, bald with piercing blue eyes. We made eye contact twice, and he decided to make his way over to me. He wasn't shy, and turns out, he was a drummer. The band that was on stage called him up to join them for a song. He was a talented musician for sure, but it certainly wasn't love at first sight for me. When he finished that one song, he came directly back to me. We danced together for a song or two, and I headed on my way. He found me online and sent me a message. I told him I wasn't ready to date, but he persisted, reaching out often and calling me as much as I'd let him. The day my divorce was finalized, I was working. I took my lunch break, went into a private office, got divorced in a Zoom call (thank you Covid times), and then went back to work. My eyes were puffy and red from crying. I excused myself to go outside for a few minutes and pull my shit together. Twisted Tea, being the great listener that he was (enter sarcasm here), chose that exact moment to show up at my office with a bouquet of red roses. Unfrickenbeliev-able. He doubled down though, taking the opportunity to hit on me. "You're amazing. Anyone would be lucky to have you. Hell, I'd date you in a heartbeat," he said. "Can I take you to dinner?" *Definitely not the moment, dude. Read the room.*

I friend-zoned him hard, which was the right call for us both while I was busy healing. Ultimately, it was the right call overall. I remem-ber him calling me for a ride home from work one day. We weren't close enough that I should be one of the first people he turned to (red flag). The commute would prove to be 20 minutes to his place of em-ployment, 40 minutes to his house, and almost another hour home. I had a raging migraine that was kicking my ass and suggested he try another friend first, but that I'd help if he was truly without another option. He said I was his only hope and happily awaited my arrival. And because I'm too nice, I stepped up. That man let me drive all that way in the blaring sun with a horrible headache for an opportunity to see me. It showed me a side of him I knew I could never date. He spent the next few months telling me about his exploits in dating and his ever increasing body count. Why do men (who tried, and failed) to date me feel the need to share details of their dating life after me? I don't need to know. I don't care. I'm not a callous person, but hearing that you got laid when I wouldn't give you a second date? Good for you.

Hoes Before Bros

We had had a lovely evening celebrating one of my dearest girlfriends on her birthday. Dinner and drinks were shared overlooking the lake while a spectacular sunset danced on the smooth surface of the water. Over-sized sun hats and shades surrounded the table, and the warmth of the late July sun kissed our cheeks and our toes. Laughs were had, too many to count, and so we decided the night was too young to end there. The birthday girl had a favorite bar, one we were sure to visit every time she was in town. With another round of 'Emily Fell off the Wagons' on order, a group of gentlemen noticed our gal group and began to circle. They thought they were stealthy in their approach and were soon part of our ongoing conversation. *Let them think they were being sneaky. Why not?* This one built fella with a dimple and perfect hair (we'll forever refer to him simply as 'Fuck Boy') took a liking to the birthday girl. His buddy was a shorter guy with tats covering every visible inch of flesh, stopping at his collar bone. Yup, you guessed it. That's the one that noticed me. *Go figure.* He was cute enough, don't get me wrong. But I wasn't single and he knew it. Under the guise of friendship, he continued to reach out for a few days, even after his group's training was done and they'd left the state. He was getting all lovey-dovey, sending me the lyrics to Conway Twitty songs and spewing romantic lines, telling me how special I was. He wanted to take things to the next level, and in this digital age, that meant nudes. I wasn't about to play the game, and after trying a few times to change my mind, he disappeared. He stopped cold turkey, not that I continued to reach out either. It was shitty how he'd ghosted me, but ultimately, who cares? A few months went by, and while he did cross my mind when my friend and I would gossip about Fuck Boy, those were about the only times that he did.

Out of the blue, I received a text message from him. And then another. And another. It seemed as though he'd forgotten how rudely he'd tossed me aside. He texted again, asking me to please pick up when he called. He called a few times, but I wasn't about to answer. What did this guy want after all this time anyway? He was beginning to piss me off, so I eventually answered, ready to put him in his place. "Please don't hang up," a soft voice pleaded. After a few seconds of silence (I was shocked and didn't know what was happening), "Um, who is this?" I asked. "I'm his wife," she said. No explanation given. None needed. I was thankful for not having indulged this creep when I had the chance and was saddened to hear what a shitbag he'd been to his wife. This sweet school teacher and mother of three turned out to be very understanding, and I quickly learned that I was only one of many he'd tried to hook up with. Although there wasn't much to tell, I answered all of her questions and was as cooperative as possible. We're still friends to this day. And the guy? They're divorced. Serves him right!

What a Handy Guy

There I was at class, watching my son practice his taekwondo patterns. I'd been taking him for weeks and had made friends with some of the other parents. One man, who was a TKD student himself, went out of his way to say hello. He was super friendly and I thought nothing of it, until one night when he spelled it out for me. "I'm trying to flirt with you," he explained. "It's been a while. Maybe I'm a little rusty." I was flattered, of course, but simply appreciated the camaraderie. Before I knew it, my son had convinced me to join him on the mat. It was a great workout and I appreciated the supportive club I'd become a member of. This guy took a special interest and was constantly checking in. I cheered him and his kids on when they tested and promoted. He did the same for us. When my son received the Rookie of the Year award and I received Most Improved, I don't think there was anyone in the room who was genuinely happier for us.

This guy was a local celebrity of sorts, owning and running his own family business for years. A devoted dad, a committed community member and a loving husband, he was well respected amongst those who know him. Apparently, his decades-long marriage wasn't all it seemed to be, and he'd grown a bit lonely. He began reaching out at all times of day and night, inviting me to join him at his business after hours. He started sending me pics... the naughties. He was very lonely and I think, hoped all his flirtiness would start paying off. I would talk him down and he'd keep things platonic for a bit, but every once in a while, he'd start back up.

He had been on his best behavior for a long time and had kept the pictures of Richard (aka dick pics) at bay. We were friends. Finally. Nothing inappropriate to fear. Then one day, I stopped in to shop at his store. It was slow and we were alone, so he gave me 'the tour'. He took me to the back room, and after telling me how much he liked the sweater I was wearing, backed me up against the wall. He put one hand on either side of me and leaned in. He tried to kiss me and I quickly turned my head to the side, preventing his lips from connecting with mine. With his forehead resting against the wall and his mouth near my ear, he started moaning. I realized then, that he had freed himself from his pants and was stroking it. His dick was fully erect and he was much closer to climax than I could have known. He begged me to touch it, or taste it. "It's been so long... Please," he cried. I refused and began pushing him away. Before I could put up a real fight or explain why I wasn't okay with what was happening, he came. Right there. On the floor of his business. Presumably, out of sight of his surveillance cameras. He'd most definitely planned this. It was calculated. I left as quickly as I could, still in shock over what had just happened. He reached out the next day, claiming that he felt so guilty and worried that his late mother could see him and what he'd done. He was ashamed. He wasn't the good husband or good Catholic he'd spent his life aiming to be. He felt terrible. And maybe I would have believed that, had he not come back months later, sending pics of bulging boxers and suggestive poses. *There is no deal good enough to get me to visit his place of business again, and it's probably for the best that I no longer practice taekwondo. If I saw him on the mat again, he'd be the one going down. Grrr.*

| 18 |

Dancing in the Moonlight...
Forever

The year was 2000, maybe 2001. He was cute. 6'0". Maybe 6'2"? He had light brown hair and a killer smile. He was new to the restaurant I worked at, washing dishes while I waited tables. He caught my eye right away, and although quiet, I could tell I'd caught his as well. It was a middle school crush, as they say, though we were both in high school. We went to different schools, and our paths hadn't crossed until we worked together. I asked another dishwasher about him and quickly learned that he lived near to the restaurant, was an avid drummer, and was a year younger than me. At first, our conversation was limited to a sentence here or there in passing. As weeks passed, I successfully navigated my shyness and our talks were far more effortless. I think we both looked forward to running into each other and dreaded the nights we'd show up to find that the other wasn't working. The flirting had ramped up, and it was unspoken amongst the other teenage boys that I was off limits.

School vacation was coming up, and he invited me to come spend some time with him at his house. His parents would be working, and all I needed to do was take the city bus to his neighborhood. Easy peasy, or so I thought. The butterflies in my stomach were on a two day bender, and when I arrived at his front step, decided to pull an all out rave. I thought I was going to be sick. The nervousness enveloped me, and had I not been spotted, I probably would have left as quietly as I'd arrived. He ushered me in (Usher, Usher) and gave me the tour, lighting up when we reached the music room. They were a family of musicians, and this seemed to be the most frequented room in the whole house. He eagerly showed me his drum set, beating his drumsticks a few times, giving me just a glimpse of the talent he had. "It suits my fancy," he said with a smirk. We didn't waste a lot of time before he led me to his bedroom. It was cozy and clean. We sat on the edge of his bed, music quietly playing in the background. Without words, he leaned in for a kiss. After giving me just enough of a teaser to make me want to continue, he rose to his feet and pulled his polo shirt off in one swift motion. He headed into the hallway and invited me to follow. When I entered the bathroom, I caught a quick glimpse of his very tall, very naked backside disappearing behind the shower curtain. He waved me in and then began singing, seemingly unbothered by whether I chose to join him or not. Self-conscious as all teenage girls are, and having never done anything like this before, it took me the entire duration of his shower to steel myself for the task. I heard the water shut off just as I removed my other sock. He pulled the curtain back to see me standing there, completely undressed and ready to join him. He smiled, whistled, and without a word, turned the water back on. This charm was embedded in who he was as a person and would later lend itself to our reboot: Scarlett and 6'4" 2.0, est. 2020.

The shower was short lived but sexy AF and led to a heavy make-out session, complete with my first... um... job. One... two... three. Three licks to get to the center of a Tootsie Roll pop. It was an impossible equation, my nerves and our combined inexperience. I didn't finish the, ahem, job, but we both filed the memory as a great 'first.' I thought for sure we had started something good, but when I returned to work, he acted as if nothing had transpired between us. I was mortified and avoided him as best as I could. Eventually, one of us found another job, and soon after, the other followed suit. I would spot him around town over the next two decades and always hid behind shelves in stores and ducked around corners to avoid his gaze. I felt foolish and didn't need to be reminded of how easily I handed myself over, pride and all.

* * *

Fast forward a few years (circa 2017 maybe), both of us in our early thirties, in close quarters at a wedding. I recognized that smile from across the field and realized there's no way I'd be able to avoid him all night. I took a deep breath and prepared myself for what would surely prove to be an uncomfortable reunion, but was surprised to be met with a smile and true excitement to see me again. We talked like old friends and reminisced about 'the good 'ole days' working together when we were in high school. "That was my first job," he said. "That was my first job, too," I said with a wink. It took him a minute to get my joke, but that didn't take any wind out of my sails.

* * *

Even though we were now reconnected, neither one of us would reach out for a few years. He was busy living his life, and I was busy with mine, married and raising two kids. He had moved to a small town in New York only a short drive away, and invited me to come see his place sometime. The offer wasn't yet valid, though, as he was adamant that he didn't want to interfere with my marriage in any way. I appreciated the sentiment, and we kept our conversations short and cordial, never overstepping the boundaries we had put in place. When 6'4" (turns out he was taller than I thought) found himself in the hospital with a mystery illness, he let down his guard just a bit. I think he was lonely, messaging me often in the wee hours of the night. He had no one by his side and wanted some love, someone to reassure him that he wasn't alone, and that he'd be okay. The hospital staff was draining fluid from his body, enough to fill jars upon jars, and had no answers as to the cause. He had been there for about a week before turning the corner. He made a miraculous recovery and was discharged from the hospital, still clueless as to what had just infiltrated his body. He had gained no further insight, but he had gained a friend. We began talking often and about most everything but were sure to keep it all above board. It was nice to build a stronger friendship than we'd ever had, and even more so to have it built upon the foundation that we laid during our teen years.

He drove the hour commute home to visit his family for Thanksgiving and coordinated to meet me for a few minutes beforehand. He wore a very respectable sweater (think Mr. Rogers, not Bill Cosby) and his hair was coiffed to the side. He was dressed to impress (his parents, not me) and only had a few minutes before heading their way to help prepare the feast. We went for a lovely walk, keeping our distance and our friendship intact. We ended with a hug that lingered about 2.47 seconds too long. There was so much love in that hug between two people who had never confessed any love for each other. Maybe I loved what he represented. Maybe he loved the newfound friendship. Maybe we both loved the ease in which we interacted and simply existed around each other. Whatever it was, I think it was the extra 2.47 seconds that widened the chasm between us once again. We weren't going to disrespect the commitment I had made, and it went without saying. When my marriage had finally run out of steam and papers were filed, he didn't wait any longer. He reached out while my boys and I were vacationing, warm weather abounding, no husband in sight. He admired the relationship I was cultivating with my sons and the relationship I was fostering between the two of them. It reminded him of his own childhood and the two brothers he thought of with fondness. They had grown apart a bit as the years passed, but the love still remained. We talked often, sharing stories from the deep recesses of our respective pasts and exchanging more recent stories, introducing each other to the many colorful characters that our families consisted of. We grew close, and with my divorce finalized, decided we'd try the romance thing again.

I can't remember our first date, but I do remember that it was basically seamless. We were more about spending time together than we were about the optics of a first date or a second date. I went to his place, he made dinner, we held hands. He was quick to warn me about the tap water, blaming the local water for having made him sick. We stuck to bottled water he purchased regularly. For a boy who wasted no time getting me on his bed when we were kids, he didn't seem to have sex on the brain whatsoever these days. It was refreshing, sure, albeit a bit odd. His house was rented to him, owned by his step-mother. She would come by, let herself in, and decorate for the upcoming holiday. The kitchen table was adorned with a pastel tablecloth, complete with eggs and bunnies. A few weeks prior, green shamrocks lined the walls and doors and made their appearance in the gardens out front. He had no issue with this, and in fact, found it to be 'sweet and thoughtful.' It was, after all, her house, and he didn't want to stand in the way of her decorating her house the way she always had. Furthermore, she had mentioned on more than one occasion that she did this for his benefit for when he might ever 'bring home a lady friend.' The bed in the master bedroom was noisy and made the loudest squeak if you so much as turned over. It was neatly made, always covered in a pale pink comforter that matched the curtains on the window. 6'4" had mentioned on several occasions that he couldn't imagine having sex there. That it'd be so disrespectful to his parents to make love in a house they owned, and especially in the bed they once shared. This was a far cry from the fifteen- year-old boy whose raging hormones convinced him to lure me into a shower with sweet talk and soft tunes.

The more time I spent with him, the weirder things got. Sometimes I got to spend time with him, the boy I'd known for twenty-plus years. Other times, he was a horse of a different color, serving spaghetti with his bare hands, majorly insulted when I called him on it. One night, I found myself singing in his kitchen and he stopped to compliment me. It was incredibly sweet, until it wasn't. "You have really great tone, Scarlett. You know that? You can sing. Ya know, just like someone else you know." He paused. He waited for what seemed like forever. Awk. Ward. "You know, like me. People tell me all the time what a good singer I am," he finished. This was only one of many compliments he made sure to pay himself. I wasn't a fan and called him out. "You know, it's fine to let others compliment you, you know. There's a fine line between arrogance and confidence. If you're as great as you think you are, your actions will speak for themselves. You don't need to." I thought for sure that was going to be the end of us right then and there, another huge blow to his ego. I wasn't looking to deflate him, but merely to help him let others appreciate him so he could truly appreciate himself through their eyes and not his own. He claimed that it had taken him a really long time to shake the darkness that plagued him in years gone by and to find the confidence and self-respect needed to build a new him. He was proud. He was loud. And he wasn't afraid to let anyone know how amazing he was, drumming, humming and all.

He would also disappear at all hours, and I'd find him in another room of the house or in the garage. He'd say that he was smoking a few puffs of a cigar or just needed to think. He would stress that when he did this, I wasn't to overthink him needing space, nor was I to come find him. One time, he'd called me no less than three times on my hour-long commute to his house, worried about my safety and impatient with the wait. I arrived there as expected, only to find him in his garage, sitting in his car. The door was shut and he was listening to something. It was an odd sound, like a loud hum, and was cranked up to max volume. This solitary note played for more than five minutes before he gestured for me to join him in the passenger seat. He sat there for another four minutes with me seated beside him and at least another 23 minutes after I'd exited his car and walked Wells. I'm not sure if he even noticed me leaving. I finally made myself as comfortable as I could in the living room, angry and confused, while waiting for him to finish doing whatever the hell he was doing. Now it was my turn to be impatient. He could tell I was frustrated, and I confirmed his hunch. An argument ensued when I called it 'noise.' He was both angry and insulted. It was apparently a note once played and recorded by his brother. 'Sheer genius,' he said. I guess I don't understand music these days.

* * *

6'4" had recently reconnected with some old bandmates and planned a revival of sorts. He was working diligently on creating some new tracks to bring to the group, hoping to book some gigs in the next few years and maybe even go on tour. Still, something was 'off.' He was always repeating himself (to himself) and repeating the same stories over and over to me. Probably to anyone who would listen. It was evident that the stories that mattered were the ones he held dear and kept on repeat. He once had given his grandmother a bouquet of flowers, beautiful and bountiful. She was tickled pink, and because of her reaction, so was he. In the several months we spent time together, I'd probably heard that story at least thirty times, if not more. Another one was a time when he was a little boy and told his mother that she looked like an angel to him. She was flattered at the notion, and clearly he was proud of making her feel good. It seemed to be a theme: the memories where he made others feel special or loved were the ones that stuck with him the most.

It was also clear that he wanted to impress his family and sought their validation in all he did. Early on he explained that he had talked to his mother about me, and eventually his father, also. What he didn't tell them was what a sweet, loving, thoughtful person I was, or that as a single mother of two, I was doing a great job raising my boys. Or that I was a hard working professional with a decent and blossoming career. What he *did* tell them was that I'd been married and divorced three times. What he *did* give them was my rap sheet, so to speak. Why lead with someone's failures instead of their accomplishments? Why not lead with accolades and triumphs? Instead, he painted a vastly different picture of who I was, and that overshadowed any other facts they'd come to learn about me. I had no chance of winning the race. Hell, I wasn't even in the race. I wasn't even in the stands. He had effectively removed me from the stadium by security. *What a gut punch. I couldn't get a refund and I definitely wasn't going to get my parking validated. Thanks, buddy. You're a real pal. In my defense, my divorce rate is 100% successful, so at least I've got that going for me.*

* * *

6'4" would often call me throughout the work day, lamenting about how he was waiting for his colleagues to show up on the jobsite. He'd recently taken a new job, and although some aspects were going well, he'd been written up in short order. Apparently, he would stomp around the office, intimidating his coworkers, especially the women. He was quick and often to tell this story, justifying his loud demeanor by his height and wide gait. He was insistent, though, that the job as a whole was going very well.

He would take laps around Memory Lane almost daily, telling me the same stories over and over again. He was apparently quite the playboy when he was younger: girls on his arm and filling his bed, groupies lining up at parties his band played at, and friends filling his family camp most weekends in the summer. Their camp was right on the water's edge, and he'd spent all summer, every summer, boating and water skiing. He held this camp in high regard and planned to take me there sometime. I'd meet the family, but he'd leave me so he could go work with the men (arrrghh, arrrrrghh, arggggh), chopping wood, building things, and flexing their muscles. With little to no introduction, he planned to leave me with the matriarchy. I'd wash dishes and dodge questions, hoping to win their approval and pass their tests. Trying as I might to explain how ass-backwards this was, he insisted that this was the only way you were accepted into the family. His mother, his aunts, and grandmothers were very protective of him, and no one would be good enough for their golden boy. He took pride in all the work he'd put into the camp and the surrounding land over the years, and he relished in the fact that someday his father's boat would be his and the camp would remain a treasure in the family, to be enjoyed by generations to come.

He was too anxious to wait until summer's arrival, so one rainy night, he surprised me with a trip into the woods. He had snatched the bottle of Malbec I'd brought to his house and packed a small backpack before we departed. Without so much as a hint as to where we were headed, he suggested that I put on something more suitable for footwear... his size 14 hikers. My size 6.5 feet struggled more to walk in his shoes than I would have in my own, but not knowing the plan, I followed his instructions. With the sky opening up and darkness descending upon us, it was too wet and too late to build the fire that he'd intended to. After a quick tour of the dock, the cabin, and its many rooms and a quick viewing of the family pictures that took up most of the real estate on the pine walls, he made one last stop. He brought me to a smaller cabin a little closer to the water and a little more remote. He called it the 'honeymoon suite' and said it'd be our love nest for the summer, on the weekends that we stayed there. Looking back, I'm glad I never joined him at camp. Surely, if the walls could talk, they wouldn't remember any of the many names either. Still, I was flattered that he felt compelled to sneak me into camp and share this huge piece of his heart with me, albeit sneaking. He didn't have anyone's permission to be there and was sure to keep my presence there, as well as his, on the down-low.

* * *

There were also good times—watching old movies on VHS, dancing like no one was watching, and the long walks we'd take. He challenged me to a game of Scrabble after shit-talking and explaining that the only person who had ever outscored him was his beloved grandmother. A family tradition at camp, he played often throughout the years. I, however, had not played in many years. We played one game, and I not only beat him, but the margin by which I won was embarrassing. He was a sore loser but came around the next day, challenging me to a rematch. Again, I left the game with bragging rights and was sure to leave our score sheets in the box, hopeful his grandmother would ask about it the next time they played. "Who's this 'Scarlett'? Looks like she's damn good. Bring her around sometime to challenge the master," I pictured her saying. It was a cute thought, but never came to fruition, and looking back, was probably for the best.

* * *

We had plans to meet up for dinner at 6:30pm—our first double date. The workday got away from us, and my girlfriend and I decided that 7:00 pm would be a safer bet. 6'4" was particularly excited about this, having known my friend since grade school. He reached out during the day, telling me he'd gotten a haircut and talking about the shirt he'd chosen to wear. Double dates can be awkward, but being the old chums that they were, it should have been damn-near effortless for everyone. We pushed back our dinner reservation, and I texted the guy but got no response. I'd tried calling him, as well, just to make sure he got the message. We were meeting halfway between his residence and mine. My friend and her boyfriend drove there in one vehicle, and I met them there as planned. We waited a few minutes for him to arrive before securing our table and ordering drinks. Then we waited quite a bit longer. I was mortified. He had been blowing up my phone all day, excited for the evening's plans, but now. Nothing. Not a peep. I hadn't heard from him in the last few hours. My friends reassured me that they knew it wasn't my fault and that I deserved better, and we moved on with our evening. Well into our meal, he finally called me. I steeled myself, not wanting to overreact or make a scene. "Are you alright?" I asked. "Yeah, I, uh… well, I'm not there," he answered. *No shit, you idiot. I've never been good at math, but even the Kevins of the world know that 2+2=4 and that 4-1= the end of a relationship.*

Since an excuse didn't immediately come, I figured I'd hear it later. "I'm going to go. The people who actually bothered to show up deserve my attention," I said calmly. "We'll talk later." He tried again to speak, desperate to salvage the situation, but I was angry and now even angrier that he was trying to interrupt my night with my friends. "Please stop," I said. I hung up and proceeded to ignore every text he sent over the next two hours… of which there were plenty. Later that night, when I'd calmed down enough to hear him out, he explained that his car battery had died earlier in the day, and he'd jumped it to get home. Once home, he could have grabbed his truck and headed my way, but instead he was hyper fixated on changing the battery on the car, I guess. So much so that he forgot to join me for dinner. He forgot to so much as reach out to let me know he'd be late. It was a terrible excuse, but after some distance for the next few weeks, he managed to talk himself back into my good graces when we did talk. He really seemed to be having issues, and I was compassionate enough to give him another chance. Maybe a TBI? Maybe a closeted drinking problem? He looked tired, more so each day, and his eyes were a constant shade of yellow. I wasn't sure, but I was definitely starting to get the feeling that something was wrong. Really, really wrong.

* * *

The weekend was approaching, and in an effort to give my family a weekend of respite, 6'4" invited us over. My sons knew him to be a friend of mine, so when he presented a platonic front, I was grateful. He was proud to be included when we took the boys driving on backroads in the woods. He and I made dinner together, and I think he truly relished the idea that that night represented... family. A family he'd never been part of and a family he'd never have. Little did I know that this was probably exactly what he was thinking. *A family he'd never have.* He took the boys to the basement and let them explore the workout equipment, coaching them along the way. He showed my younger son his electric drums, hand in hand, teaching him a thing or two and watching in pride as my son freestyled. We watched *Home Improvement*, a show we all enjoyed, but nobody more than 6'4." The nostalgia was real in a way I'd never before witnessed. He was obsessed, and we watched episode after episode every time I was there.

As evening rolled in, and we were on yet another episode of the classic sitcom, my phone started blowing up. "WHERE THE HELL ARE YOU??" it read. "WHY AREN'T YOU HOME?" Who the hell would be text—Fireball. It was that fucking loser who I thought I'd finally gotten rid of. He sent text after text in all caps. I was instantly cold then instantly hot. I was terrified and angry all at the same time. I didn't know what to do, but found myself sinking into my own skin, afraid to even look at the next messages as they came in. 6'4" grabbed my phone and was irate. I tried to explain who it was. My sons, sadly, knew exactly who it was. My phone rang. It rang again. A third time. A fourth. My son, standing 6' tall (but 6'3" in that moment), put his hand on my shoulder and sat me down. He hugged me and comforted me while sliding my phone into his pocket. When it rang again, he calmly answered. "Hey. I really need you to leave my mom alone. At least for a few days," he said. He already had grown into his facial hair and the deep voice that comes with it. Although 6'4" was happy to let my son handle this, he interjected. "Leave her alone altogether!" he shouted. Fireball hung up immediately but proceeded to reach out sporadically over the next few weeks, guessing who else it was who'd stood up to him. Knowing of and never liking 6'4", he assumed he was involved, too, and began alluding to knowing secrets about him. He would hint at following him and blackmailing him, and 6'4" grew increasingly paranoid, afraid that this guy might make his life difficult. *So much for being my protector and making me feel safe. It's all good. My fifteen-year-old has it covered.*

* * *

Another time, the boys and I were headed to see a movie, and when it slipped from my lips, 6'4" invited himself to join. Since it was a last minute decision, he left his house straight away and began the hour-long drive. We knew we might miss the trailers but should make it just in time for the movie. He rushed, we waited, and once he'd reached our car, we raced for the movie theater all together. The movie was decent, but not long into it, he grew agitated and anxious. He stepped out to take a call from his father. Not long after that, he left to use the bathroom. A few minutes after his return, he was again antsy, his leg bouncing, and asked if we could leave. Irritated, I suggested he go for a walk while we finished watching the movie. We hadn't gone to a movie since before the pandemic, and I wasn't about to make the boys leave early because this guy was bored. He wandered for a bit and ended up securing a table at the nearby Asian restaurant for dinner. When the credits rolled, we headed his way. I'd like to say that dinner was unremarkable but, of course, it wasn't. We ordered a large sampler with two or three of each item. 6'4" picked up a chicken wing then set it back down. Next, a teriyaki skewer, then a chicken tender, then an eggroll. He manhandled every food item, my sons both giving me the side-eye. They were repulsed and had no intention of eating even one bite of the banquet he'd just put his hands all over. Neither did I. He continued complaining that the food was cold, still groping the wontons and crab rangoons in a way that would make even the most acclaimed prostitute blush. Gross. And he had the nerve to act offended when I finally had the balls to call him on it. *Horrible outing. 2/10 would not recommend.*

* * *

Holding onto the memories of the guy I'd known for years, I tried again to give him a chance. We decided to meet one night halfway between our homes. We met for a drink at this rundown bar on the outside of town where only the locals and the adulterers go. He ended up running into another guy he knew. Also standing tall at 6'4", it became a competition in short order. Who's dick was bigger? Or who was the tallest? Same difference. He ended up outside with this guy and his posse, smoking and drinking. I sat at the bar alone, making small talk with the bartender and wondering what I was doing there. After what felt like forever, he finally rejoined me and apologized for his absence. His focus changed on a dime, and he ran onto the empty dance floor and over to bend the DJ's ear. A moment later, his hand was outstretched for mine, and he was pulling me onto the dingy black-and-white-checkered floor. I couldn't keep up with his pace. There must've been at least seventeen squirrels in the place that only he could see. He was so spastic and scattered. We danced to the song he'd dedicated to me, "Still The One" (1976) by Orleans. It was a sweet gesture, I suppose, though it was a stretch to say that our love story had started long ago or that I was the one who he'd been searching for all these years. He barely touched his drink, but when we were about to leave, he pounded his pint in one swift swig. Maybe he wanted it to pack a bigger punch? Who knows.

We left the bar and he decided that he had another place he wanted to introduce me to. I followed his car down to the pulloff of the basin and parked. He rolled down his windows and blasted some music from his car's speakers. We embraced in the moonlight, laughing and dancing like idiots. Some songs were special to him, others held meaning to his brothers, some were songs I introduced him to. He decided that he didn't want to head home to New York but rather would spend the evening in town at his parent's house. Being that this was his childhood home, and since he was dog sitting for them, I didn't even question his right to be there. His father and stepmother were out of town on vacation, so we headed that way.

After struggling to remember the keycode on the garage (and working hard to block me from seeing it), access was granted. Upon entering, he dropped to the floor, greeting his childhood cat. He made the cat's acquaintance for what was probably a solid twelve minutes while I, again, wondered what I was doing there. It was as if he hadn't seen this cat in years. I got a call that Wells had gotten out, so we both left in our respective cars so we could search the surrounding neighborhoods for him. Once he was safely back with me, Wells and I headed back to spend some time with 6'4". He had ended his search prematurely, so he could stop and grab a bottle of wine. Wow. We met back up at his parent's house, and again, he held that cat like he hadn't seen him in years, let alone just twenty minutes earlier. Could he really have forgotten?! Another ten minutes passed, and I tried hard to figure out what was happening. When he finally released the pussy *(the only pussy he seemed to be interested in)*, he began flipping through old photo albums, page by page, showing me every picture. And I mean every last picture. Hundreds of old construction photos where the men of the family made home renovations. Hundreds of photos of the family camp and the extended relatives that spent their summers there. It's not that I'm a callous person, mind you, but yet again, I was struggling to understand why he'd brought me here.

He joked about recreating our one memory there but seemed to forget having mentioned it just as quickly. I went outside to retrieve something from my car, and he followed me out. When I ascended the two garage steps to re-enter, I found the door to be locked. It wouldn't budge, even when he tried. There was no key stashed away, as his family had always relied solely on the garage door and its keypad. "Who the fuck locked the door?! WHAT THE FUCK?!" he screamed. He didn't just scream, he bellowed. "WHAT THE FUCK?!" he asked again. I was quiet, shocked at his reaction. It wasn't long before I realized that we weren't supposed to be there. Being the only two there, I took ownership of the mishap. Maybe I locked the door. If I did, I certainly hadn't intended to. "You shouldn't touch things that don't belong to you!" he continued. *A doorknob? This is insane. You can't possibly walk through a door without using the doorknob.* I had been extremely courteous and thoughtful the entire time I'd been there and was shocked at the audacity with which he was yelling at me.

His father's dog was locked inside, along with mine, cowering in the corner. To no avail, we searched the garage for implements to pry the door open. I pulled out a credit card from my wallet and slid it between the wooden door and the door casing. He yelled at me, told me that I was stupid, and said that it would never work. In fact, he refused to let me give it a full shot for fear that the card may break and render itself as proof to his father that we'd been there. Determined to not leave Wells for the night in a strange house, I drove home to gather screwdrivers and tools to attempt a more calculated break-in. When I returned, he was calm, telling me that he'd decided not to try anything else. He didn't want to do any damage and that his father 'would kill him' if he found out that we'd been there. Reluctantly, and knowing Wells was okay, we spent the night in my car. It was awful. Cold, uncomfortable—even painful. I couldn't even look at him, I was so disgusted at the mess he'd gotten me into. My purse and phone were locked inside the house, and although he had his phone on him, the battery was dead and refused to take a charge. We were as screwed as you could get without getting screwed. The dogs were fine, but I knew our relationship wouldn't be. In hindsight, I regret not calling the police or breaking down the door myself. It wasn't fair to the pooches or to me, and I shouldn't have let his bad decision lead to one on my part as well.

The next morning, we drove to a nearby gas station where he straight-up refused to help and disappeared into the store. I borrowed the cashier's phone and called several locksmiths, no thanks to 6'4". No one would be available for hours, but aware of the need for expedience, one gentleman suggested we try a credit card. *Gasp!* I found 6'4" outside, a hard tea in hand. He had purchased alcohol to consume before 8:00am along with a meat stick and a cheap cigar. I had developed a migraine during the night but the man didn't so much as offer to buy me a water so I could take medicine for it. We returned to the scene of the crime, and he tried the credit card. We were in in less than thirty seconds. Go figure. If only he had let me try that the night before... Grrrrr! I called work and rearranged a few things, circled to the back yard to retrieve the urine soaked tissue I'd left there during the night, and offered my phone to him so he could also call his employer. When he was done, he hid the phone from my view while he 'deleted his work number' for security purposes. I was insulted, of course, but the adrenaline kept me from thinking rationally. *There was no number to delete. No call had been made. The conversation I had heard was one-sided, and later I'd learn that no one was on the other end.*

I was done with this fool after this, unsure of what his deal was. Unsure of what he wanted. Unsure of what was going on in his brain. What he was hiding. What his intentions were. But I was sure of one thing: I was done with it all. I was done with him. We'd basically become friends and continued to talk every once in a while, never discussing what we were to each other or what had transpired. I think he knew that I was done.

On one particular night, we were chatting on the phone for a solid 45 minutes, and he hadn't come up for air. He was venting about an old friend that he was in a spat with, repeating himself and looking for someone to take his side. I did my best, letting him carry on and share details, growing more heated as he went along. When he did stop to take a breath, he redirected his anger. Out of left field, he said, "And you! What about you? You've been divorced three times! Obviously, you're the problem! I don't see a future for us. Sorry," he finished. I was in a state of shock when he hung up. The words he left me with played on repeat in my head. When he followed up with a text a few days later, he was clear. "Sorry, not sorry." I knew we were done before he did, but what a way to end it.

He reached out when he was ready and apologized, owning that he shouldn't have said what he did. I didn't cut him off or block him, realizing that something was really wrong with him and how alone he felt. His feelings weren't off base. He really was alone. He showed up for anyone in need, but I never witnessed anyone showing up for him. It sucked. And I was there for it. It's awful to feel alone, and alone but together, we both felt a little less alone. We remained friends, and every once in a while, he'd admit to regretting ending things with me, even going so far as to say that he wondered what the future might hold for us. He reached out when I had suffered an injury and even offered to support my sister through her own crisis. He was a gem in a lot of ways, and we talked as recently as a week before he disappeared from my life for the last time.

* * *

They buried him on a beautiful fall day, sunshine pouring in through the church's stained glass windows and covering every inch of the sprawling lawn outside. For what was a sad day for all in attendance, there was something very special about the weather, the air and the overall tone of the day. He was a true friend to all who knew him, and would jump at the chance to help anyone in their hour of need. This felt truer than ever, as if he was enveloping the entire crowd with one giant hug, letting them know he was still here for them. It was beautiful and deeply moving. Consoled by my girlfriend as we sat together in our wooden pew, my constantly flowing tears were interrupted by laughter more than once. These silly memories kept popping into my head, like the time when he found my lost earring by sitting on it, the post puncturing a tiny hole in his right cheek. I'll admit that the optics were less than desirable, but I knew he'd be laughing right there beside me if given the chance. We made it through the events of the day: the funeral service, the burial, and the celebration of life luncheon. His mother, a woman I'd never met (but who had told 6'4" that he was wrong for sharing my resume of divorce before allowing me to meet the family), approached me. She knew exactly who I was and held me, understanding the complexity of the relationship I had had with her son. She knew our friendship spanned the majority of our lives, and she knew how he had viewed me and cared for me and my sons. She shared words that my soul needed to hear, and I shared bits that clearly helped hers heal a little bit too. She told me that he wanted to be better for me. That he was trying so hard to do better, be a better person, be a better man, and that he wasn't ready to make me his until he deserved me. I haven't been back to his grave since that day, but he's often in my thoughts. I wish I could've helped him. I wish I could've saved him. I wish I'd seen it. He had worked hard to keep this secret from his family and his friends, trying to spare us all from the mess he'd made of himself. For what it's worth, I can respect that. He found the lord during his last few months on this earth, and I have a renewed hope that he's still dancing in the moonlight, and he's only getting started.

Rest in Peace, my friend
~ CRM ~
1985-2022

| 19 |

... Always a Liar

DISCLAIMER: One more time for good measure. Say it with me—"she did *not* date this loser." **I DID NOT DATE THIS MAN.** Which is surprising since his level of unhinged earned him three chapters in this book and could have easily earned more. *I wonder who will play him in the movie...?*

* * *

It'd been a while since the overnight trip to that concert, and although time together was (intentionally) sparse, his reach-outs weren't. I had told him that since he wasn't listening and wasn't respecting my boundaries, I needed some space from him. And some time. This didn't stop the text messages and calls, however, which were as frequent as they'd ever been.

I had planned a week-long camping trip with some of my best girlfriends and their families. We'd be staying at a local campground not far from home, one that held a good amount of nostalgia for the ladies. Even more exciting was that the next generation in our friend group was bonding. We each had teenage boys who were quickly becoming the best of friends, and they both had daughters that had long since formed their own bond. The two other mothers had been friends since elementary school and had been inseparable since. At some point in high school, I met them both and was seamlessly accepted into the group. Two decades later, these two ladies are two of my nearest and dearest, their children now lovingly refer to me as "auntie." One thing I've learned in this life is that you can't choose your family. You can, however, choose your *family*. I have been grateful enough to find my tribe, people who have my back through thick and thin. My ride or dies. People who will always answer the phone at midnight, knowing you wouldn't be calling unless you needed them. Who tell you embarrassing stories about themselves when you're a blubbering mess just to make you laugh. Who share their toilet paper in the parking lot of a Tim McGraw concert. These are my kind of people. They'll always be there, and I'll always be grateful for that.

Toothless was still reaching out often, offering to bring me dinner, run errands, and help with Wells. Anything I was willing to let him do. Anything and everything. I told him I was going camping with friends and wouldn't be available to chat much, if at all. He probably wouldn't hear from me, and if I did find time to respond, it would be brief. It was important for me to be present for these guys and to disconnect for a bit. He said he understood this, but his actions said otherwise. He was texting more than ever. With the paranoia of some emergency happening while I was in the woods with my phone off, I opted not to power down completely. I checked my phone periodically, and every time I did, there were a slew of messages. Mostly from him. It was a little overwhelming, but I did my best to respond when I could. I certainly wasn't living up to whatever expectation he had set in his mind.

His messages grew angrier in tone as each day progressed, harsher as the night drew near than they had been that morning. His tone grew angrier as the week progressed, a little more direct, a little nastier with each day that passed. When I called him on this, he denied it the best he could, explaining that he simply just missed me. He apologized if it came across as anything but. I tried to explain, again, that I was occupied with my friends and my family, and I had already told him that I wouldn't be available much that week. In what was a very obvious and transparent attempt to alienate me from my friends, he explained that I should still be making time for him. He was the constant. He'd never leave me. Friends are replaceable, according to him, and, more often than not, they end up abandoning you and leaving you. After my divorce, my fear of abandonment had taken on a life of its own. This fear of being rejected and left behind had become my 'monster under the bed' and, at times, left me feeling lost and debilitated. Toothless knew this was my Achilles heel and used it to his advantage. He tried convincing me that my "friends" would leave me: they all do. That I should turn on them before they ever had a chance to turn on me. He brought up a time that one of these ladies had been snappy with me on the phone and left me in a funk for days after. Friends don't always see eye to eye, and while I knew this, he tried to make me turn on them, trying to point out that that was only the beginning. Someday, when I didn't see it coming, for no reason at all they'd abandon me, too. But he wouldn't. Surely, I should be investing my time in him, not them. He was smart enough to not try this when it came to my sister or my children, but dumb enough to not realize that these ladies were also my family. Not to mention that they'd been in my life for damn near twenty years. I'd only known him for a few months. *Longevity takes the cake here, my friend. Unless you eat it first. I'm betting you might.*

He grew increasingly agitated that week, and I grew increasingly nervous that he might let himself into my house while I was gone or even show up at camp. He probably had made a copy of my house key. Who knows. I did my best to put him out of my mind but forces around me were making it nearly impossible to do so. I ran into some friends who were staying at another campsite that week. This husband and wife team that I'd known for years were quick to ask me about Toothless. He'd apparently run into them recently and bragged about his significant other. Me.

They'd recognized my big brown eyes on the screensaver of his phone and then were shown pictures of me that Toothless had taken without me knowing. Pictures where he was sitting next to me in bed, and I was sound asleep. The selfie from the hot tub. And other pictures just of me. Not just a few. Many. He was like a proud papa, showing several shots of basically the same pose as if the crinkle in my nose or the light in my eyes made each photo different and brag-worthy. He told them that we were together and doing great. That he loved me and that we were happy. As soon as I was able to find words again, I immediately refuted the notion. I was in shock. Utter disbelief that he was now sharing this as truth to people around town. People he'd known for years. They knew me well and knew him even bet-ter, which worked out in my favor. They knew him to be a POS, a pathological liar. They knew of his run-ins with the law and the bad company he kept. The husband of this couple had long since turned his back on those days, but he was well-acquainted with the man who proclaimed I was his. They believed me and warned me to leave him. To do whatever I needed to do to get him out of my life. As quickly as humanly possible. If I wasn't scared before, I was now. With my niece dog sitting at my house, my fear had wheels, and it drove me to check on her and the house several times throughout the rest of the week. I made sure there was no hidden spare key and made sure she was lock-ing the doors at all times. I also alerted the neighbors. They were to call me if they noticed his truck there. Immediately.

With the new knowledge of how crazy this guy might actually be and the lengths he might be willing to go to, the timing of this camping trip couldn't have been worse. I was also battling a nasty case of diverticulitis that had lasted for months (another great 'in' for Toothless, who was always more than happy to help) and was now facing an adverse reaction from one of the medications they had put me on. I was taking Benadryl daily to counteract the swelling and hives that were taking over my body every time the previous dose would wear off. One morning, I woke up with sausages for fingers. Each digit was swollen, but my middle finger was actually turning a light shade of lavender. For the last 18 years, I'd worn a sterling sil-ver band on that finger—one my father had bought me on a trip to North Carolina. It was special in that moment and had grown even more special since his passing. No $20 ring had ever held more value than this one, which was currently cutting off the circulation to my most used finger. My friends and I employed all the tactics we knew of: we researched for other methods to try and even paid a visit to the more-seasoned ladies running the camp's general store. We tried everything. The more we tried, the more swollen it got. I had no interest in visiting the ER, so I called my friend, one who worked with stainless steel on a daily basis.

My best friend drove me there, and he met us outside with a pair of tin snips. She held the ring apart with two pieces of dental floss (bless her heart) in an attempt to spare the soon-to-be-sharp metal edges from puncturing my now lilac-hued finger. *"Violet, you're violet!"* The pain was extreme as he managed to finagle the cutters between the metal band and my flesh, and the relief from the tightness was instantly replaced by the two jagged edges cutting into the swollen mass. My eyes bulged in pain, and seeing this, he swooped in and pulled the ring apart in one quick movement, providing me the relief I so desperately needed. I was so very thankful that my friends were able to save my finger but so sad the ring wasn't as fortunate. I'd have it soldered back together at some point, I told myself.

Toothless reached out later that day as expected. Let's be real. As dreaded. I didn't want to miss communicating with him for fear of upsetting him when I wasn't in a place to guard my house or surveil his every move. When we talked, I mentioned the happenings of the day, including having to have my dad's ring cut off. His reaction was unexpected and actually quite scary. "You had your ring cut off?!? Are you kidding me??! Why would you do that??" he blasted. He caught me so off-guard. "WHY THE HELL DIDN'T YOU CALL ME, SCARLETT?" He was mad. Not just a little mad. Red steam mad. "I should have been your first call! I told you your friends don't care about you! They didn't care about how much that ring means to you! I bet they didn't even try! I could have gotten it off without cutting it! I could have! WHY THE FUCK DIDN'T YOU CALL ME FIRST?! I should have been your FIRST call!" I gave him the silence I felt he needed, and when he seemed a bit more calm, tried to explain to him that we *did* try everything. At that point, it was a matter of saving my finger and time was running out. If there had been any other possible way to save the ring, I would have, but at the end of the day, it's a piece of metal. I needed my finger and made a choice, one that I didn't need his or anyone's help in making. Not to mention that my father absolutely loved camping, and some of my fondest memories with him were of our times camping—swim goggles on our faces to avoid the smoke that would inevitably chase us around the firepit. The damage was done, he reminded me. The ring's endless circle now had an end. This guy's temper had erupted, and he'd fully blown up at me, showing me yet again, his true (ugly, ugly) colors. I was the only part of the equation that hadn't had enough damage done to it. So he continued his rampage: "You think soldering that ring back together will make it the same ring? It won't. It's forever changed. Because of you. Because you didn't call me. I should have been the first person you thought of. And because you didn't, you destroyed something that meant so much to you. You can solder it, but it will never be the same. It's not the same ring your dad gave you. It's fucked up now because of you. You fucked up, Scarlett. Fucked. Up." He stopped. *Yeah, I'm the one who's fucked up. Clearly.*

* * *

We had never said our goodbyes or had any kind of closure, and Toothless had apologized more than once. He felt badly for the way he'd acted, although he still maintained that friends don't stay in your life and I should be proactive by removing mine from my life. I ended up telling him that if he continued to try to drive a wedge between me and my friends (or me and anyone), I'd have nothing more to do with him. We would cease to talk, and I'd block him on all platforms. The part of me that most resembles a doormat didn't love the idea of doing this. I continued making excuses for him. After all, this guy had been there for me when I was at my sickest. He'd helped me move. He'd always offered his services should I ever need them. We weren't talking often these days, as I tried my damndest to avoid him and keep him at arm's length (well, Shaq's arm's length, maybe). My guard was up, my senses heightened to his bullshit, and even Wells and I had had a lengthy conversation about how he was no longer welcome to drop by. Over the past several months, he had managed to meet several of my family members. I notified them all that he was no longer a friend and wasn't someone who could be trusted. If he reached out to any of them, I needed to know.

As his birthday approached, he mentioned frequently that he had no plans. He wanted to make some, though, with me. He wanted to bury the hatchet, and now that he knew he had blown his chances (not that he ever had any), he didn't want to lose me altogether. He missed his 'friend,' and more than anything, wanted to spend his birthday together. He denied any wrongdoings and claimed a misunderstanding whenever something couldn't be explained away. Or he'd say that it was "just a joke." Other friends were coming, he promised. It wouldn't be just the two of us. It definitely wasn't a date, and he triple confirmed that he understood this. Being unable to trust him, I insisted on driving myself there. Of course, I was the only one there. Apparently, the RSVPs had been rescinded throughout the day and the guestlist had dwindled down to two. Toothless. And me. He said he knew I would've backed out, too, and that's why he didn't tell me sooner. *Insert guilt trip here.* But he's right. I sure as hell wouldn't have come had I known. I did my best, seeing as it was his birthday, to enjoy a meal and light conversation. The small talk was anything but as he continued to drop hints or suggest a future for us. This went on throughout the meal, a little hint here, a little mention there. I had reached my fill and had already signaled to the server that we were ready for our check. Things had escalated quickly at his last mention of us trying again to date. And now here I was, this 5'2" brunette yelling at this big man on his birthday at a nice restaurant. He was big enough for people to have noticed us walk in, and my raised voice and finger in his face was enough to ensure that they continued to stare. This is not who I was. This is not who I ever wanted to be. But I've got to thank Toothless—he helped me to discover a part of myself that is necessary for survival. That it's okay to go into protective mode when someone threatens you or a loved one. That it's okay to stand up for yourself. That if someone is asking you to trust them and ignore that feeling in your gut, they're not the one for you. I signed the check (happy fucking birthday) and wished him a good birthday one last time. When he continued to scold me, I simply told him I was leaving, pushed my chair out, and walked away. He followed me out onto the street, clearly angry and embarrassed. I don't know if he's actually capable, but if he was, I think he may have even been hurt. I had parked further from the restaurant, and by the time I had gotten into my car, he'd pulled his truck up nearby. I didn't see him in the darkness, but later he would tell me that all he wanted was a hug on his birthday, and I almost ran him over as he approached my driver's side door in the darkness. *If I had intended to hug him, I would have. And if I'd intended to hit him, surely I wouldn't have missed. Nobody's aim is that bad. Hell, Helen Keller could've taken him out.*

This is another one of those parts that I'm terribly embarrassed to admit. Despite the glaring red flags, I gave in one more time and agreed to see him. Just as friends. Just for dinner. Despite what that little group of bullies said in the sixth grade, I've never been enough of a bitch. Honestly, being a woman this day in age is harder than ever, and I've come to believe that you need a little 'bitch' in your DNA to survive. I've since adapted this and try to continue to do so every day. But back then, I didn't yet have the gumption I needed to have. I conceded and agreed to go to dinner one last time. It was a casual meal, and he promised to behave. He dressed nicely, played the part, and didn't push the romance. He didn't even ask about my love life. He made small talk and plenty of it. We both ignored the elephant in the room (hey, I meant the elephant, not him. Cut me some slack here!). Dinner was a fine time—nothing to write home about but nothing horrible either. The food was okay, the company was okay, and at some point I must've made the mistake of saying that I was planning to go out later. He wanted to join me for a night on the town, and although I was hesitant, again, I conceded. *Ladies, go with your gut! If you don't want to do something, don't do it (laundry and taxes excluded).*

One of the most infamous murders in our area involved a young, single mother. She had gotten a call to help a couple who were stranded near her road, and against her better judgment, she went. Sadly, she didn't live to tell the tale. *Trust your gut. Always.*

He even convinced me to let him drive. He followed me to my house, where I parked my car and quickly checked on my dog. We rode in his truck to a local dive bar that wasn't quite downtown. Across the bar there was this younger guy, maybe early thirties. He noticed me and wasn't shy about it. He continued to gesture to me, trying to get me to come over to him or to follow him to the bathroom. In an effort to stop the gesturing, I paid him a quick visit. He introduced himself. "Looks like you could use an escape from that guy you're with," he nodded in the direction of the man with no teeth. Although he wasn't wrong, I replied, "Nah, he's fine. He's just a friend. But ya know, you're being kind of rude since I'm here with him." On my way out of the bar, he slipped me a napkin with his phone number written on it in blue ink. I threw the napkin out as we exited the front door. The next stop was a bar downtown, one that Toothless chose. A little club known for its live music and funky vibe, always dimly lit with a red glow. This was a dance floor that babies were made on. Pretty sure. Funny enough, this same bloke ended up at this bar too. I couldn't possibly have arranged this, as Toothless was the one who chose this as our next stop. He noticed me and, again, beckoned me over to him. I knew the bartender, not well, but she and I were friendly. After Toothless declined the invitation to join me, I excused myself for a moment and took this shady fella up on his offer for a drink. While belly-up to the bar beside him, I thanked him for the drink and explained that I wasn't interested. He explained that he travels here from out of state every other week, and we could keep our fun to a casual and discrete level, if that's what I wanted. I had no problem having this talk and putting him in his place, especially with the bartender joining in our conversation. It definitely added a layer of witness and a feeling of safety. When I'd finished the last sip of my drink, I felt my phone buzz. Looking down, I realized that Toothless had texted me. "Have fun with your friend. I'm leaving. Do you need anything out of my truck?" his message read. I looked around and behind me and didn't see him anywhere. I was fuming mad. What the actual fuck?! We'd driven here together, are NOT together. I was taking three minutes to get this man off my back. That's my prerogative. And this insecure excuse of a man couldn't handle three minutes without me by his side? Or was it that I gave three minutes of my time and attention to someone else? I stormed out of the bar and headed for his truck. He was on the street, standing near a tree, clearly waiting for his text to do its job. I noticed him but continued in the direction of the parked truck, unwilling to so much as make eye contact. He was surprised that I didn't stop to talk to him and followed me to his truck. I reached for the passenger's side door handle to find it was locked. My purse inside was the only thing keeping me here, waiting for him to unlock the doors. He refused to open his truck until I agreed to get in. I had told him several times that I just wanted my purse and to head in my own direction. He refused. When I finally told him I'd do what he asked and play nice (ya know, like all kidnap victims tell their kidnappers in the movies? Yeah, like that), he hit the unlock button on his key fob, and I opened the door. He was eyeing me cautiously and I climbed in, long enough to fool him and just long enough to snag my bag. I hopped out of the truck and started walking.

He didn't want me walking and followed me in his truck. My gait was larger than normal and my steps more brisk, as I wanted to get as far away from him as quickly as possible. There's no way he would have been able to keep up on foot, so into the truck it was. He followed me down the street in super slow motion (like in the movies, ya know? Where the child predator is trying to coax the kid into his van. Or where the couple gets into a fight and the dude is begging his girlfriend to get back into the car). He tried to convince me if I got in he'd simply bring me home. You couldn't pay me enough to get back in the truck with him. He continued to follow me down the unlit side street and into a parking garage I'd stopped in for a minute. He got out of his truck and tried again to convince me to go with him. He was doing his best to guilt me, to manipulate me. I wasn't having it and was so done with his shit. When he refused to leave, my anger got the best of me. I kicked his door three or four times, pissed that he wouldn't just leave me the fuck alone! When nothing else worked, he decided to try intimidation. *What a toolbag this toolbag had.* "Ya know, you've been drinking. The police will pick you up for walking while intoxicated, and they'll arrest you. Your name will be in the paper. You might even lose your job over it." Man, he was really laying it on thick. Reminding myself that he was full of shit, and that I wasn't even drunk, I started on my way again. What police officer would pick me up for walking away from a confrontation, not toward it? Removing myself from a toxic situation and just trying to get home? I wasn't behind the wheel, and I had done nothing wrong besides making the mistake of trusting this guy one last time. While I was still within earshot, he grabbed his phone and began reporting me to the police. As he provided my name, my address, and his version of the night, I continued walking away, tears forming in my eyes. I couldn't believe that this piece of shit was calling the police on me. ON ME! "Uh yes, sir. That's right. She's intoxicated, and I'm worried she might hurt herself or someone else. Uh huh. Right." I could hear his words as the distance between us grew. Although he was a loud talker, it was clear that he was intentionally projecting so I wouldn't miss a single word. The tears were streaming down my face at this point, coming faster and growing bigger with each sniffle. I was all out bawling, arms folded while walking past the police station and fishing in my purse for my phone. *How did I get to this point, I wondered. This creep is calling the police on me for not wanting to go home with him? How is this even a thing?* I dialed my sister's number hating to wake her, but knowing she'd come to my rescue. It wasn't the best area to be walking in so late at night, so waiting for an Uber wasn't an ideal option. Her boyfriend came to pick me up, and given the situation, wasted no time getting to me. I climbed into his truck, my hands immediately on my face, my shoulders slumped over, and the tears flowing without reprieve. I was sobbing uncontrollably, my phone lighting up nonstop.

My phone rang several times, one right after another, call after call. Finally, I answered, knowing damn well who was on the other end.

"What the hell do you want?!" I asked. He feigned concern for my safety, and after telling him I'd gotten a ride from a friend, I hung up. I had somehow managed to pull myself together by the time we pulled up to my house, but my calmness disappeared the moment I spotted that blue truck parked out front. We stepped out and confronted him together. "Why are you here?" I asked. "I wanted to make sure you got home safely," he croaked. *Ugh. I WISH he'd croaked.* "I told you he was bringing me home," I said through clenched teeth. All of the rage I had felt just twenty minutes earlier when kicking his stupid truck came flooding back. "I'm home! See?!" I yelled. It was late, and Wells needed to go out. More than anything, I wanted to take care of him and then be in bed for the night. I wanted this whole dreadful evening to be over. I asked my sister's boyfriend if he wouldn't mind handling this for me. After all, he liked to play the hero just as much as Toothless did. They were a good match. Two narcissists in a pod. (I've heard that they're still in touch to this day, Toothless still feeding him lies about me.) After he agreed he'd handle it, I let myself inside, and let Wells out, where he quickly found a bush to pee on. I hopped on my bike and rode around the block, Wells running alongside (a newer routine we'd adopted that delighted some of the neighbors. Others? Not so much). I did one quick loop, the wind in my hair helping to wash away the heaviness and regret of the night. When we returned home, Wells was eager to get inside, panting from the short run. So was I. (Well, not panting, just eager to be in for the night.) And I can barely ride a bike sober. The fact that I had made it around the neighborhood at night, in the dark, proved that I wasn't nearly as intoxicated as Toothless wanted the police to think I was. Or wanted me to think I was. They were still talking, and after thanking my driver, I headed inside and locked the door. A short bit later, my phone began to vibrate. I'd just climbed into bed, Wells curled up beside me, when I noticed the onslaught of text messages popping up on my phone. The messages grew more urgent, turning to all caps, coming in faster and faster. Eventually they stopped. The silence was deafening. About sixty seconds passed, the house eerily quiet. And then… a knock at the door. The knock got louder. It turned into a bang. He continued to bang. Wells barked and barked. My anxiety was through the roof. He began calling my phone relentlessly while simultaneously still banging on my front door. The banging was getting louder. And then it, too, stopped almost suddenly. When the messages stopped before, he'd approached my front door. Now that they stopped again, I feared he'd try the garage or would appear on my back deck. I wasn't going to spend the night living in fear or putting up with this approach of his. He called again. Stupidly, I answered. "I just need to talk to you," he urged. "I thought you left. He said you'd left," I stated. I don't know why I uttered those words, as clearly he was still here. "Please, just let me in. I'm not here to fight. I just want to talk… Please," he begged. "I need to grab some things I left here before." "You have sixty seconds. I mean it. Grab what you need and get out!" I screamed. I was so angry, and I figured letting him get what he needed and say what he wanted might actually get him to leave me alone. At least for the night. Boy was I wrong. So very, very wrong.

He followed me up the stairs and went into the kitchen first. I'm not sure what he was after, but I didn't care. I wasn't worried that he'd steal from me or take something that wasn't his other than my time. He went into the bathroom next. I couldn't think of anything he'd have in the bathroom. Despite his many attempts to spend the night, I hadn't allowed him to 'move in' or keep a bunch of toiletries there. I think he was just stalling, trying to figure out his next move. He'd spent so much time trying to get me to listen to him and to let him in, that when I did, I don't think he was actually prepared with his next move. I was so frustrated by the entire night and how what could have been an otherwise decent night completely fell apart around me. I had talked to another man, but I didn't flirt. I was respectful to the friend I was out with (though he didn't deserve it, let alone another chance to spend time with me). And even if I had been flirting with the other guy, this guy shouldn't have had two words to say about it, since we weren't together. He knew this! I was beyond frustrated and sat at the head of my bed, hugging my knees and waiting for him to leave. He came into my bedroom and stood there, hands in his pockets, looking pissed off. His stance was one of blame and frustration. I'd done nothing wrong, and he wasn't about to convince me otherwise. This was absurd.

"Scarlett, what's going on?" he asked. He knew damn well what had transpired and that he was in the wrong, though he wasn't about to show his hand. "Talk to me," he pleaded. "Please." I was not about to waste my time on him or this conversation. It was late, and he'd already caused irreparable damage that he'd never be able to undo. I'd never been followed down the street and harassed the way he'd harassed me. Or had the police called on me for deciding not to get into a vehicle with someone I didn't want to.

"I need you to leave," I said. I was doing my best to remain calm and not let things escalate again the way they had earlier. He stood there, just staring at me, a loss for words overtaking him. "I mean it. I need you to go... Now!"

"Can we just talk? Please?" he asked. "I just want to talk about everything. Talk about what happened. Ya know what I mean?" Ugh. That fucking phrase again! "YOU CALLED THE FUCKING POLICE ON ME!!" I snapped. And I did. I had turned a corner and had finally snapped. "WHO THE FUCK DOES THAT?! Because I refused to get into a car with you? Because I wanted nothing to do with you? That was a reason to call the police on me?!" I shouted. I wasn't letting him get a word in, though I'm not sure he would have had anything to say. "You're pathetic, you know that? How fucking insecure do you have to be to lose your shit over me talking to someone else? And at that, someone I was turning down. You're fucking pathetic! Ya know what I mean? Well, do you? Do ya know what I mean?!" I made sure to emphasize that last sentence and bring as much snark as I could. I wanted him to hear how stupid he sounded every time he said it.

"Well, I didn't actually call the police," he admitted. "I just wanted to help you see that getting into my truck was the right call, and I thought the fear of having the police come for you would help you see that." I was stunned. He hadn't called the police? He'd faked a whole conversation with them for my benefit? I totally lost it at this confession.

"ARE YOU FUCKING KIDDING ME?!? GET THE FUCK OUT OF MY HOUSE!" I screamed. "It was a joke. I was just making a joke," he said. "No one jokes about calling the police on someone, let alone someone they care about! You need help! You're fucking sick!" I was shaking at this point. Rage was overcoming me, and Wells was hiding under the edge of the bed, unsure of what to do.

This went on for several minutes. We were at an impasse. My volume increased, and I continued to demand he leave. He kept asking me to talk to him, to listen to his explanation. He loved me, he cared about me, and he just didn't want to leave until we talked. "We have nothing to talk about," I yelled. "Get out! I fucking mean it!" He leaned back, shifting his weight to his back leg, crossing his arms. He looked pissed off, no longer on the defensive. "If you want me to leave, you'll have to call the cops," he said. I couldn't believe he was putting me in this situation. This was absolute nonsense. Ludicrous. "So be it," I said. I was visibly shaking while I called for backup. The operator answered and I explained the situation. I had the phone on speakerphone so this creep would know that unlike him, I wasn't afraid to call the police. I hoped he'd just get spooked and leave, but that wasn't the case. When the operator asked where my attacker was, Toothless replied, "I'm right here in the bedroom with her." Although I'm sure these folks hear all kinds of things, I swear I could hear him thinking, "*Well, this is a new one.*" "Okay. Can you and your dog go to a different room, away from this gentleman?" the dispatcher asked. "He's no gentleman," I told the him. "He's a creep and I need him out." I don't know why I felt the need to say this, but I suppose I wanted to make sure he and I were on the same page. This lowlife had invaded my space and made my only retreat nonexistent. He'd taken away the safety of my sanctuary. I guess it was important for me to make sure the operator was on my side and understood my situation. There was nowhere

I could go to get away from this guy. But for the next few minutes, Wells and I hid in the locked bathroom, waiting for men in uniform to arrive.

When they did, he played the game. He went outside immediately without being asked to do so. He began talking with one officer, surely putting his spin on how everything went down. He told them I'd had a lot to drink and was being irrational. That he only came over to make sure I'd gotten home safely. That I let him in to get some of his things, and he'd only stayed because he was trying to work out our 'lover's quarrel.' He ended up telling him that he 'stays sometimes' and has his things inside. I followed him outside and pleaded with the officers to walk through, search bureau drawers, and peek into closets. They wouldn't find a single article of clothing that would fit this man. He told them he had bought some of the things that now lived inside my apartment. "Oh, a $200 TV? He can have it!" I said. I informed the officers that he wasn't on my lease and wasn't staying there, to which he suggested that he call my landlord, who would corroborate that they speak more than I do. That his connection was with Toothless and not me. The lies went on and on, and one of the officers actually started to feel bad for him, I think, and bought into the whole 'trying to fix things tonight' story. I was sobbing again, terrified that they wouldn't believe me or make him leave. Terrified that he'd convince them that he had any right at all to be there. Terrified that they'd leave but he wouldn't. I was relieved when they seemed to be finally listening to me and considering that maybe this was nothing more than a good 'ol fashioned case of trespassing. Case closed. It wasn't that simple though. He was a master manipulator and knew exactly what they wanted to hear. He fed it to them, and they kept opening their mouths for more. When I finally got one of the officers alone, I think he saw past the tale that Toothless was attempting to weave and realized how terrified I was, despite the angry facade I was presenting. I was angry, yes, but so fearful that I'd never be free of this guy. I was offered a no trespass order, should I want to guarantee that he didn't return. A no trespass is a piece of paper, though, and hardly the protection

I needed. In fact, I worried that serving him this order would only fuel his lunacy and push him beyond his breaking point. I was afraid that signing this piece of paper would be signing my own death warrant. I kindly refused, but affixed the officer's card and the TRL phone number to my fridge for safekeeping, hoping I wouldn't need to use it later.

All the uninvited guests left, Toothless included, and I locked the door behind them. I sat on my bed for a few minutes and tried to shake off the night, trails of mascara dried on my cheeks, my eyes swollen from crying. I wrapped myself in a blanket and tried to calm my nerves, a small glass of bourbon in my now shaky-hand. After a few minutes, I climbed into bed and made Wells the focus of my attention, petting the soft fur between his ears. I turned the TV on for background noise; I kept the lamp on beside my bed. No matter how hard I tried to block out the night, the same thought was on repeat: *What if he comes back? What if he lets himself in when I'm asleep? What if he's angry...* My heart was pounding, and I'm pretty sure I didn't drift off for more than twenty minutes all night.

I should've blocked him but didn't, thinking that if he was going to come by, he might actually give me a heads up first. I didn't want to move through life completely handicapping myself from seeing what was coming. Better to have one security camera than none at all. Toothless reached out a bunch over the next few days, begging me to talk, to give him a chance to explain. He claimed that he was only so persistent that night because he loved me and didn't want to leave without resolving things. I explained to him that it wasn't his call. That I had retreated into the little corner of the world that was mine, and I needed to feel safe there. That that safety that every human deserves was taken from me by him. By his actions. By his selfishness. When I refused to discuss further or see him again, he was irate. His tone changed drastically, and he insisted that I owed him money. "Do you really think I would invest money in someone if they wouldn't be with me?" His voice tinged with pain, but it was masked by extreme anger. "The way I see it, you owe me about $14,000. Sound about right?" he asked. He began listing the items he'd purchased for me, meals he'd paid for, payment for the movers, a small TV he bought. He even listed buying paper plates for my son's birthday party a few months before. "Are you kidding me?!" I asked. I told him to draft up a list of what he felt he was owed and to have his lawyer contact me. I wouldn't entertain such a ridiculous conversation with him. At this point, we were all-out screaming. A back and forth volleyball match ensued, hurling insult after insult at each other. He was hurt, and he wanted to hurt me. This may have been the first and only time he ever told me any truths. He told me that when Fireball stalked my house, he was the one driving the car. That he'd driven past my house many, many times, with and without Fireball. That he'd taken pictures of me when I was asleep. He admitted that he'd told people we were together because he fully believed we would be. He just needed me to see that too.

That's all I needed to hear. I realized there was no talking to this guy. That at some point he'd lost touch with reality and truly believed this version of his life to be real. That we were together and he just needed me to see that too.

* * *

I had blocked him on most social media, and his texting was growing less frequent. The texts were cyclical, and after a wave of harassment, it would be a few weeks before I would hear from him again. He told me he was joking. That the mention of paying him back money I owed him was simply a joke and that he just wanted a chance to see me again. Although he didn't seem to be releasing me fully from his grasp, his grip was loosening a bit at a time. Maybe he was seeing that I was truly never going to be his. Maybe.

* * *

Weeks later, my girlfriend and I had exited the theater and were spilling out onto the street along with the other theater-goers. The musical we had watched was funny, and I was glad she had talked me into going. We were headed for her car when my phone rang. It was Toothless. I shouldn't have answered, but I suppose the randomness of the call had me intrigued. I planned to snap at him in 3.9 seconds and hang up. Before I had the opportunity, he got straight to the point and blurted out that a friend of mine had died. To be more specific, a man that I'd known since we were kids. A man that I'd dated just recently (yup, 6'4"). Someone that Toothless knew I cared deeply about. He wasn't soft about it. There was no greeting and no set up to let me down easy. He fucked me without lube. His urgency in telling me was apparent, and I got off the phone as quickly as I'd answered it, hurt and angry by his insensitive delivery. I hadn't had even five seconds to process the news when my phone rang again. Fireball. WTH?! I answered the phone, and he delivered the same news in the same coldhearted and insensitive way. I hung up, shocked at their audacity. They were racing to be the first to break my heart and deliver the terrible news. I had just talked to 6'4" two weeks prior, and although we weren't seeing each other anymore, we had grown very close. We both felt alone at times, and now, I truly was. We'd always had each other, but now he was gone, and I'd never felt more alone. Could I have helped him? Was there anything I could've done? We reached the car, and before the door closed, the tears were flowing uncontrollably. I couldn't see. I couldn't breathe. My girlfriend took me home that night and took care of me, feeding me alcohol and cuddling me all night. It was a tough loss, and I knew I'd never be quite the same. And these two motherfuckers took pleasure in making sure to be the first to deliver the blow.

* * *

Months went by. My family and I were in Massachusetts for my son's rowing race in Boston Harbor. We were in line at the hotel, waiting to check in and collect the keys to our room. While my son's father was giving our info to the concierge, my phone rang. It was Wells' veterinarian. I hadn't had anything done recently nor did I have anything currently scheduled. I stepped away and answered, hoping he hadn't gotten loose or was injured somehow. It was the vet herself, concerned about the frequency in which Wells was going through his medicine. He had been prescribed puppy Xanax, a controlled substance, months prior. I had received a bottle the day he was seen and we still had more than half left. The vet informed me that it was alarming that he'd been going through it so fast and that he should probably be seen again to reassess. I let her know that I had never had the prescription refilled. She read through his chart—it had apparently been filled last month and the month prior. The request coming in for another refill just a few days ago was concerning. She wanted to speak to me before filling it again. Confusion quickly set in but passed just as quickly. Toothless. He had taken Wells to that initial appointment. The vet was able to confirm that it was a man who had requested all three refills. She also confirmed that he was listed on the account. His name wasn't just on the account, but had replaced mine as the primary on the account. His email address and phone number had been provided. They planned to investigate and press charges, and I was all for it. Once in my hotel room, I called Toothless. One call. My last call to this guy. I wasn't going to let him get away with this. He'd gone too far. At the slight mention of Wells, he knew exactly what I was referring to. He claimed that he was filling the pills for me. For Wells. That he still had the several months' worth of pills and was holding onto them for me. I had had him blocked on all platforms for months, and yet I was supposed to buy the fact that he was doing me a favor? That he was saving these for me until Wells needed them? He'd told his last lie to me. This man was completely unhinged. I'd heard that during our months of no contact, he was still telling tall tales. He was still telling folks all over town that we were together and building a future. A life. *I'm glad to hear it, because this man certainly needed to get a life. If he had the money he claimed to have, maybe he could buy one. One thing is for certain though. He couldn't buy me, an obstacle he'd never faced before.* I'm not for sale. I'm not his. I'm also not sure I've seen the last of him. But I do know that if I do, he still won't have any teeth.

| 20 |

The Vegan Saga (Part 4):
Beyond the Meat

That post-it though. I should have moved. I don't mean moved on. I should have quit my job, changed my name, and left the country. I've never had someone write something so... unhinged. And to think he'd only tasted that 'sweet pussy' once and fell asleep during. How can you write about something you don't even remember experiencing? But me being the forever forgiving, all too friendly person that I am, did none of those things. I didn't even block him. His effort was renewed, and he was coming at me full force. For the first time in our entire situationship, he was actually pursuing me. He had listened to my grievances and was finally making a full-fledged effort to make sure I knew that he was interested in more than just a physical relationship. He had flowers sent to my office. They were actually quite beautiful. They'd arrived so late in the day that I had already left the office. One of my associates texted me a picture. Not knowing who they were from was all-consuming for us both, so I gave her permission to open the card that was tucked inside. She gasped and told me they were from The Vegan. I was stunned. There was also a longer envelope tucked in, and she began to read it to me over the phone, then stopped abruptly. She was clearly embarrassed and suggested I read it myself. Naturally, the suspense was killing me, so I swung by before heading home for the night. The office was empty and locked.

I sat in my dimly lit office, reading the poem he had written for me. He wrote of being in love and the magic that comes with it. Being completely consumed with the feeling and wanting more of it. Being intoxicated by the desire to be with someone. Me. I was grateful that my coworker had stopped reading when she did. Hell, I was red-faced reading this alone. He'd never spoken to me like this, and I was taken aback. I called him that night, thanked him for the bouquet of orange roses and the poem, and made the mistake of asking if he'd just written it. He hadn't of course. Why would I expect to be the muse of his poem while he's busy trying to win my affection? *Silly, Scarlett.* He admitted that he had written it years prior, inspired by another's heart. He immediately sent me another of his works—a very graphic, sexual poem apparently inspired by another's lady bits. Awesome. *Dude, this is where you fib. I would have had no idea you didn't write it for me. Now I'm getting recycled poetry written for someone else when you were trying to get laid? Maybe she tasted like honey. Not cool, dude. That gives sloppy seconds a whole new meaning.*

He continued to make strides to try to win me over. He invited me over for dinner and made tacos. Like, real tacos with ground beef and actual cheese. I was extremely surprised at the gesture. Like he always did, he needed to tell me all about it. Every last detail. He had bought 8590. He repeated this number and finally I bit. "What's 8590?" I asked. "That's how lean the meat is. 8590," he answered confidently. I knew he was confused. "Did you happen to buy two packages of meat perhaps? One that was 85% lean and one that was 90% lean?" "Yes, 8590. Like I said," he responded. He cooked the beef in water. Water. He boiled the ground beef. He had no idea what he was doing. *A for effort, I guess?*

The Vegan continued to try to make room for me in his life. He went out and bought toiletries for me. He gave me his extra electric toothbrush and even bought my dog a dog bed. Without discussion, he added me to his Costco membership. He reached out one day while I was at work and sent me a picture of a pair of socks. He'd found them under his bed and assumed they were mine. They weren't. Without pause, he suggested that perhaps these belonged to the woman he was sleeping with before me. He had met her on a dating site for married folks who wanted discretion. I knew her personally from church. *Wicked impressive, sir. You're definitely winning my heart here. Points for integrity. Kinda wishing I HAD slept with the Plow Guy now.* He asked again about the socks, and again, I told him they still weren't mine. He suggested that perhaps they belonged to another of his exes—the mother of his son. *When the hell did she sleep in his bed?! But more so, we're talking CVS' finest socks. $5.99 at most. Let it go. Insulting three women to try and return these socks is not worth it. Toss 'em out.*

* * *

When Super Bowl Sunday arrived, I'd been at his house visiting. At the mention of the game, he was disgusted, explaining what a waste of time watching football is. I had planned on leaving to watch the game with friends, and he was more than okay with my plan. He made it very clear that he could think of many other things he'd rather do than waste a couple of hours participating in this yearly tradition of mine. When the afternoon was winding down, and the game was nearing, I grabbed my shoes and prepared to head out. He stopped me and told me he changed his mind. "I'd rather you stay than leave," he said, and he begged me to reconsider watching the game with him. I explained my interest in watching the entire event, commercials, halftime, and all, and that I didn't want him to change his mind partway through or turn the TV off early. He agreed and even suggested he make me some food. I wanted to head out to the store to grab a few things, but he was adamant that he'd whip up something for me. Options were more of the usual—rice, veggies and tofu. Honestly though, he did know how to sear that tofu, and it was pretty damn good. Wells loved it too. I further disappointed him, though, when I explained that I wanted traditional football food. He was so desperate to have me stay that he offered to run to the store for me and grab those few items. I actually enjoy shopping and making food for this yearly event, so I didn't accept his offer. And honestly, the man boiled taco meat. He doesn't ever shop for meat. He couldn't be trusted to pick up the ingredients I'd need to make homemade jalapeno poppers and chicken wings. We went together, and he followed me down the aisles. I'm not sure if he was just observing or if he was disappointed, but I definitely felt his judgment. It was stronger than the fluorescent lights overhead. When we returned to his house, he struggled to let me just do my thing, but eventually conceded and stood a few feet away with a beer in hand. He was watching, critiquing silently. Always judging. I was actually blown away that he was letting me cook my chicken wings in his cast iron skillet. He earned points in my book for this because I'm sure a little bit of him was dying inside watching me taint his most prized cooking implement with the carnage. I packed up the leftovers, and his son, who was not a vegan, would appreciate having them for lunch the next day. We watched the game, and to my surprise, he didn't interrupt too much and seemed to actually enjoy himself. I'm convinced that half of his problem was that he never allowed himself to try anything. He wasn't open to fun.

I remember getting a little buzzed one night and turning up the dance moves in his kitchen. Nothing too raunchy, mind you, but definitely not moves I'd break out in front of his son or his roommate. He was a few drinks in, as well, and joined in. He was loving my energy and matching it, much to my surprise. But when I saw him next, we were back to the same boring, monotone Vegan. The same judgy, self-righteous, self-centered man who couldn't get out of his own way long enough to enjoy himself or anyone else. *Such a shame.*

* * *

Valentine's Day neared, and The Vegan had mentioned having gotten me a gift. He mentioned it several times, in fact. I'm not sure if he wanted to make sure there would be reciprocity or if he was just proud of himself for thinking of someone else. When we were a few days out, seemingly frustrated, he blurted out, "Did you even get me a gift?!" I did, of course. Not because he was my boyfriend—he wasn't. Not because we were moving toward a relationship—we weren't. I felt obligated to return the gesture. *Please allow me to introduce to you the love child of Guilt and Reciprocity. If I'd stayed with him, surely we would've adopted this damn child.* He had been working on getting his over-sized bathtub operational since he'd bought the place, and had invested more time recently with the thought of us intimately soaking and enjoying some warm suds together. With his temperamental attitude and hard-to-read demeanor, choosing a gift damn near gave me an ulcer. I ended up creating a spa basket of sorts, complete with two loofahs, bubble bath, candles, and a book. To ensure that I gave him something that he would benefit from solely (I feared he'd accuse me of giving a gift that I too would benefit from), I also purchased two items that I truly thought he'd appreciate. With his work in the garden and his weekly mountain biking, I thought a professional massage would be just the ticket. In the time I'd known him, he'd pulled muscles in his back more than once. I paired it with a free session at a local salt cave, given that he was a meditative and grounded soul. He not only didn't appreciate the gift but told me the candles were not quality (since they weren't made of soy) and that I should just take the massage voucher back because he'd never use it. *What a slap in the face! What an ungrateful little asshole!* In hindsight, I should've taken him up on the offer and taken back the massage gift certificate. I could be venting about this joker to the masseuse right now. *Sigh.*

His gift to me was far more thoughtful. He presented me with a set of three candles. Yes, they were soy. Perhaps he forgot that he already told me he had ordered these for his house. Either way, he changed his mind and made these my present (yup, after brazenly asking me if I'd even gotten him a gift). Grrr. We're not done though. He had one gift remaining. To my surprise, he gave me a ring. Not just any ring. The ring was made of wood and was several sizes too big for me. He handed me this ring and explained that it was a commitment ring… for him. He wanted me to place it on his finger. He wanted the world to know that he was 'taken.' He explained that I didn't need a ring since I sometimes still wore my old wedding ring. (In my defense, it was custom-made designed by me, and no longer held any sentimental value.) He went on to share that the purpose of this ring was to also remind him that he was committed to someone and to keep him from straying, or even considering it. *Dude, you need a ring to remember you're seeing someone?! Oh, right. I almost forgot that you were banging a married woman before me. I'm not the morality police, but still, eww. Must be hard to remember boundaries. And it must be hard to remember the woman whose pussy tastes like chocolate. You could've saved your money and tied a string to your finger instead.* I'm sure nobody is surprised, but yes, I refused to put that ring on his finger. I'd been married and wasn't about to make that mistake again. And I certainly wasn't going to be tricked into joining into a committed relationship with someone who wasn't being his true self and ignoring my true self. *No. Fucking. Way. And honestly? Let's start with a cock ring, not a commitment ring. You're doing it wrong, babe.*

* * *

The Vegan's roommate moved out. It'd been long overdue, and by the time he left, the two were not living as harmoniously as they once were. There was tension and resentment, and they never spent time together in any capacity. He took time to clean the carpet and repaint the newly vacant room, and it showed. This was the biggest and nicest bedroom in the house, and I strongly encouraged him to finally be the master of his domain and move into the master bedroom. The room was large, had a gorgeous old wood stove, and let in the perfect amount of natural light. Honestly, I don't know why he had ever chosen the smallest room in the-paying roommate to make this gorgeous space his own. Wells always found his way into this room, and on two separate occasions, he and I (The Vegan, not Wells) built a fire and enjoyed its warmth while sitting on the carpet of this empty room. Even so, it was lovely, and he began considering relocating downstairs. He suggested that we move in, citing that my dog loved that room and that it would be perfect for us together. He hadn't spent much time with my sons, but since the roommate moved out, he made it clear that there would be room for my sons to have their own spaces too.

The gesture was sweet but completely blindsided me. He wasn't my boyfriend. In fact, we weren't even dating! And I had refused his commitment ring. *I think your gears are busted, sir. Zero to sixty with no in-between.*

I didn't move in (thank God) and started distancing myself. He mentioned marriage and the fact that he had recently realized that it was something he'd want again someday. I'm sure he felt my hesitation, but decided to ignore it. He began putting the pressure on hardcore. To be clear, we still weren't going on dates. We still weren't hanging out with each other's families. We weren't moving forward in any way, yet he was clear that he wanted to get married. He wasn't in love with me or near to taking a knee, but he wanted to get married. It seemed like he was setting the expectation so I could bow out if I wasn't ready to commit. I've been proposed to more than once, and the lamest proposal was better than whatever this was. He approached me with a proposal of its own kind. I had refused to move in. I had refused to be his girlfriend or to give him the commitment ring he gave me to give him (you followed that, right?). So, to say I was shocked at his next suggestion is an understatement. He suggested that we become engaged. He wanted to be engaged for a year and see where we stood at the end of that year. He wanted me to commit to spending a full year with him, for the good and the bad, after which I could leave if I wasn't ready to marry him, or if he wasn't ready to marry me. We'd have to stick it out for a full 365 days, even if we weren't thriving as a couple. It gets better. He wanted me to sign a contract agreeing to this. He wanted me to be contractually obligated to be his partner for a full year, while he wore a commitment ring so he would be reminded not to sleep with anyone else. He wanted me to be committed on paper to stay with him and ignore the things I didn't like about him. Great plan. *You've pleasured me once. Only once. The sex is vanilla. I miss steak. And I have better taste in socks, and you should know that. Do you even know me at all? Can't marry you, sir. I'm already in love. I love cheese, and cheese will always win. No contract necessary.*

* * *

I hadn't managed to fully break it off with The Vegan, though I kept coming up with excuses to not see him. I was busy with anything and everything. He had put on the full court press, and I couldn't keep facing him. It was getting suffocating. The man wasn't even in love with me. I think maybe he had begun thinking about his own mortality or wanted guaranteed sex for his workout routine. Maybe the house was quieter without the roommate, and he knew that his son would probably move out within a year or two. Maybe he was being proactive so he wouldn't be alone. Maybe he wanted help with the rent. Who knows. My disappearing act wasn't quite flawless though, and he was noticing. I knew I wouldn't be able to keep it up much longer.

* * *

My girlfriend and I had decided to take a burlesque class on Sunday evenings. I was nervous at first, but it ended up being so freeing and empowering. I loved every minute of it, including the bruised knees. *Now, I finally had a reason worthy of bruising my knees. Sorry, Vegan, maybe you should've cooked me a steak once in a while. Maybe bacon with eggs. Just a thought.* All the students wore lingerie and lacey things for class. It was out of my comfort zone but was evident that I wasn't the only one who felt that way. These women (and men), would show up for class in spandex athletic wear; strip down to heels, thigh highs, and corsets for the floor tease, and leave class the way they arrived. When you entered the studio, you came out of your shell. You were this fierce animal whose sole mission was to entice and discover. Often after class, a group of us would negate the workout and head across the street for a cocktail and an appetizer. That's where you'd really get a chance to meet these ladies. One that we really connected with was a woman who was very quiet and shy. Since class really opened folks up, after a few weeks she was sharing more, and we had really begun to learn about her. Turns out, she had an ex-husband who she wasn't much a fan of. My girlfriend shared the tattered journey of her love life. I shared my recent adventures with The Vegan as well. The ladies couldn't believe this man was asking me to sign an engagement contract. The more I shared, the more appalled they were. They told me to run, that he was unstable. This one particular night, our new friend was venting about her ex and it all came together for me. I panicked. My heart was pounding and my palms were instantly clammy. "Wait, what did you say your son's name was?" I asked. "And your ex. He gardens? Grows and sells his own weed? Did he recently move into a tiny house on a farm?!" Her eyes grew big, and I knew she had come to the same conclusion that I had. I didn't need anything more than the look of shock she gave me, but still, she offered confirmation. "Oh my God!!! The Vegan! The Vegan!!!" Turns out, her ex was The Vegan's roommate who had recently moved out. Before I could make it the twenty feet to the bar, she yelled over to the bartender, "Pour her a shot!!" Before I could tell the bartender what I wanted to drink, she had a shot poured. She, like most women, understood that in that moment, anything would suffice. *Just make it strong.* I learned so much more about The Vegan that night, and running was absolutely the right call. She gave me so much insight about his past relationships and how unhinged he really was. I left that night, determined to end things immediately. Whatever there was to end.

I tried one night, but his son ended up being home that evening and made polite conversation as he usually did. I didn't get a moment alone with The Vegan. It made it impossible for me to broach the subject. I tried again the next day, and again, something got in the way. I couldn't keep avoiding his passive-aggressive text messages nor could I keep visiting him, pretending everything was fine. In his world, we'd bypass dating, and I'd move in with him and marry him. Maybe someday he'd even grow feelings for me. Fingers crossed. Legs not. I tried one last time to meet up with him, but our schedules were not cooperating. I knew he was headed to the hardware store, so I decided I'd head that way and try to see him for a minute so we could set up a time to sit down and say our goodbyes. The Vegan was intuitive and smart enough to feel me pulling away, and when he saw me in the parking lot, he refused to talk. He threw his hat on the ground multiple times like a child. The seagulls circled around him, just as confused as I was. He stormed off toward the entrance to the store, then came back, marching angrily my way. He stood there, in a populated parking lot, screaming at me, telling me how awful I was, and that if I was ending it, to just end it. He did this three times, repeatedly throwing his hat on the ground and causing a ridiculous scene. (He was in his late forties, in case you were wondering.) I was able to convince him to call me later so we could talk. Instead of calling, I received many text messages from him over the next few days, unapologetic but rather demanding AF. He needed more frequency. He wanted me at his house at least four times a week, or he wanted to end it. I was preparing to leave for a trip with my sons and received one last text from him, reiterating just that: "This isn't working for me. If you can't commit to seeing me more than half the week and being physically intimate with me most, if not all, of those days, then we should move on. At this point, I don't expect to hear from you until you get back from your trip. It's up to you." That was the last I heard from him. I didn't respond, nor did I reach out when I returned from Mexico. I wouldn't be surprised if he already had someone else in his bed the moment our ship hit open water. I'll bet they love their tofu burritos and scheduled sex. Hell, they're probably already engaged. I'm sure Wells misses his mountain biking adventures, and I know I miss the free shishito peppers, but that's about it. I don't miss the constant criticism, the oh-so-bland sex, or being encouraged to be quiet rather than share. And damn it, if this book proves anything, I'll never be one to tell the 'abridged version.'

| 21 |

So Much for a Grand Finale

Facebook for the win again, bringing another asshat my way, one thirsty for some cooch juice and an ego boost. He thought I was cute (yada yada, same script, different day). There was something different about this guy though. His charm was so thick and so tangible that I swear I could feel him reaching through the phone and caressing my chin with his thumb. We were inseparable right away, our phone calls lasting into the wee hours of the morning, five to six hours at a time (red flag alert!—I know this now, but was blind to it at the time). The connection strengthened as we realized the similarities we shared and the past hurdles we'd both had to endure. We had both been through a lot over the years, and though his struggles different than mine, they were no less real. "We've both been through so much," he said. "Maybe we were meant to be each other's 'Grand Finale,' he added. He was the first and only person to stop me from making self-deprecating jokes about my track record of divorce. He reminded me that it's better to have tried than to have never tried at all. That three men loved me enough to promise me forever, and that I loved hard enough to commit fully three separate times. That despite a journey ending, it never jaded me or deterred me from putting myself out there again. That I didn't owe anybody an apology or an explanation, and if anyone deserved an apology, it was me. I needed to stop being so hard on myself and holding myself to a standard that no one else was.

Our conversations were so deep, and I looked forward to whatever the next topic might be. Sometimes he'd lead, sometimes I'd branch off completely, and other times, our minds were in the same place at the same time. It was like a beautiful ice dancing routine, two partners gliding gracefully, each taking their moment to stand out. He throws her in the air and she lets him, trusting the power and the landing. He kneels behind her as she takes a bow, her moment to shine. It was effortless, and my face hurt from the perma-grin I sported each time we talked. We had discussed a first date, and suddenly it all became a little too real. I snapped back to reality, remembering how my ex-husband had destroyed me, and how I had taken time to heal and find myself. *Was I even ready to give this a real shot? He wasn't a booty call, this I knew. But was I ready to put myself out there again?* I was terrified of getting hurt and very vulnerably shared this with him. "Life is short," he said. "Let me make you happy." The confidence and sincerity in his tone made me weak in the knees. Despite the overwhelming uncertainty that he represented, I agreed to dinner.

Grand Finale (spoiler alert—he wasn't) picked me up for dinner. He was dressed in a blue long-sleeve button-up shirt and khaki pants. He had three stargazer lily stems in his hand when he came to my door. I quickly put the flowers in water and followed him out to his truck. Like the old-fashioned sweetheart he'd presented himself to be, he held my door and closed it after I'd taken my seat. We drove to dinner, holding hands. It seemed long overdue, given the intensity of the conversations we'd had. In some ways, I felt like I'd known him forever. He took me to a nice restaurant and insisted on paying, saying that it makes him feel good, and that he'd never let me pay for dinner. He copied my choice of cocktail, seeming to be rather inexperienced when it came to spirits. I'll admit, it was pretty cute. A girlfriend of mine was at a mall just around the corner and suggested that we come by so she could meet the guy I'd told her so much about. It was on our way home, so he agreed. She was standing in the parking lot, waiting for her dog to relieve himself. She's one of those women who all men drool over, and all women either hate or want to be best friends with. Sexy in ripped jeans and a trucker hat, or glowing in skintight alligator pants while doing the splits on a pool table (true story). And here she was, wearing the most ass-hugging seafoam green leggings, bent over to tend to her four-legged friend. I fully expected his eyes to be tracing her curves, but was surprised to see him smiling at me, completely unaware of what was right in front of him. Or maybe, for once, a man saw exactly what was right in front of him. And it felt damn good to be seen.

With a few more dinner dates and late night chats under our belts, we were anxious to see each other again. Although I already had New Year's plans with a couple of girlfriends, we made plans to spend the night together once the night's festivities were done. He'd spent the day buying provisions, a bottle of my favorite whiskey, a bottle of red wine, a set of rocks glasses, a mold to make large ice spheres, and coffee with a variety of creamers for the morning. While I was out shaking my sequined tail feathers with my equally sequined gal pals, he was busy setting out candles and fluffing throw pillows (okay, well, maybe not, but it was a nice thought anyway). When the ladies headed for home, I grabbed Wells and headed his way. He greeted us at the door, grateful we'd made it. It was well past midnight at this point, and my hair had turned curly from the sweaty mess I'd become on the dancefloor. He complimented my dress, but the only thing on my mind was getting out of that golden ensemble and freshening up before he got close enough to smell me. He obliged, leading me into the bathroom and providing me with a towel and the necessary toiletries. He waited patiently while I made sure I was ready for what was about to be our first time being physically intimate. I emerged from the bathroom in pajamas and we spent hours together, dancing in the living room, playfully talking and laughing, all while repeatedly topping off our drinks.

At some point, there was a lull in the conversation and in that moment of silence, we both knew it was time to retreat to the bedroom. There was passion and ease in the way that we moved in the dark, exploring each other's bodies. It wasn't mind-blowing by any means (thank you, whiskey) but a new closeness was formed, our vulnerabilities taking the lead. When I woke the next morning, I was alone in his bed, but I could hear him rustling around in the kitchen. He entered the bedroom and sat on the edge of his bed, turning his body to face me. "You stay here, beautiful," he said softly. "I'm coming back with coffee for you. Just rest." Although there's something to be said for the burnt toast and undercooked bacon served by your children on Mother's Day, 'coffee in bed' had its own ring to it. Definitely something I could get used to. I rested my head back onto the pillow, the sheet tucked under my arms while I took in the details of the room. He had motorcycle helmets on his dresser, a hamper in the corner, and one window shade that needed replacing.

The apartment was tidy, otherwise, with minimal decor. His daughter's room was the only colorful area of the house, bursting with hues of orange and yellow. It was organized and minimal, but it looked like she had everything she could want. It was clear that she was the center of his world. Just one weekend together gave me a glimpse of what that must feel like, and it was amazing.

He returned to the bedroom, coffee in hand, and told me to stay in bed until every last drop was gone. He took Wells out to use the bathroom, keeping true to his word, so that I could relax without interruption. He started the shower and laid out a fresh towel. To my surprise, he climbed in behind me and began washing my shoulders and back, moving the loofa in a small circular motion. It was incredibly sweet and reassured me that he wanted me for me. That he wanted me for more than just a romp in his bed. He didn't attempt to make our shower a sexy one, but rather couldn't stop kissing the back of my head. When I looked back to see his face, he was covered in shampoo, lathered foam taking over his cheek and his lips. Even the threat of a mouthful of soap didn't deter him from showing his affection.

He offered to buy me the shampoo of my choice and keep it on hand for when I was over in the future. He made it known that as the owner and landlord of that house, he didn't allow dogs, however, he liked me so much that he'd make an exception when I visited. He even insisted on keeping a pair of my socks at his place so I'd be comfortable the next time I came by. Everything pointed to the beginning of something that could be great.

We spent the next several hours together, rolling around on the couch, playful and giddy. I was worried I was overstaying my welcome, but he seemed to be enjoying his time just as much as I was, so neither of us rushed the day along. When it was time to bring Wells out for a walk, I decided to call the date to an end. We both had our own to-do lists and agendas for the rest of the weekend, and I knew I'd be seeing him soon enough anyhow. I grabbed my things and set them in my car before walking the perimeter of his yard, hand-in-hand, Wells leading the way. He seemed just as focused as he was when handing me that cup 'o joe, just as taken as when he'd laid out a towel for my shower, and just as smitten as he had been while smiling at me from across the table on our first date. I kissed him goodbye and drove off, watching him grow small in my rearview mirror, appreciating the last 16 hours of my life... with a huge smile on my face.

Prior to our slumber party, he had messaged frequently. Not more than a few hours would go by between texts, but now, it'd been hours. Not two hours. Not three. I hadn't heard a peep out of him all day. I reached out, thanking him for a good time, but making sure to play the game. I was careful to stay between the yellow lines of assuming it was a one night stand and assuming he viewed it as more. I didn't want to scare him away, but I wanted him to know I was willing to see where this could go if he was. He didn't respond.

No response the next day.

Nothing the day after that.

A few days later, I saw that he had posted something on Facebook. Still nothing.

I'd been ghosted before, but this time, it hurt. It more than hurt. He broke me. This man had asked me to let him make me happy, despite my fear of letting another man close to my heart. He promised me that he wouldn't let me down in the ways that others had before, but he'd done just that. I'd entrusted him with my past, and he used it against me. He played me. The oldest game in history. *The classic #dick-and-dash*

After a few days of text-bombing him, he finally responded. Turns out, men don't like being called cowards, a fact I'd learned previously and used more than once. If you insult a man's ego, his inability to bite his tongue is all but guaranteed. *I'll tell you that for free. You're welcome.* His excuse was one of the lamest any man had ever fed me—he thought he was ready to date, but he wasn't. He needed to focus on building his empire and taking care of his daughter, not his love life. He hadn't healed from the death of his previous marriage, and spending time with me made that glaringly apparent to him. I'd like to tell myself that he felt so strongly about me, that it scared him. That he could see the future that he'd hoped for in my eyes, and that it paralyzed him. But at the end of the day, that day specifically, he had used me. He had played me. He'd gotten exactly what he'd set out for and shattered me in the process. It had taken me so long to let my guard down and let anyone in again, and after he disappeared from my life, my guards went back up, more fortified than before.

He reached out months later, telling me he missed me. He said he wasn't sure what that meant, but that he wanted to see me. He was clear to say he didn't want to date, but that he no longer had joy in his life. That spending time with me brought him joy, and he wanted that back. But he wanted that without any commitment or title, no exclusivity, no rules, no obligation. I agreed to meet for a drink, nothing more, but expressed that I was still afraid he'd hurt me again. He tried to convince me that he'd proven to me he wasn't going anywhere (from one long phone call, mind you), but after we'd agreed to meet up, communication once again ceased. Grand Finale once again disappeared from my life just as quickly as he'd entered it.

He was like a pair of waterproof boots in your favorite brand, made with the best materials, in the perfect shade of cognac brown. The laces taught and precise, the footbed keeping your foot warm and snug, the stunning fur edge tying it all together. *Chef's kiss.* The pair of boots you knew you always wanted but never thought you'd find.

Boots you'd paid the price for. But boots that weren't waterproof at all.

| 22 |

No Strings Attached

Disclaimer: This guy wasn't unhinged. Did he end up being superficial? Maybe. Shallow? I'd say so. Selfish? Absolutely. But was he good with his tongue? You better believe it. This chapter lacks any surprise twists or turns (except the ones he made with his appendages). Take this as the palette cleanser it is. Everyone deserves a fun, commitment-free chapter, and he was mine. Enjoy.

* * *

I imagine it felt how a speed dating round must feel. We were both rattling off information about ourselves and asking questions about the other. Sparks had flown instantly, heavy at first. As a troop of daycare children passed by behind him, it was clear that we had different views on children. Watching these little tykes walk by and splash in puddles with their bright-colored rainboots made me smile. He cringed and asked if I had kids. He was clearly unimpressed when I said I did. He returned the favor, admitting that he wasn't a fan of kids in any capacity. The sparks were fizzling out as quickly as they had started. Despite our glaringly obvious differences, I found him later online, and with a little liquid courage, reached out. My DM was simple, not overly aggressive, and stayed in his inbox for a few weeks, unopened. I'd honestly forgotten that I'd even reached out to him until randomly, he finally read my message and decided to respond. We exchanged a few messages back and forth, and I soon learned that he was in a relationship. He'd been with the same woman for seven years, on again, off again. It was a long-distance arrangement, and that was his preference. He liked having time with her and thoroughly enjoyed his time without her as well. But learning he wasn't single was enough for me. He wasn't trying to step out on his old lady any more than I was trying to be a homewrecker. With that, we bid each other adieu.

Months passed, and he reached out. Apparently he and his girlfriend had finally decided to end things, and this time, there was no return. I was still single. Thank goodness. He asked me out and almost immediately reached back out to confirm that this was not a date. We'd be going out on Valentine's Day, and he wanted to ensure that I knew it was just two friends grabbing drinks, not the start of a love affair. I'd received a four-page card from one guy, and a commitment ring and some serious attitude from another. A casual night out with a charismatic guy over some drinks sounded like a decent change of pace. Hell, it couldn't be any worse. I parked outside his apartment building. He met me outside, and we walked to one of my favorite spots nearby. He was very casually dressed (a hoodie and some nice jeans), but all items were in perfect condition and his shoes were pristine. They looked like he'd just taken them out of the box. He smelled great and his hair had the perfect coif. You could tell that he put a lot of time into how he looked. Not long into our non-date date, he had mentioned again that it wasn't a date. We soon learned that we had a few things in common. We enjoyed similar music, going out dancing, fine dinners, and a good scotch. But that was pretty much where our similarities ended. I had kids, he didn't want any. I had been married, he never had any aspiration to. Without question, he was interested in me. He had even told his father about me when he first met me, but knew I was off-limits back then. He may have even been up for exploring a relationship, had it not been for my membership in the motherhood club. He was extremely selfish, however, and made sure I knew it wasn't me, but the fact that I had kids that would prevent him from exploring things further. I was enjoying his smile and our conversation, and it was easier than ever to accept his answer. He admitted that he'd probably passed up on some really great women throughout the years simply because they had baggage. It was unfortunate, and he knew it. All the same, he wasn't about to change his ways now. Not for me. Not for anyone.

I walked him back to his corner and we parted ways, him into his building, me, across the street and into my car. I was leaving my spot when he called me. "You haven't even left the street yet. Come up. Doesn't have to be long. I'd love to show you the place," he said. The angel on my shoulder was off on a bathroom break, and the devil had consumed two energy drinks. She was ready to go. Which meant that so was I. I was nervous, of course, but going up to his apartment wasn't lost on me. I knew what I was getting myself into. Or rather, what he was about to get into.

He showed me around his fancy downtown apartment. It was immaculately kept. He had old movie posters and vintage memorabilia framed on his walls. His place was clean, and on his counter a bottle of scotch sat atop a live edge cutting board. It was lovely. Even his dog's toys and blankets were neatly organized. His dog was named after the designer cologne he was wearing the day he picked him out as a puppy. Another sign that he was maybe not the family man I would someday want in my life. He worked for a radio station. When I referred to him as a 'DJ,' he quickly corrected me. He was the Vice President of Programming. My bad. His home office was neatly kept, and it was evident that he would often broadcast from home. It was all fascinating and so simple at the same time. He tried sharing with me, talking about the area he grew up in, and in a rare change of events, I became the world's worst listener. I couldn't stop focusing on what might happen, and it was making it extremely hard to pay attention to his words.

I was near the door, slipping my stocking feet into my boots, about to leave. He leaned down and kissed me. We'd made it through his entire apartment with no attempt from him, so I honestly assumed I was in the clear. He kissed me hard, knocking the framed picture of Frank Sinatra off the wall. I trapped it against the wall with my ass. He freed the picture and lowered it to safety with one hand while pulling off my jacket with the other. Details aren't important, but the next thing I knew, he had convinced me to have a night I wouldn't soon forget. Surely, I could get past the fact that he was a fan of the Yankees fan (Go Sox!). He gave me a more in depth tour of his bedroom. High thread count. Nice. I left, my legs shaking, the smile on my face huge. The text messages that followed were hot and heavy. He reached out several times a day, making sure I knew how badly he wanted me. Emojis were used. Filthy, filthy words. He loved the noises I made, and I loved him inspiring me to make them. There was nothing vanilla about what we were doing. And I fucking loved every fucking second of it. (See what I did there?)

* * *

Our time together was always fun. We only connected a few times, but after exchanging pleasantries, we got right down to business. After all, we didn't always have a lot to talk about. This one time, we couldn't seem to make our schedules align. He would be starting a several-hours-long conference call just before I'd be getting out of work. We were both disappointed, but he offered an ingenious solution. He wouldn't be able to step away from his call for more than ten minutes or so, but he promised he'd make it worth my while. I texted him when I arrived, and he buzzed me in. He excused himself from the meeting, and with no time to waste, met me at his door. He didn't even allow me a chance to take off my strappy wedges. He had me flat on my back in mere seconds, my legs hanging over the end of his bed. In one fast motion, he'd slipped my panties over my shoes and gotten started. That man didn't waste one second of this brief ten minute window of opportunity. He didn't take my shoes off, but that didn't stop him from enjoying my toes. He'd pleasured me well, sent me on my way, not expecting anything in return. He'd left me speechless, and not just because I was out of breath.

* * *

The sexting continued, each message dirtier than the last. I'd called his bluff, inviting him to join me broad day in an alleyway. He called mine and showed. I held up my end of the agreement, meeting him outside wearing a dress with easy access. He'd held up his, removing my panties with his teeth. After sliding that lacey blue thong into his pocket, he stayed on his knees, the skirt of my dress draped over his head. This was one of the hottest encounters I've ever had. If PDA isn't your thing, that's fine. If your sex life has become bland, add some sprinkles. Maybe some hot fudge if you're into a little pain. Point being, everyone deserves a chapter like this one. No strings attached. Fun. No shame, no regrets. When I decided to give love a shot with someone available, we called it quits, no hard feelings from either of us. He was out of my life just as quickly as he had come into it. I never did get those panties back though. *Sigh. #pantybandit*

| 23 |

Borrowed Time

T his one didn't start too dissimilar from other chapters. I met The Puerto Rican online. He found me, thought I was cute, and reached out. And yes, he's Puerto Rican. (This is only really relevant because he was constantly breaking into Puerto Rican Spanish, talking about family traditions and traditional PR foods.) I could just as easily call him "The Aquarian," as his astrological sign was his other security blanket. I didn't know him to not bring up one or both of these identifiers on a daily basis. The Puerto Rican reached out, we began talking, and we were basically nonstop right from the beginning. He would message me daily—text messages, Insta, Facebook Messenger, FaceTime, and phone calls. When we weren't FaceTiming, we were together. In the time that we spent together, we didn't have an abundance of outings, but when we did connect, we'd occupy a booth at a restaurant for four-hour lunches, or spend six hours at my place for dinner and a movie. Our time together was carefree and silly, and it was refreshing for a change. We walked through clothing stores and window shopped for cute clothes (in hindsight, I see why he has female best friends but struggles to find real love interests). Our conversations were enthralling and seamless. And his messages throughout the day were admittedly dumb, but entertaining nonetheless. He'd even FaceTime me with his sister in tow. I never met her in person, but she knew that I was special to him, and it seemed like something could really blossom in that realm too.

He'd explained his set up pretty early on. He was a family guy who met with his parents weekly for a meal. Sometimes this was at his parents' house, and other times, at restaurants. He was a creature of habit, and the restaurants were the same week after week. Even when we went out, he preferred we go to one of those same spots. His teenage sister (who was still living at home) seemed to be his personal mission. He had made it clear that he was her saving grace and felt that he was the only real advocate she had. He was her only escape from the smothering helicopter parents they shared. He had two groups of friends: the friends he routinely went to the bars with on Fridays and played trivia with on Tuesdays, and the short list of female BFFs that he held dear. He didn't come out and say it, per se, but he did make it very clear that he would always put them first. All of them. It was an uneven first step to say the least.

For our first date, it was last minute, and the snow had begun falling heavily. I was honestly a little worried about driving in what was quickly becoming a blizzard. The temperature was dropping rapidly and the roads were getting sloppy, but I was so eager to see this guy, I decided to rough it. I met him at a restaurant somewhere centrally located between our homes. Neither of us had been there, so it was a perfectly neutral spot. He had come from a family birthday party for his grandmother and brought me a cupcake. It was a sweet gesture. He looked sharp, snow gently falling on his dark gray wool peacoat. We took our seats at an open table inside and were quickly greeted by our waitress. She was very pleasant and even laughed at his 'coke' joke. "I'll take an eighth." This made way to conversation about his past, which was apparently riddled with drugs, sex, crimes, and bad influences. Sounds like he'd left some demons in Puerto Rico and brought a few back to the States with him. Although he'd left the drug trafficking behind, he came with a darkness he couldn't seem to shake. He'd been married once, and the carnage of his divorce left some scars that he couldn't hide. Even though he'd presented himself as the prodigal son and ever-present family man, it turns out he felt like the black sheep of the family. He even took it so far as to get a black sheep tattooed on his hand. I'm sure this was a perfect conversation starter, and surely got him pity-fucked more than once. *"Oh, what's this blob of black ink that probably used to be something of significance..?. A black sheep?! Why??!" "Oh, you poor thing. Maybe your mamma doesn't love you but I will, at least for tonight..." On second thought, imma get a stray cat tattooed on my shoulder in hopes that men will think I feel lost, like the world has turned its back on me. Truth is, they won't notice my shoulder. Maybe I'll get it tattooed on my boob. Yup, that's what I'll do.* He knew exactly what he was doing when he pretended to be vulnerable and shyly admitted to me that he had a hard time having a hard time (if ya know what I mean). So naturally, when we kissed for the first time, and he told me he'd felt something he hadn't felt in a long time, I was proud. I was hopeful that perhaps this was a good sign.

* * *

I had traveled out-of-state for work, and we'd been in touch the entire time. He even helped me pick out an outfit to wear to go to dinner with my coworkers. It was actually pretty cute. Snow flew as soon as I hit the road to head home, and about thirty minutes into my drive, the interstate was covered. It was a complete white out. Although I was driving for the conditions and had snow tires on, I don't trust other idiot drivers. The drive home took a solid two hours longer than it should have, and I white-knuckled it the entire time. The Puerto Rican stayed on the phone with me most of that time, talking me down and keeping me distracted from the ever-mounting anxiety. I made it safely into town, and instead of going home, decided to go see him. He was at trivia and had invited me to go if I made it back in time. I surprised him and walked into the bar, definitely worse for the wear. He didn't seem to notice, though, and was an affectionate and proud man. He kept kissing the side of my face, and when his arm wasn't around me, his fingers were interlocked with mine. It was incredibly sweet, and his friends seemed to be eating it up. This group of friends was the group he saw weekly for trivia and beer. Every Friday, he'd go to this hole-in-the-wall dive bar (where everybody knew his name) and follow it up with a larger, more popular bar for drinks and sometimes dancing. These friends were great, and honestly, they might be the only thing I miss about this guy. I had become fast friends with this one couple who later went on to encourage me to stick with it. That he pulls away. That that's what he does. That I'm worth it. That I'd have to try hard. This trivia night was so wonderful and inclusive that I took him up on his offer and decided to join him again the following week. To my disappointment, he seemed like a completely different person. He actually seemed annoyed that I was there and barely spoke to me. I don't know what I did wrong. To this day, no idea.

He reached out again the next day, back to his old self. I helped him pick out new glasses, and he said it was important that I liked them on him. If you saw him in the mirror, though, and in subsequent social media posts, clearly HE liked the way he looked in them more. This continued to be a more frequent theme I saw in him. He was pretty full of himself, and until this point, he'd hidden it well. Some days, he'd blow up my phone. Other days, I'd barely hear from him, and when I did, his replies were cold and short. (Cold and short, ha!) *I feel like there's a 'that's what she said' joke to be made here.*

* * *

We agreed to go on another date, and he agreed to break out of his comfort zone. We opted for something a little more upscale and went with one of my favorite restaurants. Mmm, picanha for two. Never gets old. He nervously got ready, shopping for a new shirt days before. He later admitted to me that before our date, he had talked to his grandmother about his 'physical' attraction to me. Since they were oddly close, she knew that he'd had problems with that in the past. Apparently she was thrilled for him and told him to 'go for it.' He'd also shared with his mother how nervous he was, and she, too, told him that obviously any girl would want him. So, he arrived to pick me up for dinner with not one, but two feathers in his cap. *Thanks, ladies.* This was a completely different experience. He was dressed to the nines (he broke out the peacoat again) and held the door for me. We were seated near the fireplace and enjoyed some lovely conversation. He was handsy on the way home, and this time it was welcomed. We arrived back at my place, and the action in the car continued to heat up. He'd previously made it clear that he wanted to take things slow, so when, in the heat of the moment, he suggested we move it to my bed, I gently pumped the brakes. We had had an enjoyable evening and I didn't want to end it by doing something either of us would regret. If we were a good match, there was no harm in waiting. *It was a nice change of pace to have a man want to get to know me on the inside before getting to know my insides.*

* * *

I was confused, though. Our date was lovely. He was constantly telling me he wanted to take things slow in all ways, but then spent big chunks of the day with me, followed by more time the following day. He was chatting live with me often and calling me at night. Our conversations were much longer than I anticipated they'd be. I was filling a void for him, I see now. He just liked to talk. I'm not sure it had anything to do with me at all. He claimed none of his coworkers liked him (but based on the amount of time he spent posting random memes and links on Facebook, and the time I knew he was reaching out to me, I'm not sure he was getting any work done). I wouldn't be a fan of his work ethic either, and by extension, him. The stuff he would post was so random and all over the place. And so much of it was superficial. I've never seen a grown man post so many astrological memes. He had made it clear on more than one occasion that, since we were both Aquarians, we might not have longevity. He said that two Aquarians have trouble together in romantic situations because they're both super opinionated and have to be right, but that traditionally, they tend to be great friends. *If you're not into me, just say so. Why hide behind a water sign?* This guy just needed to realize that the real world exists, and that you are responsible for the decisions that you make. He lived life with his hands perpetually in the air, shoulders raised in confusion. As if everything just happened to him and he was a powerless participant on this ride. As if he had no say in dictating his life or the happiness he longed for. His words and his actions constantly contradicted one another. It was getting really old and was hard to follow. When he wasn't working, or with me, or with family, he was with his girlfriends. He had three beautiful women who, respectively, were his besties. He was also still in touch with an ex-girlfriend and her daughters. She lived locally but was often out of town, so he'd check in with the two teenage girls and even take them out to dinner, the movies, and for pedicures. He loved getting pedicures too. It was getting harder and harder to figure him out or see him in the way I once had. The line was blurring more and more, and I'm pretty sure I was dating a teenage girl trapped in a man's body (minus the scrunchie and lip balm). Hell, he'd even interlock our pinkies and kiss his own, while making a promise. *Thank you for kissing your own pinky while locking fingers with mine. That definitely means more than an actual promise or good intentions that you deliver upon. I wonder if I could have offered that binding agreement to The Vegan when he wanted a signed contract of engagement. Damn it, missed opportunity.*

* * *

One night we were on the phone and I was home alone. He began talking about the evil spirits at my place, saying that he felt a strong presence when he was there before. The chair I was sitting in had its back to the stairway below, and he told me that the doorway area was where he felt it strongest. I was frozen in fear. I couldn't even turn around to look. He was legitimately freaking me out, and I asked him to stop. He continued. *Asshole.* He told me he was trying to warn me, but that unless I gave them power (fear), that they wouldn't harm me. Probably wouldn't harm me. He told me he felt that a dark presence would stare at him from that landing. He had me too freaked out to even leave the chair to grab my keys and leave the house. He finally stopped but swore that he truly felt something unsettling there and that he had always had a thin veil with the spirit world. We didn't stay on the phone much longer, and I ran through the hall to my bedroom and jumped into bed. I'm not even ashamed to admit that I neglected to take my contact lenses out, nor did I brush my teeth. Not sure I even fell asleep that night. I had the TV on all night for light and sound. *Fuck you, Puerto Rican. Who does that?!*

* * *

I was frustrated with this little game that he played but I decided to give him the benefit of the doubt. Boys will be boys, I suppose. Not sure that gives him license to be an asshole. Maybe he had no idea how much it actually bothered me. Over lunch, we had a good talk about it. He told me that he had meant every word even though he knew that's not what I wanted to hear. In his time in Puerto Rico, he had begun shedding a bunch of weight with no real explanation. He grew sickly in a very short time, and it turned out that he had been exposed to some really severe black mold. He was losing weight faster than he could put it on, and with everything else going on in his body, the doctors didn't think there was any hope for him. Somehow, he made a miraculous recovery. "I didn't think I'd make it. I'm living on borrowed time," he said. "I could die at any moment." "Aren't we all," I joked back. He was not impressed with my lack of seriousness. He began explaining that when he was born, he entered this world with the faintest heartbeat. It was so slow that he shouldn't have survived. The doctors and hospital staff were able to nurse him to a healthy enough point to eventually leave the hospital, but he was still quite ill. He was only four days old when his mother paid a local witch a visit. This woman was well-known within the black magic community, and well sought-out. Together with his mother, she performed several spells to bring him health and life. These spells were to bring him extra time, extra life. Of course, this extra life has to come from somewhere. He began to thrive. He was healthy and became well adjusted as he grew. His parents tried multiple times to add to the family. They had miscarriage after miscarriage. They had one child who was born and passed away as an infant of only a few days. To this day, he believes in order for him to live as long and as healthily as he has, he stole life from oth-ers, his unborn siblings included. He truly believes that because of this dark magic, he is haunted by so much more than the rest of us. Dark-ness follows him wherever he goes; he is extra sensitive to spirits and forces around him. He is aware of supernatural elements in the uni-verse and that his clock could be punched at any given moment. *Great. Another man afraid of commitment. Could drop dead at any moment. A likely excuse. Wow.*

* * *

Although our time together was becoming overtaken with horo-scopes, mean ghosts, and talk of black magic, I wanted to try one last time. In my mind, we had become friends, though the handholding and sweet touches were confusing as hell. He kept me on the hook just enough to think he was interested, but by and large, his actions indi-cated anything but interest. One last attempt to see if I'd been friend-zoned: I offered to cook him dinner (and had all these elaborate ideas). He was particular and vetoed most everything I suggested, so I ended up making his favorite: spaghetti. I even had to dumb down my usual recipe, as he wasn't a fan of all the veggies I would normally include. I had the skillet heating up when he arrived, but then he took over. He began hurling insults, one right after the next. It was like one big insult fart, cheeks flapping until he was done. "You don't know how to cook, huh?" "I'm self-taught, actually. I think I do pretty well, con-sidering," I replied. I was mortified. He kept going, "So, to conceal the fact that you can't cook, you just throw all kinds of seasonings and spices to mask it?" "You don't put pasta water into your sauce?! What is wrong with you?" I reached a point where I wouldn't allow him to continue a second longer, so I retreated down the hall to my bed-room. I closed the door and sat for a minute, trying to calm down. He quickly realized he done did fuck up and came to apologize. It was evident that his apology was only half sincere. *And ya know what? He fucked up the sauce too! You don't add pasta water when using a jarred sauce. Amateur.* I pushed past my anger, and we put on a movie. *Grease* was on, and I was hella surprised when he decided he wanted to watch it. Apparently, it's his favorite movie of all time. I thought maybe that was just a line, but no, he knew all the lines, all the songs. It was actually both impressive and intimidating. He was putting my *Grease* knowledge to shame. My couch had seen better days, so I suggested watching the rest of the movie in my bedroom. Now, I do see how this looks. I mean, if a guy had done the same thing, I would've assumed he was trying to get me into bed for scandalous endeavors. I, however, was not. My couch was anything but comfortable, and I thought we'd have a better time on a cushy mattress. The Puerto Rican was instantly angry. Blood-boiling angry. He reached for me as if he was going to make violently passionate love to me right there just to prove a point. He was clearly upset. I stopped him before he did anything he would regret, and although he calmed down a bit, he left frustrated with me. He had wanted to take things slow, and I thought I'd been more than receptive and respectful of that. And I wasn't trying to make things happen. I wasn't trying to get him 'into my bed,' just on it. Oops. Over the last few weeks, he'd become very depressed. He hated his job and had almost walked out more than a few times. He was constantly getting into heated arguments with his peers. He was helping out a friend by taking on shifts at her family's convenience store. He barely messaged me anymore, and he hardly ever called. He was in contact just enough to keep me from fully walking away from whatever this was.

* * *

It was St. Patty's Day. And it was a Friday. I hadn't seen him in more than a week. I was (mostly) over it. (Doesn't mean I didn't want him to see me looking good if I happened to run into him). A guy friend of mine reached out and invited me out for some fun. I didn't have plans and was up for some green beer, so he came by to pick me up. This was someone who had previously been interested in me but had accepted his place, prominently located in the friend zone. He hung out while I picked out an outfit. He helped. It was fun. I put on some cute shorts, and with nothing green to wear, decided my Red Sox jersey was the next best thing. I put a white wrap-around top underneath and unbuttoned the top two buttons. It was showy, yes, but plenty modest at the same time. We headed to my usual spot, knowing it was more than likely The Puerto Rican would be there, but I didn't let it deter me. Sure enough, he and his friends were exiting the bar when we arrived. I caught their attention as they were descending the stairs, and we stopped for an awkward hug. His friends were down to stay for one more drink just to visit with me. Begrudgingly, he agreed to stay as well. When we got inside, and I introduced him to my friend, he refused to shake his hand. Clearly I was not on a date and even introduced him as 'my friend.' The PR showed his ass and wouldn't speak to him. He looked back at me, buttoned my two top buttons without so much as a word, and then took off in the opposite direction. He was outside and on the street before I made heads or tails of what had just happened. I ran outside to catch him, upset by this little stunt of his. I got him to stop and talk to me long enough to tell me that I'd fucked up again. This was basically the third time he'd told me that I messed up, and this time, he wouldn't even humor me with what I apparently did wrong. He stormed off across the crosswalk without even looking. *With a scrunched-up face, I watched. I waited for a bus to come out of nowhere and take him out,* Meet Joe Black *style. I waited for him to drop right there and have a sudden heart attack. Or hell, even for a bicycle to come by and knock him over. He was on borrowed time, right? Maybe now's the time...* He reached out the next day, telling me that in due time, he would explain everything. He couldn't have been more cryptic or more frustrating. It was infuriating, but I no longer gave a shit. My give-a-fuck meter was busted. I cared about him, sure. Clearly, he was in a dark place, but I knew one thing. I didn't deserve the ping pong match he was putting me through. I deserved to be treated so much better, and after kissing so many frogs, I wasn't about to put up with it from him. Or anyone. I'll never beg a man to want me or to show me he wants me. The promise of an explanation meant jack shit to me, and although I would've loved closure, he wasn't worth my time. I didn't need it. And more importantly, I didn't need him. About a week after he showed me his true colors, he had tagged me in a post about how Aquarians can't be lovers with other Aquarians. I was so over the astrological bullshit. I wish he had just owned his ED or the fact that he wasn't into me. The best part was that it had been only about a week since he told me to be patient… and here he was, posting on social media that he was in a relationship with 'the love of his life.' But of course, he wrote it in Spanish. In the beginning, he told me that I was the first non-Puerto Rican woman he'd ever dated, but that it wasn't going to be a problem. He was now dating one of his own. Honestly, I don't think he ever planned to give this basic white Aquarian bitch a chance. *It's all good though. My horoscope shows that love is on the horizon.*

* * *

The last time I intentionally saw him, he'd reached out, super down and feeling lost. He hated his job, felt alone, and didn't know where his life was headed. I offered him words of encouragement, albeit at arm's length. I knew better than to get involved with him, and

I sure as hell wasn't going to bite and let him string me along again. All the same, part of me did feel bad for what he was going through. I was passing the store, and knowing he'd be there closing, decided I would stop by just to offer my support. He hadn't locked the doors yet and spotted me outside. He invited me in and locked the doors behind me. It was awkward. I stood there as he counted money. Maybe he was distracted, maybe bothered, but he recounted that money at least five times. He was really struggling. He walked me to my car and gave me a big hug, telling me to be careful. Apparently the gas station next door was notorious for drug deals and drama. He thanked me for being a good friend and being there for him when no one else was. Within a few days, I noticed that he'd unfriended me online. *Great friend, huh?* I've seen him out and about a few times since then, usually at trivia. I've got nothing to say to him, and he's clearly got nothing to say to me. *Hell, I don't want him to put a spell on me or anything.*

| 24 |

The Vegan Saga (Part 5)

I ran into The Vegan's son again. That was awkward.

| 25 |

A Breath of Fresh Air

DISCLAIMER: The Bartender forbade me to use the term "cooch juice" in this chapter. He was also aware that I'd tell the truth, not sugar coating any shortcomings on his part. And he also thinks you should know that I have a very aggressive affinity for vegetables when I'm drunk (and that it's on an "abnormal and disturbing level"). And spoiler alert: his bedsheets came in that damn box. *Sigh.*

* * *

I was done. I had had my vanilla sex (see The Vegan Saga). I had tried to take it slow (see Chapter 23: Borrowed Time). I had run from stalkers (see Chapter 2: Fireball and Chapters 3, 10, and 19: Toothless). I gave myself permission to have fun (see Chapter 22: No Strings Attached). I buried a friend (see Chapter 18: Dancing in the Moonlight). I had tried to let my guard down (see Chapter 21: Grand Finale). I shut down all my online dating profiles. I had been rejected, ghosted, hurt, played, crushed. I'd been used, abused, and slapped across the face. I was out a pair of socks and a pair of panties. I'd been scared, and at points, downright terrified. I'd been lied to and led on. I was done. Defeated.

And then there he was.

This bar has been around for as long as I can remember. I'd been a patron for years, sometimes going with friends, sometimes alone. They had live music on the weekends, and it was a great place to go dancing without the chaos of the downtown scene. The bar was always busy, a row of customers filling every seat, another line spanning across the room, people waiting to order their drinks. I never had to wait, though. I'd walk in the door, and no matter how busy it was, the strikingly handsome bartender would notice me and make his way over. We had exchanged names at some point, and to my surprise, he never forgot mine. "Scarlett, what can I get you?" he'd ask with a smile. I never had to search for a spot to belly up to the bar. I never had to wait in line. With my drink in hand, I'd mosey on over to the dance-floor, and he'd return to his spot behind the bar, tending to the next patron. He was always friendly, never creepy. I suppose I'd never taken the time to ask exactly what his role was but assumed he was a bartender and sometimes a bouncer. He was 6'5", large and in charge. Turns out, he was actually in charge. He wore many hats, including that of 'manager'.

* * *

I met up with a friend one night; a social butterfly who is always the life of the party. In true fashion, he was always introducing me to friends of his, both men and women. This one particular night, a gray-haired buddy of his seemed to take a liking to me. This silver fox bought me a drink, and before I could finish it, placed another in front of me. In short order, I was feeling it but not feeling him. He seemed like a great guy, don't get me wrong, but there was no spark. *All the shots but sadly, he never had a shot.* I don't remember the route that the bourbon train took that night, but it led me to the end of the bar, away from my whiskey dealer and over to The Bartender. "We should hang out sometime," I proclaimed, the liquid courage fueling me. After he agreed, I followed that up with, "But don't do that thing where you leave it up to me to figure out when. I hate that." The next morning, a text came in. "Leunig's? Wednesday? 7:00pm?" I grinned from ear to ear. Handsome, killer smile and interested enough to take the lead? Yes, please. "Leunig's sounds great," I replied. "Honestly, I'm surprised you chose it," I said. "Oh yeah? What'd you expect me to say? Olive

Garden?" he asked. "No, I guess I was picturing Roadhouse," I said. "You may not believe this, Scarlett, but I'm quite the bougie bitch." We both laughed and eagerly awaited our date. I hadn't stopped smiling. Wednesday couldn't come soon enough.

* * *

He arrived a few minutes early to pick me up for our first date. It was refreshing to be able to give him my address, as I didn't have any fear of him knowing where I lived. No fear of being stalked. No fear of being followed or harassed if one date didn't turn into two. He had always been kind and respectful, and I knew he wasn't someone I had to be worried about in the slightest. He was dressed sharply in a long sleeve button up shirt, its collar framing his strong jawline. He was 'dark and handsome,' a phrase I never fully understood until I met him. He parked his Jeep, and we walked toward the restaurant in the rain. I hadn't thought to bring an umbrella, nor did he, but he did offer me his jacket. I declined, trying to tough it out. I'm no passenger princess, after all, and wanted him to see that. After we reached our table, he took my jacket and walked all the way across the restaurant to hang it up near the entrance. I was tickled pink by the gesture. The hair I'd spent a half hour washing, drying, and straightening was now a soggy, unruly mess. We're talking a 'do that mimicked Frankenstein's bride. I looked a fright, but he pretended not to notice. What a gentleman. Dinner was tasty, the company even more delicious. I liked everything about him. We shared stories back and forth, and I was immediately drawn to him. The twinkle in his eyes was what did me in. I was a sucker for his lips, his eyes, his smile. It wasn't the wine or the candlelight. For the first time in a long time, it wasn't anything but the guy himself. He was impressing me at every turn, every bit the intellect, not a hint of the meathead (his words, not mine), that I thought he might prove to be. I didn't want to like him. I wanted to cross his name off my list and move on—go back into hiding from the myriad of men who had yet to break my heart. But I couldn't. There was something different about him. Something real. Something un-deniably real.

He didn't push for sex. In fact, he suggested we wait. He'd been hurt before, just like I had. He had been wronged. Used. Unbe-knownst to me, he'd hung up his dating hat too. He had decided, like me, that he was done. So done. I didn't know where he stood on this, and he didn't know where I stood. Something compelled me to press on and give this a real shot. On a subsequent date, I'd shared with him snippets of my dating experiences. In the two years since my divorce, I'd met some real winners and joked about writing a book (and here it is). I teased that all the men had nicknames, not because I needed them for the book, but that they'd earned these nicknames when I was seeing them. I didn't want to get attached to anyone, so real names were only a hassle. It would be much harder to get hurt by Skater Boi or Plow Guy than it would be Jeremy or Chris. "What will your nickname be?" I joked. He didn't miss a beat. "Your boyfriend doesn't need a nickname." Damn he was good. "What will your chapter be called?" I continued, entertained and curious for his response. "The End," he proudly stated. I was hooked. He was good, real good. And I was falling, falling hard and fast. There was no stopping what had been set in motion. And to be honest, I didn't want it to stop. Not one bit.

I frequently stopped by the bar, hoping to spend a little more time with him. Early on, he decided to get something out of the way. "I have no problem with you dancing," he said. "You've never been a wallflower, and I'm not looking to change that now," he continued. "Dance, visit, have fun," he said. "I'm good with it. I trust you. I don't want you to change." I'd say it was refreshing to find someone who wasn't overflowing with jealousy or control issues, but that would mean I'd experienced it before. I had never experienced someone so willing to let me be myself, oozing sensuality, my flirtatious nature leading the way. He was confident in who he was, and confident in my desire to be with him and only him. I was taking burlesque dance classes at the time, and he was supportive, with no hint of judgment or dismay. He wasn't phased at the thought of me moving about in slow and intentional ways, crawling on the floor with my ass bouncing for the audience or running my hands slowly up the curves of my body. It was empowering, and instead of worrying about what that could mean, he embraced it and loved the confidence it gave me. With a mutual love of our pets and a combined three sons between us, we already had some common ground to build upon. We realized early on that he knew my ex-husband and wasn't a fan (another commonality), but didn't hold it against me or my children like another ex of mine once had.

The Bartender understood that before him, I spent some time dating casually, and with that, had some loose ends to tie up. We wanted to make it official and be exclusive, a notion that scared us both but excited us even more. The Plow Guy was still smitten and was struggling with the idea that I really didn't have any interest in giving him another shot, hence the four-hour non-breakup breakup. There were a few others who needed to be let down gently via text, and still another few who's injured egos escalated the goodbye, resulting in being blocked in every way possible. *Ain't nobody got time for that.* I had already planned to go on a cruise with a girlfriend of mine and our children, and our departure date was fast approaching. The Bartender was understanding, of course, but even more so, supportive. We made sure to talk everyday, but we were careful to not overstep or take time away from my boys or the trip's festivities. My girlfriend and I had planned to step aboard this boat single AF but ended up each with a boyfriend waiting for our return home.

My decision to give this a real shot was the right one, confirmed by the small gray slippers he'd ordered to keep at his place for me. The more time we spent together, he took it upon himself to buy the toiletries I needed to feel more comfortable staying over. He bought a straightening iron and a blowdryer to help with getting ready for work in the mornings. He bought a heating pad to support my old lady back, not once picking on me or making me feel as old as I sometimes feel. He even purchased the cheapest phone charger that Amazon sells. Then the second cheapest. Then the third (that one was the winner). He even sprung for the $3 upgrade for white. I'm a lucky lady. But seriously though, the one that won me over was the keychain. He presented me with a small white box one morning, containing a single key adorned with a heart-shaped keyring. It was engraved with the letters 'S + J'. Ever the cynic, I found myself challenging him. Maybe it was recycled from his last girlfriend. Her name began with an 'S' also. *Maybe he has a type. This relationship is brought to you by the letters S and J.* Always matching my sass and snark shot for shot, he was ready for his rebuttal. "Nah. It's a new one. I got it from my key guy on Etsy. He makes all my keyrings." *Asshat. That made me smile though. Still does.*

* * *

Only a few months into dating, I ended up sick. Real sick. There were too many symptoms and not enough answers. The pain brought me to the ER more than once, and each time, the Bartender did the driving. He stayed by my side, asked questions, and advocated for me. He took me to procedures and stayed by my side for testing. I felt like an absolute imposition, but he reassured me that I was anything but. We talked about poop on the regular. *Talk about shitty.* I went from never being able to 'go' at his place to praying I would. He even celebrated my return to regularity with an 'I pooped today' cake. He held my hand during my iron infusions. This vulnerability brought us close really quickly, and looking back, was the first glimpse I've ever had of having a true partner. I'd never had a "partner," but here he was, owing me nothing but showing me love and support in a way I'd never fully experienced before. To be honest, I had almost given up on its existence. The idea that there might be a true partner for me out there, with fewer and smaller red flags than most, was a welcomed discovery. I even got along with his ex-wife and her family and friends. Hell, we met every week to play trivia, and right from the first time I joined them, I felt included. He wasn't perfect, but who is? I know I'm certainly far from it myself (despite how Toothless viewed me).

We enjoyed our fancy dinners and shared a mutual love (and respect) for dad jokes (the worse the better). Still, there were times that were less than ideal. As compatible as we were, his baggage and my baggage weren't a matching set. He came with a past that often left him quiet and reserved. He wasn't the best communicator to begin with and had the strongest RBF I'd ever seen. I, however, am blessed with a palpable fear of abandonment. When he'd get quiet, I'd assume he was growing distant and was getting ready to leave me. When he didn't ask me to come over or to stay, I wondered if he wanted me around at all. And worst of all, when I tried to ask him about these things, he was defensive, which I internalized. We couldn't seem to get ahead no matter how hard we tried. Two steps forward, three steps back.

Even though he wasn't the jealous type, I had men reaching out to me often, and between naivety and kindness, I didn't shut them down often enough or quickly enough. This has been my battle to fight for years, and I wasn't used to having someone by my side, happy to help handle things. And working at the bar several nights a week put him in a fantastic position to flirt or cheat. Not that I thought he would, mind you, but it left room for paranoia to creep in. This one night, he'd finished his shift and was seated behind me at the bar. He stepped away for a minute, leaving his phone unattended. In an attempt to tease, I grabbed his phone and planned to take a quick cleavage shot for him to find when he returned. When I opened his phone, there was a new text message waiting for him. A woman. Big smile, confident pose. She was winking and wearing glasses. The caption read, "I look so cute in these!" I put his phone down immediately, feeling disheartened and foolish. When he returned to his seat beside me, I did my best to pretend nothing was wrong. It didn't last long though, my foolishness turning to concern and anger. I asked him about it, wondering who she was and why she was texting him. "We're just friends," he said. "She's actually here tonight. I saw her earlier on the porch." I had no reason not to trust him, especially since my only ask had been that he tell me if there was someone he was talking to, or introducing me to, who played a romantic part in his past. We all have a past, and although I don't need a complete roster for everyone he had ever dated, I don't want to be made a fool of when someone is around, touching his arm, smiling, laughing, and joking. Worst of all, I don't want her to know that we're together but for me to have no idea that they used to be. It's only fair and right that I'm in the loop too.

A little while later, I spotted a familiar face from across the bar. She was smiling right at The Bartender, who was seated beside me. She was giving him 'fuck me' eyes and although he didn't seem to notice, I sure as shit did. "Are you sure there's nothing going on with her?" I asked. "You never dated?" He paused for a moment, seemingly nervous to respond. "Well, yeah, we used to date," he answered. "But that was years ago." I didn't make a scene but I also didn't waste any time getting the fuck out of there. I was furious. I just wanted to get Wells and get home. *Unbelievable.* He met me at his place and convinced me to stay so we could talk things out. He needed to be more forthright. I promised to be receptive if he was.

* * *

We were in a decent spot for a while, albeit with patches of miscommunication and ambiguity plaguing our journey. The quieter he was, the more I pushed. The more I pushed, the more defensive he got. The more defensive he got, the more I wanted to cut and run. He'd convince me to talk it out and I'd have a change of heart, deciding to stick around. I wanted so badly for it to work out. I wanted to give it a full chance, but something just wasn't lining up.

My 29th birthday (okay, 40th, shhh) was fast approaching. About a week before, I spotted a pile of boxes under his bed. There was a white-hinged box tied with a built-in satin ribbon. On top of it, a boxed game that read "intimate game for couples." Next to it, another box, and beside that, a floral duffel bag. I wasn't assuming they were for me necessarily, but I knew that for Christmas, the space under his bed had become his hiding place for gifts. Surely, there were no Nikes in that box, and with few women in his life to buy gifts for, I assumed that box would be headed my way shortly.

My birthday arrived on a Wednesday. I'd spent the day with my twin sister and nieces, getting our nails done and celebrating our birthdays over lunch. When I arrived at The Bartender's house to get ready for our weekly date night, he immediately handed me a birthday card. Before I had even taken my shoes off, he was insisting that I read it. Before I had taken off my second shoe, he was asking that I check my phone as he'd texted me my gift. He had purchased concert tickets for us for an amazing stadium show later in the summer. I'm sure he spent a pretty penny on the pair, and although I was thrilled at the concept, my mind wandered back to the box that lay under his bed, untouched, unopened. Much like the movie *Love Actually*, I wondered where the gold necklace had gone. *If he didn't have that box tucked away for me, who was it intended for? Was there someone else he was talking to? Seeing?* I thanked him for the generous and thoughtful gift, but it was clear that my reaction wasn't what he'd hoped it would be. We got ready for dinner and he took me to Leunig's—the site of our first date. Our meals were delicious as always, but something was off. He was quiet, more reserved than usual, but I was distracted, as I'd made a friend. There was a lovely girl at the table next to us, celebrating her 23rd birthday with her friends and her boyfriend. She had turned her friends down for a shot but agreed without hesitation when we realized we were birthday buddies. It was the highlight of dinner and seemed to break him out of his funk, at least for a few minutes.

The drive home was quiet. Upon entering his place, I sat in his recliner, lifting one foot and then the other, while he removed my heels. This had become a date night tradition and one of my favorite parts of the night. He sat down shortly after, looking a little defeated. He questioned my reaction to his gift, something he'd been extremely excited to give me. I had assumed he had handed it over so quickly to get it out of the way, obligatory at best, but in reality, he was so damn excited to see my reaction. I had presented as underwhelmed, when really, my thoughts were racing, wondering if he was emotionally or physically involved with someone else. We talked. We fought. I cried. He felt accused. I felt like I couldn't even ask. It was a milestone birthday, and here I was, bawling my eyes out, trying to make heads and tails of the night and how it so easily got derailed. Again. He convinced me to stay, a choice I'm now glad I made.

We talked into the early hours of the morning, reconciling, hurting, loving. Most of all, loving. I laid it all out on the table and told him what I needed from him. I needed to know where he stood. Maybe he'd grown complacent. Maybe we were both too comfortable, too soon. I needed him to tell me he loved me first, not just reciprocally. That he wanted me around. I missed having him stand to greet me at the door, and the busy-ness of our day to day was hindering our sex life. I missed his advances, him taking the lead. I no longer felt desired by him, and it was crushing me. His love for me had never waned, so he was oblivious to how I had grown to feel. For the first time, he wasn't defensive. He listened. He showed he cared. He heard me. Every. Word. And he was respectful and receptive. He didn't challenge me, but rather owned his part in allowing me to feel less than. After my failed marriages, I was finally with someone who made me feel amazing... sometimes. Fewer and further between, as of late. I told him that I was excited that this would be the last time we would fight. He understood precisely.

* * *

Valentine's Day was only a few weeks away and we were stronger than ever. He was intentional with his words and his actions. He would correct himself when he said something that was less than clear. The words coming out of his mouth still occasionally contradicted those of his inner monologue, and luckily, he listened to the latter. He was trying hard. And I was there for it, appreciating every effort, every gesture. Even before our most recent tear fest, he had decided to come visit me while I was out of town for work. The timing happened to work out well, though, just when we needed it most. He took two days off from his government job and drove to New Hampshire to be with me. He wasn't about to let me spend our first Valentine's Day alone in a hotel room. When I finished my work day, I came back to find him in the room alongside an adorable stuffed bunny and a beautiful bouquet of flowers. He took me out to a scrumptious dinner, to a place he'd made a reservation at weeks prior. We brought dessert back to our room—carrot cake for me and cheesecake for him. We snuggled in bed, grateful for each other's love and company. For the first time in a long time, I felt... home. I know that's a funny way to feel while out of state and sleeping in a strange bed, but he was back. We were back. It was incredible. I felt loved, wanted, appreciated. I hope I made him feel half as loved as he made me feel. It was amazing to fall asleep in his arms and downright orgasmic when he made love to me the next morning, and again the night after.

The next few weeks were incredible, and we struggled to keep our hands off each other. I'll never forget the night I was doing my best to keep quiet, my hand draped over my mouth while the pleasure was overtaking me. He removed my hand and demanded, "Don't you dare cover your mouth!" He was sure the apartment was virtually soundproof, so I indulged, holding nothing back. Seconds later, a loud pounding came from the upstairs neighbor. Oh shit. It was 4am. I'm sure they haven't forgotten that night either. Oops.

* * *

I'm not about to say that The Bartender is my 'forever after.' Nothing is predictable, and in a world of constant change, it's easy to lose your footing. But I can say that he and I want this. He will gladly shine a light on all the red flags that he is aware he has. I'll stop and ask, he'll listen and answer. We both want a forever where we feel loved and safe, respected and wanted. And while he's not perfect, I have many flaws myself. You don't need to find someone perfect. You just need to find the one who's imperfections compliment your own. I am more in love with this damn bartender now than I was when I first realized I'd fallen.

And with that, dare I say,
'The End'?

Hindsight

Hindsight can be a terribly beautiful thing. What a gift to be able to see where you've been and to learn from the mistakes you've made. To look back and know what you'd do differently if given the chance. But how awful it is to look back and watch the past version of you endure things you didn't have to. To put up with being treated poorly, taken for granted, manipulated, lied to, stalked, used, abused and abandoned by people whose minds you haven't crossed even once since they left you behind. I just want to hug her! The past me who didn't think she deserved more. Who didn't hold out for better and walk away from the men who treated her like she was as insignificant as yesterday's newspaper. The past me who measured potential partners to the level of her exes. *Obviously, they were keepers. 'If he's not worse than my ex, let's give him a shot! Or seven...' Have another glass of wine, Scarlett.* If you found yourself passing judgment as you read this, I don't blame you. I struggled to write it, revisiting the chain of bad decisions I made. But give me a little credit, please. I ran away from the red flags a little faster each time and put up with a little less. I hope you learn from my horror stories of dating and spare yourself a smidge of what I went through. *If he doesn't check your boxes, don't let him near yours!*

Following my last divorce, I made myself a few promises. I promised to love myself, to show myself some grace, to take my time, to rediscover myself, to stop apologizing, to put myself first, and to be open to love only when I was truly ready. As scary as love is, dating is scarier, and I wouldn't wish it upon anyone. Dating as a single mom to two teenage boys? Nope. Dating in your thirties? No, thank you. And dating in this modern age of social media, where it's more common to be ghosted by someone than to politely be let down? Fuck no. So be guarded, be calculated, have standards, and don't ignore the red flags. How can you expect anyone to treat you with the love and respect you deserve if you don't demand it? And that starts with holding yourself to that same standard. If they think you're high maintenance or too demanding, let them. It's their loss, not yours. You just saved yourself a whole lotta time and frustration.

*"If a man doesn't want you at your worst, then he sure
as hell doesn't deserve you at your best."*
~ Marilyn Monroe ~

Although I've since bought stock in mouthwash and toothpaste, I don't regret kissing all the frogs I did. Kissing them, okay, yes, but I've learned so much about so many things that I wouldn't have otherwise. I've learned about myself—what I'm capable of and how I'm stronger than I ever gave myself credit for. I've learned what to watch out for and what to walk away from. And what to dead sprint run from. I've learned to have higher standards for myself and to hold my friends, my family, and my children to higher standards too (whenever they'll listen to me anyway). I'm thankful for the experiences I've gone through, if for nothing more than to share them with all of you. I know you've all been there too. You've had similar experiences and dealt with the same guys. And since I protected their privacy by using nicknames, they might actually be the same guys! Sorry. I hope that if you were able to relate to what I've gone through, it helps you to feel a little less alone or to feel somewhat validated. Even better. Thank you for reading my *#slutography* and not judging too harshly. At the very least, I hope you found yourself laughing (and at least once, spitting out water at the absurdity of what you read). At least a good 'ol fashioned snort when you were trying to read this discreetly while at work. Just remember, don't kiss frogs because you think you have to... you don't.

Acknowledgements

Everyone needs a little support along the way, and I was blessed enough to have a boatload of encouragement from my nearest and dearest. To my friends and family who faithfully read each chapter as I wrote, I wouldn't have had the motivation without you. Trista, Alex, Misty, Katrin, Leah, Spencer, Steve, Matt, Mike, Chris, Thea, and Jennifer—thank you for keeping me going and laughing at my words. Photography by Matthew Gustafson—thank you for humoring my silly idea and bringing it to life. You made my vision a reality and gave me a photo of myself that I don't actually hate. Kudos.

To my sons, I pray you read this only when you're adults and understand how women should be treated... and that I've taught you better than these fools. You deserve the best and your partners do too. Run from the red flags that appear in your path and don't look back.

To J, thank you for being the most supportive and understanding partner throughout this process. I know I sure wouldn't want to read about my lover's previous exploits. This proves that you're not just my guy, but also my best hype man.

To my big-eared pooch, B, you had to tolerate all these frogs with me. I owe you infinite dog treats and snuggles!

Lastly, and maybe most importantly, to all the thirsty boys, without whom I wouldn't have had the material needed to write this book. Thank you for sucking so badly and raising the bar without even trying. You've left the boxes unchecked so I could find someone worthy of holding the pen, and for that, I'm forever grateful.

About the Illustrator

Lin Hoerner is a multimedia artist and illustrator currently residing in Burlington, Vermont. Her work aims to capture humor, childlike wonder, transcience, and natural elements. Lin has done murals and other architectural art for local businesses, and sells prints and stickers at local shops in Burlington. Much of her work uses mediums such as ink, colored pencil, and screenprinting, with overlap in these areas exploring new potentials and perspectives.